Praise for *The Year o*

"Horowitz's goal is to think and write about dogs in a way that is distinct from usual pet-related fare about how to teach a puppy not to lunge at children and not to increase your household paper-towel budget. Instead, she aims to try to better understand a young dog, from Day One to day three hundred and sixty-five, as a being in transformation."

—Rivka Galchen, *The New Yorker*

"What Mr. Rogers was to children, Alexandra Horowitz is to dogs: a wise and patient observer who seeks to intimately *know* a creature who is fundamentally different from us adult humans. . . . Horowitz's writing is as simultaneously buoyant and precise as Quid's zest for catching tennis balls—over, and over, and over again. Her chapters, packed with close observations about canine cognition and behavior, are mini mood lifters."

—Maureen Corrigan on *Fresh Air* (NPR)

"Horowitz takes science writing to the next level in this stunning exploration of what the world looks like through the eyes of man's best friend. It's a blast to join her as she tracks a puppy's development week by week for a year. Come for the heartwarming anecdotes about her pandemic pup Quiddity, stay for the constantly surprising takeaways."

—*Publishers Weekly*, "Best Books 2022"

"Equal parts science and doggy diary, this new charmer from the author of *Inside of a Dog* charts how our irresistible fur babies develop personality."

—*People*

"Horowitz (*Our Dogs, Ourselves*), head of Barnard College's Dog Cognition Lab, charts the first year of a puppy's life in this splendid dog behavior explainer. . . . Animal lovers will eat this up."

—*Publishers Weekly* (starred review)

"Keenly observed . . . With her characteristic sharp eye for detail and vast knowledge of canine-related scientific research, the author expertly guides us through Quid's critical early development. . . . This book provides a science-based, honest look at the ups and downs of raising a puppy. . . . A detailed, highly illuminating portrait of puppies and our relationships with them." —*Kirkus Reviews*

"A fascinating beauty of a book that will add immensely to the world of dog research and will thrill dog owners." —*Library Journal*

PENGUIN BOOKS

THE YEAR OF THE PUPPY

Alexandra Horowitz observes dogs for a living. Her research began more than two decades ago, studying dogs at play, and continues today at her Dog Cognition Lab at Barnard College. She is the author of *Inside of a Dog: What Dogs See, Smell, and Know* and three other books for adults—*On Looking*; *Being a Dog*; and *Our Dogs, Ourselves*—as well as two books for young readers. She lives with her family of *Homo sapiens*, *Canis familiaris*, and *Felis catus* in New York City.

ALSO BY ALEXANDRA HOROWITZ

Inside of a Dog

On Looking

Being a Dog

Our Dogs, Ourselves

The
Year
of the
Puppy

HOW DOGS BECOME
THEMSELVES

ALEXANDRA HOROWITZ

PENGUIN BOOKS

PENGUIN BOOKS
An imprint of Penguin Random House LLC
penguinrandomhouse.com

First published in the United States of America by Viking,
an imprint of Penguin Random House LLC, 2022
Published in Penguin Books 2024

Drawings on pages 243 and 263 by Ogden Horowitz Shea.

ISBN 9780593298022 (paperback)

THE LIBRARY OF CONGRESS HAS CATALOGED THE HARDCOVER EDITION AS FOLLOWS:

Names: Horowitz, Alexandra, author.
Title: The year of the puppy: how dogs become themselves / Alexandra Horowitz.
Description: First edition. | New York: Viking, an imprint of
Penguin Random House LLC, [2022] |
Includes bibliographical references and index.
Identifiers: LCCN 2022015113 (print) | LCCN 2022015114 (ebook) |
ISBN 9780593298008 (hardcover) | ISBN 9780593298015 (ebook)
Subjects: LCSH: Puppies. | Puppies—Growth.
Classification: LCC SF426.5 .H6725 2022 (print) |
LCC SF426.5 (ebook) | DDC 636.7/07—dc23/eng/20220706
LC record available at https://lccn.loc.gov/2022015113
LC ebook record available at https://lccn.loc.gov/2022015114

Printed in the United States of America
1st Printing

Set in Sabon LT Std
Designed by Cassandra Garruzzo Mueller

for Ammon, at last

Not to have known him as a frisky young dog, to have missed his entire puppyhood! I don't feel just sad, I feel cheated.

SIGRID NUNEZ, *THE FRIEND* (OF DOG APOLLO)

Contents

PART 3: QUID YEARS

PART 0

Gestation

I peek in the rearview mirror and see her asleep in the back seat. She's outgrown the little donut-shaped dog bed she first used and now she is more lying on it than in it: her head and shoulders are fully on my son, O.'s, lap.

It's slowly changing with her. It's that she folds her ears back against her head as she greets me. It's her new, rabbit-legged sitting posture. It's her sitting beside me in the car en route to the city, just the two of us in wordless conversation. It's that she will now jump fully onto my lap, and then snuffle pig-like for a kiss. She chases her tail. She digs into the shoebox of toys and takes everything out, batting a ball around and flipping the long-legged and spindly Grinch around her head, banging herself on her sides. She has a way with each of us in the morning: *aroooo!* she calls, when we enter the room where she's sleeping. She has a way with each of the dogs. She and the cat are working it out, licking each other in turns. It's that even as she outgrows her dog bed she is fitting into the family.

I met her right after she was born.

Our family did not need a puppy. We are three humans, two dogs, and a cat; our days are rich with interactions, and our home is replete with animal fur. Sometimes, though, an idea grips me. It appears from thin air, as though I simply walked into it and breathed it in. And once I've taken it in, it circulates in my mind, gradually and then relentlessly breaking through the hum of my brain's background noise. This time, the idea was simple: *puppy.*

It's a popular idea, puppies. But it was as distant a notion to me as the prospect of hand-raising a snow leopard. As attracted as I am to puppies' guileless manner, to their clumsy gait, and to the bigness of their excitement to see a person or their alarm at a bird taking flight, I was not attracted to the idea of *living with* one. For one thing, there are plenty of puppies about. I need only walk out of our apartment in New York City to see puppies—to see people with puppies, the people blearily standing in attendance with an over-long leash waiting for a puppy to remember to pee. For another, one of the satisfactions of adopting dogs from shelters, as our family has always done, is knowing we are taking home a dog who needs a home. Often, that dog is not a young puppy, but a dog who has already lived some life. I did not want to be implicated in *making* a dog who would need a home.

So a new puppy was off the table—or so I thought. Our last adoption, eight years earlier, was of three-and-a-half-year-old Upton, already eighty pounds of hound, candor, and goofiness when we met him. He arrived at our home needing ACL surgery for an injury long suffered and never addressed. And he arrived with a mysterious set of fears—of noises, of his shadow—and with, it seemed, no experience at all of the things that were to become the substance of his life with us: walking on leash, sidewalks, elevators; people wanting to pet him, dogs wanting to sniff him. We met him at a shelter to which he had been returned as a three-year-old (*Reason for return: have too many dogs*) after having been adopted from the same place as a puppy. Thus, included in the paper trail of his life that was delivered to us was a photo of baby Upton, all ears and smile.

I think that is when I first breathed in the idea. *Who was he as a puppy?* I wanted to know. The only sorrow of coming to know Upton was the great mystery of his life before us: of where those fears came from; and of not being able to reach back in time and make it right. This sentiment is not uncommon. Few of us meet our dogs at Day One. The dog who will, eventually, become an integral part of our family, our constant companion and best friend, is born without us, into a family of her own. Her parents contribute genetically and, in the case of the mother, substantially after birth, to what kind of dog this young wiggly grub of a puppy will become. Her littermates, the world around her, the sounds and smells and sensations she is exposed to, all will influence her personality. By eight weeks of age, she is developmentally equivalent to a year-old human baby—with all the walking, chattering, world-exploring milestones in her past—and she still won't be meeting her human family for weeks or months. When she first sniffs the human visitors who pack her into the car at the breeder's, or whisk her off from a shelter and bring her home, she is already partly who she will be.

Years went by, and the puppy idea was displaced by louder and more urgent ideas. But it bubbled up again as our dogs passed their eleventh and twelfth birthdays, officially well into "geriatric," in veterinary terms. We could not avoid the inevitable ending of their lives, but we might let them influence the next dog we got to know. Who better to teach a new dog about the world—about *our* world—than our crazy wonderful dogs? My son and husband made approving noises when I let the idea float out of my mouth and into the room.

I have no dearth of dogs in my life. Not only do I live in a city bursting with dogs—many of them so completely socialized to urban living that they will not even break stride if you reach down to tickle their head as they pass—but I live with two already. In addition to Upton, our family includes Finnegan, a charming and endearing character who has endured the introduction of a child, another dog, and a cat with only the rare dagger-filled glare at us for so ruining his life. And I am a scientist of dogs: I study their behavior to try to understand their minds. I founded and run the Dog Cognition Lab at Barnard College, where researchers and I observe dogs who come onto campus with their people to participate in our experiments, or who submit to our gaze at their homes or in the parks. As a scientist and author, I have surely typed the word "dog" tens of thousands of times.

As this nascent idea was bouncing around in my consciousness, I found myself thinking of Jean Piaget. As a father of three, as well as the father of developmental psychology, he famously observed his own children while wearing the hats of both parent and scientist. While I can bear no puppies, it occurred to me that I might bring a scientific eye to puppy development. As a bonus: I'd get to live with a puppy.

I had trepidations. Committing to taking on a lifetime of responsibility for another creature is no casual matter. Moreover, I was hesitant about a puppy's untrammeled enthusiasms disrupting the dynamic between us and our current dogs. At the same time, though, I wanted in on this mystery: if I couldn't know my own dogs as puppies, perhaps I could at least know this puppy into doghood.

The mysteriousness of this period of dogs' lives is accidental—an artifact of our society's way of thinking about dogs. Two hundred years ago, we had a different relationship with dogs. They were rarely living inside people's homes: more likely on the farm or on the street or underfoot than in our beds. The business of purebreeding dogs had not developed, and neither had the idea of a young puppy as something to be bought at a store (with accessories to match). Unchecked breeding had not yet led to severe overpopulation, necessitating the development of dog pounds, then shelters and rescue groups, which usually negotiated the re-homing of a dog whose puppy days were waning or past. Two hundred years ago, people knew puppies. They witnessed births. The life course of animals, from beginning to end, was woven into humans' lives (not always to the animals' advantage).

No longer. And a secondary result of how we live with dogs now is that most people miss not only the birth and first weeks of life of their puppies, but also effectively miss the first months of their puppy's life *with* them. The quick development of the dog—from underdeveloped newborn to overdeveloped teenager in a year—happens while their person is simply trying to both acclimate the dog and be acclimated to them. We get caught up in the housetraining, walk training, bite training, don't-chew-everything training that is the typical contemporary approach to a dog's first months of life with a new family. In focusing on training a dog to behave, though, we mostly miss the radical development of puppies into *themselves*—through the equivalent of infancy, childhood, young adolescence, and teenagerhood—until it's already happened.

Most books about puppies are instructional: *Here's a complicated, furry, adorable piece of machinery you just carried into your home; how do you get it to run?* Instead of following an instruction manual for a puppy, I wanted to follow the puppy: through introductions to a new world, meeting suspicious older dogs, a playful feline with long claws, and an adolescent boy who, in his enthusiasms and energy, bridges the world between dog and human. By slowing down to observe the changes in our new charge from week to week, I hoped to make new sense of the dog's behavior in a way that is missed in a focus only on training. I wanted to keep a lens firmly on the puppy's point of view—how they begin to see and smell the world, make meaning of it, and become themselves. And at each moment and developmental stage, I stepped back to consider what the science or history of dogs tells us that can shed light on the behavior of puppies. I wanted to compare our puppy's early days to those of wolf pups, and to compare her development to that of another group of pups being raised among people, but with the aim of becoming working dogs: professional detection dogs. The ample research into young humans also helps make sense of what was happening with this new young creature. In other words, this puppy was to be my subject and my dog; her actions experienced, scrutinized, and contextualized. Should we all get through it, I hoped to know her as I have never known a dog before.

She is here with me now; come meet her. In following that idea, I became a witness to the transformation of a mewling splodge of fur into an exquisitely sensitive, preternaturally agile, sweet, loving creature. Into a member of our family.

PART 1

A pup is born

Dear God, that's a lot of puppies

Time is moving in an irregular, disconcerting way now that we no longer have the regular cadence of leaving the house every day. During the pandemic, whether it's Friday or Monday hardly matters. But time moves apace in the season and in the puppy. She's our circadian rhythm now, as she races through the long day that is a puppy's first year. Against the sameness of our Groundhog Days, she is different every day, sometimes even from morning to night. I could measure time by her ears, which have been inching ever up, and then, one morning, dropped under their own weight, becoming floppy triangles again. I could track time in the speed of her behavior changes: first she comes when we call her, then she doesn't come. She learns to sit in a place; she learns to sit right near but not on the place. She stays on the first floor, then she learns about stairs, then she learns of the fun of running up and down stairs. She learns about squirrels, she learns about trees, she learns about squirrels in trees. She loves the water, she retreats from the water. The only thing that doesn't change is that every single day she seems surprised about the cat.

The young dog was surrendered to a shelter when her owners realized she was pregnant. "Surrendered," as in given up, handed over, abandoned. The dog herself has not given up. She wears the expression that many pregnant dogs seem to: of vigilance. Her amber eyes follow the motion of people nearby, while she keeps her back against a wall. Catching a glimpse of her head-on, I note the blaze of white between her eyes, the merle, mottled coat; the ears that aim up but fall down. She is winsome, her bearing stolid. In profile her belly is swollen downward, making her legs look unnaturally short. Inside are unknown numbers of pups, visible on X-ray as a cacophony of snaky vertebrae overlapping one another and round nuggets of skulls. The dog was probably due several days ago, Amy suggested, but held out while being transported from Georgia. Amy is her foster mom, one of the many miraculous folks who agree to house dogs in the interstices: going from homeless to homed, from scared to sociable. She is tall, dressed practically, with a shy smile and glance that mirror some of her charges. The dog she has named Maize. Not only has Amy agreed to take in Maize, she's taking in indeterminately many Maize puppies, committed to raising them all to be dogs who will not be surrendered to a shelter.

Maize arrived in the middle of a rainstormy night, having been driven up the Hudson Valley, in New York, traveling against the current of the river just to the west, working against her body's drive to birth her pups. From the car she was walked in the rain to the house, where, though it was full of the smells and sounds of several other dogs and birds, she finally found a warm, dry spot and collapsed, relaxing into sleep.

The next morning Amy was due at work early, so she left Maize in a comfortable setup with plenty of room to move around, soft spots to lie, water to drink. We cannot know, but it is likely that even with her stress at being in a new place, with new faces, canid and human, the sensations of her body began to take prominence, and she paced, panting and restless, finding no place to quell the tremors of muscular contractions beginning to ripple through her. She might have felt at once hot and cold, and as her cervix began to dilate, she worked to find a place to nest, digging into one surface after another until she finally settled.

What we do know is that when Amy returned several hours later she found Maize settled on a soft bed placed in a plastic kiddie pool, her body curled around six small furry forms. Strictly speaking, of course, people don't need to be present for the birth of a litter. Most dogs are born without human assistance. Of course, dogs also get ill in delivery, bleed to death, fail to aid their puppies after birth. When people are present, they are there to help in case of one of these emergencies, and to be a redundant mother, in a sense. Watching a dog deal with a handful of puppies suddenly appearing from her bum, it is hard not to wonder how she does it. But she does, whether we assist or not.

Six puppies: still just suggestions of dogs, with all the parts but not yet themselves, their fur sleek with the remnants of the amniotic sac that had been Saran-wrapped to them, keeping them alive in utero. Amy settles down outside the pool, talking admiringly to the mother, and lifts up one after the other, each one fitting comfortably in her hand, legs dangling, toes sprawled, as her hand envelops the belly. She towels each one in turn and replaces them by their mother, setting them near her belly, encouraging their mouths to a nipple with her finger. Everyone dried and at a spigot, she leaves the room to gather more supplies. When she returns, another pup has joined the six. An hour later she steps out again, and returns to an eighth puppy.

Then she stays put. Maize is panting, looking entreatingly at Amy, at the space in front of her, and then suddenly lifts her top rear leg high up and ducks underneath it, licking her nether regions. There is a head there. It is an unsmiling head, thoroughly wet from the rupture of the amniotic sac, the nose bright pink. A front leg appears, and then another, all attended to by the tongue of the new mother, relentlessly licking each part. With each lick the form is paradoxically less wet, as the remains of the sac around it are removed and its very short, fresh hair is smoothed back by the mother's tongue. The pup, a boy, is motionless except as the tongue jostles him, and as he is expelled in spurts from the warm safety of mother's womb. With most of him out, she grabs more forcefully and pulls at him with her teeth—she has gotten hold of the umbilical cord and placenta, the organ of fetal-puppy life providing oxygen and nourishment that has just this second expired its usefulness. She drags it—and the puppy—over in front of her, gently pins him to the ground, and pulls off the whole thing, consuming it. The huddle of puppies along her flank mew plaintive sounds: *errms* and *uumphs* and tiny screams.

The newest puppy has started to squirm: he is being jostled and pushed, and there is a strong pulling at his belly. Lying on his back, he does his first recognizable dog act, stretching his hind legs out long and pawing the air with his front legs. I can see each tiny finger of his paw: a miniature webbed hand drawn by a child, raised up in a herky-jerky wave to the world. Mom is back at her own bum, cleaning up, and the pup rests between her front legs. When the tongue stops its attentions he lies there, stunned, the muscles of his face working to operate each of its early tools—the eyes (which will not open for weeks), the nose (which will soon lead him to a meal), the ears (the canal closed, with the outer ear flap pressed back against his head), and the eyebrows (furrowed as though in deep concentration).

His tiny heart—running the length of just five tiny vertebrae—beats strongly, up to 220 beats a minute, each beat visible through his skin. His breaths come irregularly, faster than one a second, as the lungs take the first of their great bellows-blows of life, then slowing to one every few seconds. He is otherwise still, exhausted from his launch into the world. His mother's nose nudges him to movement. With her tongue she tumbles him around, and only when she relents for a moment does he curl his nails into the soft ground and get enough traction to pivot his body to almost turn over to his belly. Now he is working his limbs, swimming through this new water. Three minutes from the sudden expulsion from his home, he is breathing, moving, and making his way to rejoin his siblings on the other side of the belly they just left.

The next pup appears rump first, the tiniest of tails a quotation mark on this announcement. Maize ducks her head under her foot and is licking, and suddenly the pup is plunged out in a rush of bodily fluids, rolled into her siblings by the persistent, long licks from her mother, who is alternating between cleaning herself up and licking madly around the new pup's tiny face. Somehow the pup gets free, grips the ground, army crawls right under an older sibling, and beelines as best she can toward mom's belly. Another appears, headfirst—especially noticeable as the head is completely green (probably meconium—waste matter—which can contain the bright-green pigment biliverdin, making for a harmless but shocking hair color). Soon the puppy opens her tiny mouth and gives an early-morning stretch, even as she is still attached to her mom. Maize keeps at it, her eyes wide. When not tending to a pup she rests her head on the lot of them, her eyes darting around her.

By midnight there are eleven puppies sharing a birthday, five boys and six girls. "Whelp" is the very specific word used for female dogs giving birth—and that is just about the sound that I made when the final puppy appeared. "Dear God," Amy says, sitting back, "that's a lot of puppies." The oldest, several hours into their lives, seem impossibly mature compared to the new ones: their bodies are dry, their fur plumped, and they are all directed toward their momma's belly, rumps mooning the world. The newest are scraggly and still moist, their bodies looking more fragile, just put together. They are on their backs, straining with the effort of just turning over.

There are three fewer nipples than there are puppies. In their first exhibition of mathematical understanding, the pups who can right themselves aim for a nipple, scrabbling over one another, and, finding it occupied, just take a nap. The end result is a towering puppy pile, making it hard to tell where one ends and another begins, despite their different colorations becoming more visible as their fur dries. Unlike piglets and kittens, who not only compete for nipples, but also have strong allegiances to *particular* nipples—like the student who spends the semester sitting at the same desk in the classroom she chose on the first day—puppies nipple-search willy-nilly. They "show no evidence of teat consistency" at all, researchers into neonatal behavior say somewhat dismissively—although if there is a surplus of nipples for the number of puppies, they prefer the middle ones. The only time I saw a newborn replace another on a nipple was when Amy removed a pudgy one and wormed a skinny one into their place.

When any one of them falls off the pile, they lift their heads in an earnest probing motion, jerkily searching the air for wherever their warmth and comfort and food have gone. Pup legs are always gently pedaling, trying to pull them forward, closer, into. When a full eight are latched on, they completely span the length of Maize's belly, from forelimb to back limb. They fall asleep that way, suckling in gasps as Maize adjusts herself, then finally dislodging themselves. When Maize next rises, the puppies stay where they have dropped. Their limbs splay and their heads rest heavily on the ground. They look completely spent.

As I watch Maize manage one pup after another, I find that I am holding my breath. I haven't changed posture at all, as if movement would break the spell. I am in awe—not just at the matter-of-factness with which she handles this turn of events, and her impressive skill at it. I am watching life generate life. To see a new being go from *not born* to *born* feels as big as if I were witnessing that puppy's whole life. At one point I glance outside, unsure whether while I have been watching the trees will have gone from barren to blooming to dropping their leaves.

Maize raises her head, panting, looking momentarily stunned, and then goes back to tending her new charges. I finally take a breath and something in me turns. Our new family member is in that pile.

• • •

Let's get this out of the way: every science paper on dog mums and pups refers to the mum as "the bitch," the accredited term among professionals. I will not be doing so. Even with my scientist cap snugly on, it is hard to read "He [the male dog] might 'lose interest,' and cease altogether to interact with a bitch that repeatedly threatened or attacked him," without thinking, *Well, yeah, she sounds like a bitch.* I would like to have a word with the person (or cat) who decided that a female dog is a "bitch" whereas a female cat is a "queen." To add insult to injury, the male dog used for breeding is considered a "stud."

In the last year I have seen several dogs give birth—perfectly independent creatures one moment, experiencing this surprising and dramatic turn of events the next: small dogs coming out of their fundament. There is nothing bitchy about them. Not only do they, to a dog, turn and help the puppies out, clean them up, and then spend weeks feeding and tending them; they largely do it with steady attention and patience—and without assistance from any stud, for the most part.

Litters are five puppies strong, on average—more in free-ranging dogs, for whom the pup survival rate is lower, and fewer in smaller-sized breeds. The largest litter recorded, by those who record such things, was a litter of twenty-four, to a Neapolitan mastiff. Producing such a gaggle might have taken that mother more than a day in labor, as the interval between births can be up to or beyond an hour.

Pups are birthed alternately from either side of the Y-shaped uterus. Where they are situated in utero affects their sexual development:

right before birth, fetuses are exposed to a surge of hormones, especially testosterone and other androgens, which can tend a puppy toward maleness. In mice and pigs, and probably also in dogs, females who are jammed between male pups experience this surge and may develop male-like traits. Pups who are at the far end of each uterine horn get the most nutrient-rich blood and are likely to have a higher birth weight. The fetuses are also affected by what their mom has eaten: if an unusual flavor is added to her diet, it passes into the amniotic fluid. The newborns then prefer water or milk with that flavor added over the unflavored version. So are they affected by their mom's travails: stress during pregnancy can lead to more reactivity—essentially, overreaction to stimuli—in the puppies. In the uterus, and at birth, the different head shapes that so distinguish various breeds—the long face of the greyhound, the short face of the bulldog—have not developed yet. Everyone looks more or less like a wee pug.

Birth stimulates reflexes that the new mother likely did not know she had. She will consume the placenta and amniotic sac, which not only clears the newborn's airway, but also is thought to avoid attracting predators that could be drawn by the odor. Eating the placenta, referred to by the unfairly ugly term "placentophagia," also appears to alter the mother's hormone levels in such a way that her milk production is increased. The fluid from the amniotic sac functions as a prompt for the mother not just to lick, but to begin to accept and bond with these strange forms that have just appeared. When researchers remove the pups and their afterbirth straightaway, returning them after washing them, their mothers fail to interact with the pups, or reject them outright. The licking also prods a newborn puppy into action, just as the fright of cold air and glare of bright light on emergence from the warm womb helps to impel the human lungs to breathe for the first time. And the mother's saliva kills off *E. coli* and *Streptococcus canis*, which could be fatal to the newborn. Being born vaginally, puppies share the microbiome of their mothers, a useful start to a bacteria-filled world.

Pheromones also appear to prompt the mother to lie down—in the position called "lateral decubitus," or "on her side"—and allow for nursing, as well as providing her body heat to warm the puppies. One French study exposed new dog mothers to a blast of dog-appeasing pheromone product (or a placebo) that was intended to reproduce the odors naturally produced by a lactating mother in the intermammary region around the nipples. They found that the mothers who got the extra pheromone nursed more lying down, paid more attention to their puppies, and had a better relationship with their pups.

Just as human babies born in hospitals are subjected to a test within a minute of their entering the world, so are puppies. The test for babies is called the Apgar score (after its creator, Dr. Virginia Apgar), and gauges the health of the newborn. The puppy Apgar also tests for viability. Are their gums a healthy pink, or blue? Is their heart rate the speedy 220 beats a minute, or slower than 180? If a paw is pressed, do they whimper and move it? Flex their limbs and move their heads? Do they cry? Crying is, perhaps paradoxically for those who have lived with a newborn, always good: it is the proper reaction of a nervous system to the new, startling experience of being cold, hungry, and outside the womb. Absence of crying is a warning sign. Is their weight in the normal range? Pup size varies by breed, from a single ounce (Chihuahua) to over two pounds (Newfoundland), but a cross-breed average is six tiny ounces. More important than approximating the average weight at birth, though, is whether they gain weight in the next week.

For that, the pups have some responsibility. They need to muster their early reflexes and capacities to make it to mom's belly, and fast. Pups will push into anything warm and soft, their bodies rocking, their heads nodding. By kneading their front legs against the warm, soft mom they have found, they help to encourage the flow of milk. They will soon each be drinking about five ounces of milk a day—the quantity of a glass of wine. The kneading-suckling rhythm seems to stimulate a reward center in the mother, the same one that cocaine animates. Researchers studying lactating lab rats have found that they prefer being near their pups to pressing a lever that gives them a jolt of intravenous cocaine. The pups are themselves the reward. So mom is inclined to stay put—good for both mom and pups.

Sweet potatoes

I pull into the driveway on a cold day. The sky is the kind of fathomless gray that makes you forget it could ever be blue. A fence abuts the driveway, framing a front yard with two dogs statue-still inside it. There is no clear gate into the yard, and no door painted a bright welcoming color. I approach the fence, and the statues animate, barking a greeting, then tearing toward the fence, rearing on their hind legs to try to reach my face with their tongues. On closer inspection the fence is two fences thick; the paths worn in the grass indicate where they open. To get in, I need to pull up a dog collar that is ringed around the fence posts and lever open a section of fence. The collar, and the smiling dogs now leaping into the air in turns, are just the first indications of the level of dogness I will find at this home.

I have come to see the puppies. The dogs show me where a door is. As I knock, a commotion erupts inside: a chorus of more barks, mixed with the sounds of dogs running and scratching the door. A dog nose appears suddenly from behind a curtain, then just as quickly retreats. As the door opens, more dogs dart out: Kelpies, wagging and barking and jumping up. Two older Border collies saunter among them, calm schooners surrounded by crazed motorboats. There are eight dogs here, plus two more, I learn, that Amy is fostering, in another room. And then, too, the puppies.

Amy lets me in, and we step gently through the carpet of dogs. A radio is playing, an appliance hums; the smell of a birch fire greets me. One wall of the room is lined with shelves of trophies and ribbons from dog competition events: agility, sheepherding, disc, mushing. Another wall has a giant cage in which a cockatoo who is missing her back feathers side-eyes me warily. "I'm bird-sitting," Amy explains, "and the people haven't come back." She gestures to another room which has been given over completely to her own two parrots. At the same time, a calico cat saunters in and checks me out before sitting down to clean herself. Boxes of food and supplies donated for the fostered pups tower to the ceiling like modular furniture.

The new mom, Maize, is just visible outside the back of the house, staring intently at the screen door. I follow her gaze inside to the kitchen. I approach and navigate a baby gate, then climb over a makeshift wall segregating the kitchen appliances. Beyond that wall is a smaller pen, and within the pen is a small-dog dog bed, and on one half of the bed is a pile of eleven puppies curled around one another. That pile is the object of Maize's gaze.

Amy opens the door, and Maize runs in. Spotting a new person, she crouches submissively, and I, in turn, sit down and turn away to assuage her. Amy places a large sausage of dog food on a plate for her, and she is assuaged. We step into the pen and settle beside the dog bed.

The pups, only several days old, are not quite dog-shaped yet: lumpish forms the eye registers as living but whose species one cannot quite place. They appear to be perfect sweet potatoes with ears, feet, and a tail. A white sweet potato adjusts herself and morphs into a piglet, short of snout and pink of body.

We scoot the bed onto a heating pad. The pile shifts. It is just above freezing outside, and the puppies will not be able to maintain their own body temperature until they are four weeks old. They lack the necessary extra fat for insulation, and they cannot shiver to warm themselves. Each pup's body temperature is still several degrees below where it needs to be, and they instinctively keep one another's close company. In the pile they form, they can get close to the 101.5 that churns the adult dog's blood through her body and powers her muscles.

When Maize finishes eating she steps into the pen. Her smell steps in with her, the odor of milk and the pheromones of mom wafting over the pups. They stir as a heap, gently pulsing and morphing in her direction. Maize pokes her nose among the pups, licking and rousing them. She suffers my presence there with grace and even, guardedly, lets me pet her. Tiny heads lift and mouths open, aimed mom-ward. At this age the puppies spend their lives mostly sleeping or nursing, and over the three hours that I am there they do both, sometimes at once. The pups make soft squeaking, whimpering noises, shimmying over one another in the general direction of their mother's belly. As they make their way over to Maize she licks each one's behind clean without comment. "She's a good mom," Amy says: patient, deliberate, and rump-cleaning.

When they fall off her belly they collapse into the pancake-like posture typical of animals who cannot yet lift their heads for any length of time. We pick them up gently to rotate them through suckling, giving the littlest extra time at the nipples. After birth and their first meal they weighed between just eight and thirteen ounces. Eight ounces is scanty: a simple cup of coffee. (Coincidentally, I have seen many a wee pup weighed by being put *in* a coffee cup set on a kitchen scale—a sight that is off-the-charts adorable.) Now, only a few days into life, some have doubled their weight while others are struggling. The tiniest pup, whom Amy has named Chaya, with a head smaller than my fist, is half the size of Pawpaw, a merle puppy—his coat marked with patches of black, white, the gray called "blue," and a copper called "red," with moody dark makeup under each eye. I grasp Pawpaw and lift him toward me. He is heavy in my hand, but I can

nearly circle his body when I close my fingers. Save for the more enthusiastic gymnasts, their limbs reaching in all directions, most of the
puppies can be palmed. Pawpaw squirms and utters a small gurgle,
his paws outstretched, every toe reaching for ground. Each plump pad
is an almost fluorescent pink, completely new out of the box. I set him
down and grasp Chaya, settling her between her siblings, where she
has a chance at breakfast. A tan puppy with expressive eyebrows and
a blaze of white, Pumpkin, coos at me, and I coo back to him as I
stroke his soft back.

I gaze at them with astonishment. I feel let in on a secret, as a witness to this time in the lives of puppies. Until now it had been simply
the indeterminate blank space that came before I met my own dogs.
The turn from unliving to life was quick, and these pups are busily
getting on with the process of becoming themselves. For now, it is not
clear who is who; it is not clear that there is any "who" in there at all
yet. In these early days of their puppyhood, eager to know them, we
gather facts about their size and weight; comment on their colors;
study whose ear is starting to stand upright. Later, when they begin
showing distinct behaviors, we will note them all, collecting them like
baseball cards—as though with each new fact or description, their
true essence will be revealed to us.

We prod softly at the bodies to try to identify them all. Amy has
named them for indigenous North American foods: here is Fiddlehead, a blue merle with extra black markings; and three other merles,
Calais Flint Corn (Flint), Blue Camas, and Persimmons, each with a
distinguishing spot or fetching stripe of color. Underneath them we
reveal Cholla Cactus, Acorn, and Cranberry, whose colors vary from
gold to white as a sunbeam enters a high window and moves across
their backs.

The final pup is not among the pile at Maize's belly. Wild Ramps is
a tricolor merle but mostly black, with a snout dipped in a white paint

can and gold eyebrows. She is marooned on the puppy bed, the last one to whom it occurred either that "Oh, the smell of mom is near" or "Oh, the warmth of siblings is missing," directing them toward mom. Her eyes, like those of all her siblings, are sealed closed in quiet protest at this bright world. Her ears, like those of all her siblings, are sealed closed in bright protest at this noisy world. She scooches herself on her belly, using the tools she has, pursuing warmth or smell, until she reaches the rim of the bed. At maybe two inches high, the rim is as tall as she is, and she pauses, her head writhing for a nipple. Nothing. She skates along the bed edge, midway between a slink and a crawl, with a leg making an occasional step-like gesture. Tracing one corner, then another. Even at this age she knows to keep her body hugging another surface—the thigmotaxis that leads her at last to the corner closest to her mother's body. Heading over the great wall she topples dramatically, somersaulting and whimpering. Maize turns at her cries and licks her entire body in one long swipe, sending Wild Ramps onto her back. Righting herself, she heads straight for my knee, clothed in soft corduroy, and tests it for milk. I feel her tiny mouth puckered against it, and am vividly aware of the inadequacy of my knee's offerings. I pivot her lightly toward the rump of another puppy. Then she need only climb him, creep up the length of his body, and at last nuzzle her way in to the desired belly.

•   •   •

While a human baby has a few years to make sense out of what William James described as a sensory "bloom of confusion" that they encounter on exiting the womb, puppies have a scant few months to figure out how to see, eat, communicate, move, deal with others, and find their way. This learning process started in the womb, influenced by choices their mother makes. Once born, they need to make sense of not only other dogs but a whole nother species, *Homo sapiens*—enormously different from them in anatomy and behavior.

It starts small. To puppies at this age, the world is made up of the smells and the warmth of their mother and of one another. That's roughly it. They neither see nor hear. They cannot understand corduroyed knees, hands appearing from nowhere to lift them mom-ward, the sounds of our voices above their heads. They can *do* almost nothing: lifting their giant, wobbling heads is a great effort; their wriggly crawling barely qualifies as forward movement. They cannot stand up. They can't lift a paw or wag a tail. They cannot roll on their backs. None of the small dog gestures so familiar to people who live with dogs is yet in their repertoires: they can't lick their tiny felted jowls, perk their ears, raise an eyebrow, lick a paw, or even pant. They do not sniff or blink. They can't stretch out, they can only knead their forelegs toward a nipple or smell of milk. They don't bark, growl, yodel, or howl. They can't pee or poo on their own; finding themselves cold, a plaintive whine spills from them, directed at the great beyond. Their mother's role is to do for them what they cannot do for themselves, and to keep them safe within their tiny worlds. As if to demonstrate, Maize grabs a wayward pup fully in her mouth and drops him by her belly; her licking prompts him to urinate and poo, and she cleans him up once he does.

They're in their neonatal stage, the period of about twelve days postbirth when, their capacities limited, their reflexes are tuned to keep them close to mom. But even in this bloblike state, when they are less *dogs* than *furry lima beans*, the puppies are having experiences. If they find themselves far from the smell of milk, or the warmth of their siblings, their yelps broadcast their discomfort. Their motor skills are few: though they can nurse enthusiastically, they are just lifting their heads when three days old, and not even standing upright for another week. They have modest preferences: they creep toward warmth and away from a chill; sensible creatures, they will choose sleeping on cloth over sleeping on a wire surface. They find some smells disgusting (anise oil, quinine) and others lovely (milk). Some, it is instantly clear, have terrific nipple-locating skills: these are the pups who, over the first five days, double their body weight. We find others regularly stuck under one of mom's legs, or fast asleep upside down, facing away from the belly while all their siblings nurse on it greedily. Even so, they are still less individual agents than they are a gradually differentiating life-form. As they pile on and over one another in pursuit of the holy nipple, not one puppy stirs or cries on being climbed over by her brother. They sleep with limbs braided together, one pup's head on another's back, whose head is on another pup's back—and so on, a daisy chain of pups.

For the first seven days of life especially, the puppies' brains are still getting organized. By putting tiny nets with small electrodes on their furry heads, researchers determined that the electrical activity in neonatal brains is about the same when waking and sleeping. The connections between the more ancient, subcortical areas of the brain and the cortex, where much of experience happens, are still being formed. Their sleep is active, visible in twitchy, dreamy kicks and shudders, and their waking time is sleepy. Studies on human infants have found that growth hormone is secreted in bursts in slow-wave sleep—deep sleep—so frequent deep, long sleep sessions lead to growth spurts. So, too, with puppies. Especially in that first week, a daily weight tally is informative about their health: a sudden decline in weight in the first two days is linked to a risk of early death. The best science suggests that puppies of all breeds should double their birth weight by the time they are a week into life. It is no surprise, then, that neonatal pups spend the majority of their lives asleep.

Even so, they are definitely doing things—eating, scooting, yawning, rooting, stretching, reaching—and with that, they are learning things. If puppies are exposed to a little of that repugnant anise oil on mom's nipples for the first few days of their lives, they come to know what the smell portends, and soon will turn their head toward that odor on a Q-tip, instead of turning away. The ease with which they can learn to associate odors with positive experiences prompted one researcher to suggest that prospective owners spread a little of the odor swabbed from their own armpits onto a puppy's fur. I decline to so anoint these pups—but I let a few puppies suckle on my little finger, hoping to prime their preferences to me, should we come to live together. The strength of their suckle reminds me of slipping a finger into a latex glove: a persistent pressure surprising for a creature whose velvet lips are soft and small. Just as their mom's diet during pregnancy did, her diet in these first weeks of their lives will influence the puppies' food preferences even after they are weaned: their bodies tune in to the tastes of infancy.

In these early moments they are already learning about the great unfurry animals who will be in their lives: persons. Puppies who are gently handled for just a few minutes a day from soon after birth grow up to be less reactive and fearful than puppies who are not gentled. In the 1960s and 1970s the U.S. military developed a "Super Dog" program which specified daily neurological stimulation protocols for young pups, in the hope of making them more successful working dogs. From the third to the sixteenth day of their lives, the puppies were run through five handled poses for three to five seconds apiece, each one intended to stimulate them in ways outside of what their mom could provide. In one, a person holds the puppy head up, legs dangling, and tickles their toes gently; in a second, the pup is held vertically, their head supported in one hand, their rump in another, as you might hold a plant and its roots as you are repotting it. A third carefully sends the pup into a head-first skydiving position, firmly gripped with both hands. The fourth lays the pup belly up in your palms, completely at your mercy. And the last places them on a slightly refrigerator-cooled damp towel, to try to prompt their metabolism into action. Those super puppies who went through the program turned out to later have stronger heartbeats, improved cardiovascular functioning, more tolerance to stress and a more effective adrenal response, and greater resistance to disease than unhandled pups.

Since that program, a not small amount of research has looked more carefully at the effects of early handling of newborn animals, particularly in rats, whose young pups, apart from being especially small and hairless, look quite a bit like newborn puppies. Handled briefly every day for their first three weeks of life, little rat pups are less stressed in new settings, producing lower levels of corticosteroids, and are more eager to explore. Brave researchers have handled dog puppies for science: massaging their bodies; palpating their ears and muzzle; kneading their back, tail, and toes; and then flipping them over to belly-rub them. Surely this was arduous work. At eight weeks of age these manhandled pups were slower to vocalize when alarmed, explored a new space more, and were calmer when left alone. Just as they can learn calmness, pups can learn to be anxious during this period, too: weaned early, they are more likely to become compulsive blanket-suckers later in life. Knowing this, I take care to scoop up each puppy in turn, running two fingers down their spine and lightly squeezing their delicate mouse paws, each digit a plump noodle finished with the tiniest and sharpest of claws. I for the briefest moment set them on their backs in my open palms, their tails jutting just past my wrists. Each of the pups squirms a bit, stretching their toes to try to reach safe ground; one hiccups, and another sticks the tiniest tongue out at me.

These manipulations of the puppies are perceived by their nervous systems as small "challenges"—something exogenous and new they need to react to—and while small, they appear to make the pups better prepared for the inevitable challenges of life. Similarly, another research program found that puppies whose moms lie down for nursing turn out to do less well in guide dog training than those whose moms stand up while they nurse. The latter, "vertical" nursing style is harder for the pups: they must reach for the nipples, and it is easier to get detached than when lying snugly against mom's belly. The kind of maternal care pups receive will influence their response to stress, their endocrine system—an influence that will last their lives. The puppy's mother does her own sort of "handling"—licking, sniffing, nose-poking. Those pups who receive higher levels of maternal contact become more exploratory pups later, and even at eighteen months old are more engaged with people and objects. Every dog will be confronted with the need to adapt to an uncontrollable world, to live with a different species; some will encounter the challenges of specific working roles.

Already we can see gestures that will evolve into familiar dog behaviors—into features woven into their personalities. Bunting—gently head-butting their mother, trying to find their breakfast—appears later in their repertoire as a sweet greeting of another dog or person. Your dog's nose-bump of your leg as you are idling at your laptop is a remnant of her entreaties to her original parent. Similarly, early whines and cries aimed at getting mom to find them and carry them back to her eventually become the similarly high-pitched "alone" barks that come out of dogs left by themselves in your home: pleas for safety and companionship. They are becoming who they will be.

Anyone who has met a very new person may see analogies in their early life. Infants, too, spend most of their time asleep, interspersed with regular bouts of enthusiastic nursing. They, too, are completely dependent on their parents for care. They cannot yet move anywhere, hold themselves up, or communicate. Their eyes are open, but their vision is poor. They have virtually no color vision, the world is blindingly bright through their transparent lenses, and they are wildly nearsighted to boot. They cannot even decide where to look: vision is involuntary, driven by subcortical parts of the brain. They are creatures of taste and smell, though, and will wrinkle their noses in protest at bitter tastes, smack their lips and tongues at sweet. Just as with pups, flavors in their mothers' diet influence their own preferences: in one study, infants whose moms started drinking carrot juice regularly during pregnancy or nursing showed a preference for carrots six months later compared with babies of non-carrot-juice drinkers. And they are like puppies in the use of their noses: both newborns and their mothers recognize, if subconsciously, the smell of each other, and prefer it over the smells of other babies or moms.

A puppy's life is structured around a few survival-related behaviors; similarly, a small set of reflexes organizes pretty much everything that a baby does: they turn their head toward a touch on the cheek—"rooting"; they will suck on a finger placed in their mouth; their limbs move reflexively when they are turned, tickled, or startled. Every parent who has wiggled each of their newborn's toes in turn, or played "This little piggy went to market" along their fingers, is essentially doing the baby equivalent of the "handling" tasks that benefit young dogs, too. When we pick up a baby, we support their head, but swoop them gently through airplane postures: challenges to the new nervous system, the size of the challenge inversely proportional to its newness. At its center, the newborn brain is hurrying to get things in place, and in its rush, it mixes wiring up: a visual stimulus, presented to the eyes, may prompt brain activity in, say, the auditory cortex, and vice versa. Overall electrical activity in the infant brain is maintained at every level of wakefulness: the neonatal city that never sleeps. But for pups, this will change in a blink.

Young blue eyes

J ust one week and about seventy of their milk meals later, I see the puppies again. They form a great pile on a far corner of the dog bed, collapsed on each other willy-nilly as though a puppy pyramid suddenly fell asleep. One pup—the top of the ill-fated pyramid, presumably—is completely upside down, her nose poking out between a line of stout rumps. Even en masse, they are clearly changed from last week: now they look like a heap of honest-to-goodness guinea pigs. Well, guinea pigs of mixed zoological heritage: they have tiny pink noses, more feline than canine; their heads are rounded and foreheads broad. The small noses of some of the pups are peppered with dark splashes; their white whiskers, grown out a centimeter in a week, sport a hint of black dye. The largest puppies dwarf the smaller. I gravitate immediately to the tiniest, Chaya, a tawny piglet lying off-pile, and place her on the others. Her breath is malted milk and hay.

Within several minutes I have called them by five separate nicknames: little squibs, blobs, nuggets, puddle pups. Fuzzballs. They stir to none of those names. I gaze at the sleeping pile of fuzzballs. It heaves slowly with their breathing. Though I know each puppy is becoming themself, for now they are a group self. They have spent two months in a uterus packed tightly, and now are just beginning to unpack themselves. Even at first glance, the puppies are clearly plumper, and their bodies longer—gently taking up their space in the world.

When I look closely, I can glimpse small individual changes: this one's head is rounder; that one's brow is long and flat. They have expressions: Persimmons is calm, her face unperturbed; Flint rests with a slight gape of his mouth, as though continually amazed; the eyebrows on Pumpkin read worry. The scale tells us that almost all of them have doubled their birth weight, and now the heaviest is twenty-eight ounces, the lightest only fourteen.

It takes a few minutes before I notice the real change of the week. Maize rises, glances at me with full amber eyes, and pokes her nose into the pile. At her touch, the pile begins to stir, squeaking and grunting. And then I notice it. To see the slits of a puppy's eyes suddenly open is to see them transform: one minute they are fetal—their heads circling around, rooting, enacting a time-lapse video of the stem of a flower aiming for the sun—and the next they are vividly puppy.

Newborn dogs' eyes usually open around two weeks, so at ten days these pups are a little precocious. Amy suggests that if, as she suspects, Maize actually held off birthing until she was settled, the pups might have been ready to be born a few days earlier. To be sure, not everyone's eyes are fully open. Amy lifts up one of the tawny pups, Pumpkin, to take a closer look. He has only one eye sleepily open: the left. A second tawny, Chaya, first has only the right eye open, then manages both, her eyebrows working hard to wrest the lids apart. The merle Blue Camas gazes calmly, as though having eyes were the most natural thing. Wild Ramps gives a big blink, re-closing her right eye at the sight of this new world.

And it *is* a new world. For the world as a pup smells it in their first few weeks changes shape when they can see it, too—when the odor, which spreads in all directions, turns out to have a focal origin with a shape—navigable, explorable, and measurable.

All of the opened puppy eyes are blue, the lightness of a tentative spring flower. My heart leaps at this striking color, but I know it won't last. For most dogs, blue is only the first color of their eyes—it is the color of new irises, not yet darkened with melanin. The front of the iris, the stroma, will generally turn brown, or hazel, by the time they are adults. The pups' temporarily clear eyes feel like a fleeting gateway into who they are. It is the first moment that I feel that there is someone *in* there. And they are, it appears, looking back at us, starting to see us just as we see them. This observation is completely human of me, of course: even with their eyes newly open, they cannot see much—they are heavily nearsighted—and the brilliant light of the world surely blitzes out any details they can see. Their brows are furrowed, their expressions much like what I expect I wear when just awakened and reluctantly encountering morning. But for us, the eyes are the window to the soul, the access point to the mind, the carrier of warmth and humor and gentleness. So it's the moment the puppy becomes a person.

Sight is not the only sense coming on line this week. I zoom in on one of the white puppies, Cranberry, whose snout is especially wrinkly, and who twitches softly in sleep. Her ears are tiny triangles, each a small felt flap, a chad not quite punched clean of its paper. Today they have flopped forward, covering the ear opening. This is about the 'time that the ear canal begins sloughing cells—the beginning of the possibility for the pup to notice noises from this bright new world. In another week the ears will be completely open—albeit temporarily protected by the tiny chad. Their hearing will still be developing for several more weeks, but for now they can begin to register sounds. Some of the first things they must hear are the sounds they are making themselves. The literature on early dog vocalizations tells me that they cry and whine. But these words do not conjure up the range of noises rising from the pile. Sure, they cry and whine—exactly the noises that pups *should* make when they find themselves beached in outer space, far from their mother. The overall chorus of the puppy pile, though, consists of squeals; squeaks; various moans, groans, and moany groans; tiny bird squawks, chirps, and chatters; and the precise sound that you would expect a toy hyena would make. Most of these are mouth sounds, but the whine is a noise that comes from the nose, not just the mouth, giving it a special rumbly resonance. I swear I hear one puppy making a moan with a contented grunt motif inside it—early modern dog music. Happily, even puppy yawns make a (very small) sound.

Maize steps into the pen, panting lightly. She is keeping an eye on me but somehow manages not to step on any puppy tails. Soon a few swim her way—nearly crawling, but bent under the weight of their great bobble heads. I stay still and quiet, and Maize lies down cooperatively on her side, earning a charge at her belly. Several pups give me quick views of their tongues, making small forays out of their mouths en route to breakfast. The sounds of greedy suckling drown out the pile chirps. They have advanced considerably in the strength of their suckle: latecomers to the belly find the first pups difficult to dislodge. I watch one puppy, eyes shut as if in concentration, try to burrow in among her nursing siblings. Her tiny nails grip the ground and she launches herself forward. The muscles of her shoulders contract as she wedges herself between bodies. The burrower clambers up the fortress of rumps and completely mounts another pup. I can see her tail vibrating—less wagging than outboard-motoring. She slides into a full-body embrace of a brother latched to a nipple, and stretches her neck toward an unattended one. By ramming her head into both mom and her brother, she manages to untether him from their mom's belly; he lifts his head high, quietly howling a complaint. Everyone's eyes close as they take in the warm milk among warm bodies and soon they are nearly all asleep again, some with their mouths still suckling in fits and starts.

•   •   •

Hundreds of miles south, there is another week-old litter, born of Pinto. One side of Pinto's trading card shows a photo of a slim, smiling dog; the other, her stats: date of birth June 6, 2014; breed, Labrador retriever; job: human remains detection. Pinto has a trading card because she is a working dog, trained by the Penn Vet Working Dog Center, or WDC. And her job now is doubled: she is a mom to eight pups, seven female. They are sleekly black, the color of their dad, a search-and-rescue dog from Arizona with whom she had been paired. Their puppies, too, are destined to be working dogs, trained generally to find people and odors, then placed where their skills lie and where they are needed.

In other words, they are destined for greatness. Which prompts the question: When is their destiny determined—is it foreordained by their parentage, or is it in their raising? Certainly they will get an extraordinary amount of trainerly attention in their first year, quite different from most companion dogs. For now, though, they are one-week-old grubs living next to the kitchen in a house in Bryn Mawr, Pennsylvania. Alice and Keith, a nurse and physician, are fostering the litter for the birth—whelping—and early weeks. They are not dog trainers; they are just people who, like Amy, were ready to extend themselves to welcome chaos in the form of puppies in their early lives. In Alice's case, she started fostering working dog litters after her mother passed away from ovarian cancer and she discovered the WDC's ovarian cancer detection dog training program.

I see the litter for the first time at one week old. I FaceTime in, feeling like the grandmother video calling to see her grandchild, even though my connection to these dogs is not familial but professional—assessing how much of their development is due to their upbringing and how much to their dogness. I have met Pinto several times before, when she was only a year old, a svelte adolescent with soft eyes and energy more controlled than one would expect of an oversized puppy. Like grandmothers everywhere, I am surprised to suddenly be visiting her babies: the V litter, as the WDC calls them, for the first letter of their future names. Like all the center's litters raised to be working dogs, they will be named for those who lost their lives in the World Trade Center collapse on 9/11: first responders, people who worked in the towers. For now, they are called by the colors of the bright collars that have already been placed around their necks.

Amritha Mallikarjun, a postdoc at the WDC working on training dogs to detect the odor of COVID captured on T-shirts, greets me with her mask on. We chat as she settles down near the puppies, and I itch to reach through the screen and tickle their chins. As with Grandma, there is not a lot to do by video call other than smile widely and make happy, agreeable cooing sounds at the eight black potatoes with round head appendages. More accurately, I am smiling at an undifferentiated mass of puppies: just like Maize's litter, they are bodies on bodies, distinguished only by their collars. To get to Yellow to weigh her, they needed to remove Pink, Purple, and Orange from on top of her. It is not yet clear who they are, or even if they are whos yet.

Look past the collars, though, and they look like any other litter. I cannot yet see, at this stage, that they are meant for working-dog greatness, that each will flourish with a different handler, detecting a different drug, or disease, or missing soul. They grunt small contented grunts and squeak creaky-rocking-chair squeaks when someone abruptly levitates them from the warmth of the pile.

Red is lifted and set far, far away from her siblings: about a foot. Facing away from them, though, she may as well be in a different dimension. For Red, the world has gone colorless: she probes her nose around jerkily, not yet able to coordinate movement with sensing. She is confronted with air, with the side of the puppy crib; she finally pauses, exhausted, her body pulsing with each breath, until she is levitated again back into the warm-smelling pile of home.

I catch a glimpse of my image in the video call and find I am making ridiculous wide-eyed faces at them, as I would at a baby confronting her two-dimensional ancestors. Pinto wanders into the screen, keeping a worried eye on the person near her pups. She noses each of them in turn, counting them with her snout. At Orange she stops and delivers long, body-cleansing licks to her belly, tongue outstretched measuring her length. The puppy submits completely, powerless before Big Tongue.

•   •   •

Puppies are born with relatively giant heads and broad foreheads; their eye orbits are large and their mouths are wide. During their first weeks everything grows, but different parts grow at different rates— the mouth, or palate, gets longer much faster than it gets wider; the body grows faster than the head. By adulthood, the average dog has a long and narrow snout and a smaller forehead. That is an average, of course, and among the hundreds of dog breeds there are examples on the extreme in either direction. Indeed, some—like the short-nosed, large-eyed French bulldog—are snapshots of early dog development: frozen in their puppy-like shape.

The dog's growth is quite different from the way that some other domesticated animals, such as cats and horses, develop, with their adult proportions much more similar to their infant ones. But young pigs show changes similar to those of dogs, in at least their skull proportions, as they grow: born with short, broad faces and wide palates, they will grow up to have longer, narrower heads (though they also have the breed variability that dogs do, with some retaining the proportions of juveniles). This may be partly why calling a puppy "piglet" feels right.

This time in young puppy development is called the "transitional stage," as they move out of the group self into themselves. And "moving" is part of it, literally. Getting the motor system running is a major advance in the story of who these puppies will be. The tiniest movements of eyes, mouth, nose, and ears allow puppies to start to tune in to the world; movement of limbs allows pups to start exploring it. Each sound they hear, taste they collect, smell they sniff, and sight they see begins to shape them; their reactions toward—or away from, or interacting with—each of those aspects of the world shapes them further. Their limbs are filling with energy. Their tails are gearing up to wag, instead of just being wagged by an insistent mom tongue licking their rumps. They begin tentative explorations, not fully upright, but under their own steam. It takes days to get their front legs to move voluntarily, then more days for those legs to power them forward. The hind legs come on line several days later, so by twelve days old they are less swimming than they are wobbly crawl-walking. To be sure, their main preoccupations are still sleeping and nursing. But even their sleep is more animated now.

The puppies' development has taken a sharp left away from babies'. In contrast to the activity of the pups, the two-week-old human baby's movement is still entirely reflexive. Several dozen reflexes are meticulously described in child development literature, appearing in the first days to first months of a baby's life. The reason they are so well described, no doubt, is that for babies, that is all they've got. At two weeks they can root and suck, they can move a foot away from pain or a tickle—a withdrawal reflex—and they show several other so-called "primitive" reflexes tailored to keep them alive. While their legs might pedal through step-like movements, they are still months away from stepping anywhere, at a crawl or walk.

Both species are designed to spend a little intermediate time between being a fetus and becoming fully person or dog. Just like humans, dogs are altricial, unable to care for themselves and dependent on parents for their very survival after birth. In other words, they are not fully cooked in utero, and need a little more time to get the entire body running smoothly. The brains of all newborns are still developing, but the brain of an altricial animal is raw—light on myelin, the insulating covering for neurons that enables rapid nerve signaling within the brain and through the body. Pups, though, are on a radically speedier path than human babies. By this week in the puppies' lives, a new round of myelin is developing. It is going to coat the neurons that change the puppies from slow-moving, rooting potatoes to recognizable dogs—while their peer babies still kick idly into the air.

While human babies are still trapped in their slowly developing bodies, puppy bodies are already ramping up the peripheral—but key—details: the eyes are opened, the ears are opening; the tongue starts tonguing, the voice starts voicing. With open eyes, dogs make a huge step into what will be the foundation of their bond with people: looking at, watching, and learning about us. Opened eyes allow for expressiveness—side-eyes, sleepy eyes, let's-go-for-a-walk eyes—as well as blinking. Dogs have, researchers determined, three spontaneous blink types: fully closed, half-closed, and one-eye. On average, an adult dog will fully blink about thirteen times a minute—just about the rate of human blinking (but half the rate of the average gorilla, and considerably more than the nearly non-blinking guinea pig). Dogs vary less in blink rate than in how quickly they reopen their eyes after the lid descends. Incredibly, this is detectable—and detected—by the adoring human eye, for we rate those dogs who unblink most quickly as the most intelligent dogs.

With opening ears, puppies not only hear one another; they are also now able to be startled by sounds. Being startleable may not seem like a useful development, but it is one way that the world starts becoming perceptible to the newborn animal. Each puppy finds themselves in a world abuzz, among fellow creatures, adding another layer to their growing understanding.

The tiny puppy tongue has a way of sticking just out of the mouth—a "blep," in the nonscientific literature—but it is more than just cute. Mammalian tongues, described by tongue scientists as "a tethered limb without an internal skeleton," are remarkable in the shapes they can take on and motions they can make. While they will never work to help form speech sounds like the human tongue, dogs' considerable tongue musculature enables them to groom themselves; explore the taste of an object before ingesting it; and even, by curling backwards, pull a column of water, adhering to the front of the tongue, neatly (okay, messily) into their mouths. It is full of capillaries to help in lowering body temperature when panting. But the tongue also winds up being used meaningfully in interactions with others (face-licking is part of the most enthusiastic greetings of other dogs or people); as an investigative organ (licking a surface brings odor molecules to the vomeronasal organ, above the roof of their mouth, to be smelled); and as a sign of stress (the tongue-flick, a short in-and-out of the tongue tip, is a clear signal of uncertainty or fear).

Their voices have grown louder and are getting more specific. Puppies who have their tails docked (the tailbone literally cut short)—a barbaric act often done before the pup is a week old—shriek, an "intense, strident, and prolonged" sound, as researchers describe it. Soon they will be listening to the world around them, and barking back. As their closest relatives, gray wolves, rarely bark, it is thought that domestication brought out the bark in dogs. Indeed, a guard dog with a strong bark would be desirable. The many kinds of barks in every dog's repertoire are used in different contexts—from social play to when left alone—and have different meanings: as an alert, goad, warning, or plea. I bend down over the puppy pile, inhale a heady smell of milk, fur, and bodies, and try to hear what they're saying.

The week of poop

Three weeks into the pups' lives, I open the door to visit them not knowing exactly what I'll find. The distinctive odor of many animals living in a small space greets me first. I hear a fan thrumming somewhere, the radio chattering to an empty room. The warmth of the wood stove reaches my face as I shut the door on the winter chill. The cockatoo losing all her back feathers side-eyes me warily; barking is in stereo.

In the puppy room Maize wags at me sweetly. She is just outside the pen with a cluster of puppies, and as I approach she pokes her head over the gate, almost visibly counting each of her offspring with her nose.

The pups are fat dumplings with tails, tossed in a heap. A dream-surge radiates through the pile, ears and legs twitching, bodies inflating and deflating. The pulses of breathing and rumbly snores coming from the other bodies in the pile are suddenly upstaged by a bigger vibration as a mountainous figure casts a shadow over them. They groggily stir, some of them tumbling off others as they stretch into awakedness. And then the mountain is making high, friendly sounds, and it smells of foods and warmth and outside air, and they lurch toward it, over and under one another. Reaching the mountain, some attempt to scale it, others pull at it, grabbing at soft bits that do not quite pull off, and fleshy appendages that move quickly out of their mouths and cover their bodies. Every once in a while they are magically levitated with a gentle squeeze and set down farther away, and must head mountainward again.

For the first time, they are sensing me. They may see me as more mountain than person, just a foggy morass of new stimuli; still, it is hard not to feel immediate gratification at being the focus of interest of these little dough balls. Their interest is expressed using all the active verbs available to puppies: they are biting, mouthing, suckling, kneading. I squat down among them and experience the full onslaught. Mouth first, they lick my sleeve and one another, trying to take bites of my knees, grabbing a sibling by the head. This is the week their teeth have come in, and they seem fascinated by what they can now secure with their tiny mouth knives. My watchband is fully examined and tasted, at one point, by five puppies at once. At the pups' current size, my outstretched fingers can entertain three of them. Flint chomps my pinkie, Wild Ramps licks my ring, and Acorn rests his head on the other three digits. A new sound is coming out of a puppy somewhere in the jumble: a high, almost cartoonish squeal. If it were coming from a baby, we would be completely confident in translating the utterance as "Ruh-roh."

Maize looks around with worried eyebrows as her tidy bunch of puppies distributes itself around the pen. I find myself talking out loud to her puppies: "Oh, you're biting my finger!"; "You're a very fat one . . ." as I tickle Pawpaw's head; ". . . and you're a very little one," of the tiny Chaya. She's shivering, and I trace full, long warming strokes down her body with my hand. "Here's a yawning one," Pumpkin, "and tiny lamb belly," Cholla Cactus, lying on his back, pink limbs reaching upward, with ears and mouth flopped open. Persimmons starts nosing her way up the cuffs of my pants; Cranberry, the prodigious noisemaker of the litter, is whimpering. Even as I watch her, she adds some consonants to the whimper and suddenly comes out with the first legitimate bark I have heard. Wild Ramps sneaks behind me, worrying the heel of my shoe, and as if by prearrangement, Blue Camas takes on the other shoe. Fiddlehead is trying to get, as far as I can tell, inside my knee, mouth first. There is a lot of puppiness happening.

They have definitely hatched this week, and the nest, such as it is, will soon be left. Trying to scale my legs, they claw over one another, stepping on heads, licking and mouthing anything in front of them, including one another's faces. Each movement is there in its rudimentary form: to climb, one must first paw at; to step, one must first lift a front leg off the ground. It is the next step where they falter, but they are not deterred long. The pure resilience to *keep at it* is present in each of them. I see a few tails gearing up to wag, managing only erratic, asymmetrical flits, as if the tail is not sure how to go both back *and* forth. It is also the week they have begun eliminating on their own: there are tiny poops on every surface and in every corner, and erratic golden lines that track where they've been while peeing—including on their siblings' backs. The reflex to eliminate has begun to mature, but the urge to eliminate at the edge of their own nest has another week in development.

All are much larger than the week before, except Chaya, whose fur is matted and who is not at all robust. Everyone's ears flop down, jiggling gaily with each tumble. They all have the wee pug nose, the flattish face; the fatter ones have rolls of skin forming around the eyes and nose. Their nails are also precociously sharp, I learn as one navigates up my jacket sleeve.

This week I have brought props. I pull out several tiny bottles and a fistful of Q-tips. The bottles are essential oils with distinctive scents: cherry, vanilla, smoke, banana. I hover a Q-tip doused in banana odor in front of Wild Ramps, who is worrying my shoelaces. She pauses, as if momentarily hypnotized, then drops the shoelace and walks away.

Persimmons also freezes at encountering a vanilla Q-tip in front of her face, then toddles on. Each puppy seems to notice the odors, pausing as if in thought, but few animate their nostrils and really sniff them. When Maize gets interested, and I offer her a Q-tip smelling of smoke, she gives it long, investigatory sniffs, her nostrils flared with the effort.

After snorting out, she then hops neatly into the pen. Within seconds everyone stops what they are doing and heads mom-ward. As she stands, a few of the merles—and Cranberry, the largest—can just suckle while upright. Their suckling has turned noisy and vigorous, more zealous than the rhythmic nursing of weeks past. I grab Chaya and direct her head to a swollen teat, holding her there as she drinks. Some nipples are bloodied and all hang low, hard but disconsolate workers. Maize looks to be questioning her choice herself, to be wolf-mom to Remus and Romulus—and their nine pals. She abruptly jumps out, and the pups fall off. This week she may begin weaning them from her milk, a process that takes one week or several, depending on the breed and the individual. I realize that it is just as their mom is starting to distance herself from them that the puppies have started to notice me—as though, ultimately, all movement, all behavior, is in search of mom, even as she just gets farther and farther away.

With Maize's retreat, the puppies settle into a pile again, burrowing into and under one another, and are quickly asleep. Dreams cascade down Cranberry's body as she dream-barks. There is a kind of puppy topography, the ways puppy hills and puppy valleys best fit together; which size pup can pile on the others; which precipice tumbles off, creating a new fault line. Their urge not just to be near but to be fully in contact with one or four others puts the lie to any dog-keeping that segregates a single dog from others, and from people. It makes me want to reproduce that comfort for them. I think of sad dogs "parked" in a box on the sidewalk, or poking a nose out from behind a curtain, looking out at the world that has left them alone. Might they be remembering back to this time?

•   •   •

At three weeks old the puppies have toddled into a key developmental period. Not to put too fine a point on it, this stage has been described as "the most influential nine weeks of a puppy's life." Until now their mother has been the sun around which their world revolves. She is the puppies' main source of food, warmth, and comfort; the one they talk to, they search for, they yearn to touch. While it is still sunny, at this age the puppies start learning about the rest of the galaxy. For the next several weeks they will be in a "socialization period," or sensitive period, during which they are open to learning about everything that might be in their world. What they learn in these weeks is the foundation for growing up to be happy, healthy, well-adjusted adults; without this foundation, their happiness, health, and adjustment-tuning can be challenging or unachievable. Indeed, the higher rate of behavior disorders in commercially bred or puppy-mill dogs is linked to insufficient stimulation during these weeks. These weeks lay the groundwork for how puppies deal with others socially and sexually, for how they play and when they are aggressive, for how to solve problems, how and whom to imitate, what to fear, and when to explore. They form the basis of a pup's trainability and emotional stability— all the things that a new pup owner will encounter in the first days of living with them. It is when they learn to trust and bond with people, or learn a suspicion of people. So, yeah, a big deal.

The Austrian ethologist Konrad Lorenz famously introduced the public to the idea of animals' "critical periods" of social development, during which the growing youngsters need exposure to others of their species to learn, essentially, how to be the animal that they are. Lorenz demonstrated both the flexibility and the rigidity of this period by making himself, and not an adult goose, the first large moving thing that a brood of young goslings saw when they hatched. While flexible enough to accept that a middle-aged Austrian was a model goose, they were not flexible enough to rethink that decision when he behaved more human than goosey. They followed him around dutifully, and he, in turn, took the geese on swimming expeditions in the Danube, trying to help along their development into actual swimming birds. Alas, learning flying was particularly tough with a land-bound model.

Unlike Lorenz's geese, puppies do not imprint rigidly on the first living thing they see. Instead, the socialization period lasts for several weeks. That it begins at about three weeks is not accidental. Their bodies are rapidly developing: at three weeks their nervous systems have matured enough for them to learn by association. With eyes and ears joining the other senses in transmitting information about the world, the sensory and motor cortices of the brain mature rapidly, helping to forge those connections between what they experience and what they do. Humans have a socialization period as well, but unlike dogs, who have gone through a transitional period of rapid development, human infants are still incredibly immature and completely dependent on their mothers. As a result, the infant's primary social figures are their caregivers; for dogs, the primary relationships will be with their siblings—or any other animals they encounter.

And I do mean *any* animals. For puppies the sensitive period of development is a time when they can be exposed not only to dogs but also to people, cats, rabbits, horses, cows—to any species with which they might need to peaceably interact—in order to impress the idea of their familiarity on the pup. Remove a puppy from her litter and raise her exclusively with sheep, and she won't grow up to be a sheep. She will, however, forge a relationship and way of interacting with sheep—treating them as normal social companions—that other puppies of her litter will not have. This is not to say that she will act like a sheep: she won't. She will act like a dog whose friends are all sheep-shaped. And, relatedly, she won't be as skilled in dealing with other dogs, or with people, if she didn't grow up with them. One researcher, Michael Fox, raised Chihuahua puppies with a cat and her kittens; when faced with a mirror, the pups did not wag, gaze, or bark at the image, the way pups raised with their own litters do. Raised among felines, these Chihuahuas must not have recognized the odd-looking cat looking back at them. I don't think it has been done, but raise a puppy among porcupines, and you will get a porcupine-friendly adult. (I cannot vouch for the friendliness of the porcupines.)

As an extreme example, consider livestock-guarding dogs. They must live primarily with their charges for the first months of their lives; being a member of a breed that has traditionally guarded sheep does not make a dog a natural shepherd. It prepares them for the gig, should they meet the sheep early. While they stay with their birth litter for the first several weeks of life, before they are nine weeks old they are removed to a pen first next to, and then among the animals they are to guard, be they sheep, llamas, goats, horses, chickens, or ostriches. Then, the types of play and social interactions that the pups would usually engage in with other dogs, they develop instead with their charges. They will sleep with their heads on a soft ewe, or let a ewe use them as a pillow; they will lick a sheep's face as they would their mom's; they will later let young lambs suckle from them. Literature on livestock guarding does caution against allowing a pup to play over-aggressively with the herd, chewing the ears of lambs or play-slapping a chick—a possibly chick-fatal move. But in general, dogs come to treat these non-dogs as their social group, and will repel any potential predator who threatens the group.

The pups also have to learn to deal with one another now. Their littermates have transformed from warm sleep buddies to increasingly independent other beings. While they have long been aware of one another, they are now coming to a different level of awareness: of others as separate puppies. At this age they are perfectly able to recognize their siblings by smell, and if given the choice of lying on bedding with the odor of their siblings on it, or bedding with the odor of an unknown pup, they choose to sleep with their sibling smell. The first two weeks of living in and around one another, with no equipment to make an escape, creates a bond that makes the social experimentation of the coming weeks possible. All that biting of one another's body parts could be described as a safe, if poorly controlled, experiment on what happens when they bite. The reaction from some of their targets—biting back—is the beginning of learning to inhibit their own bites. Without this daily or even hourly experimentation and feedback, puppies might bite more forcefully as adults—too forcefully for most people and dogs they will encounter.

Dogs' cousins, gray wolves, have a briefer social window to be exposed to other species: if they have not met a human, say by about nineteen days, they will never come to live safely among people. At Wolf Park, a sanctuary in Indiana where wolves live outside in their own natural enclosure, but with daily care and interactions with people, the staff will remove a wolf pup from their den at ten days, even before their eyes open, and then handle them around the clock until they are five months old. They live in a nursery, an indoor enclosure whose floor is covered with all manner of soft and (for small pups) climbable substrate: futons, blankets, pillows, comforters. Agreeable adult wolves who will suffer pup behavior are eventually brought in to spend time with them, too. The idea is not to tame the wolves, or make them non-wolfy. Instead, this intensive socialization program is what Wolf Park curators have determined works best to ensure that the wolf pups not only can live with wolves but can also attach to people. Should they not have this exposure, young wolves would not grow up accepting food from humans, or allow even their presence, let alone happily greet them or offer their heads for scratching or paws for toe-clipping—as they do.

This longer phase is called the socialization period because it is the time pups can learn how to be social with other beings, but this time from three weeks to twelve or fourteen weeks is also when they can be exposed to new noises, smells, textures, contexts—"novel stimuli," as the research likes to call them. For a brief window, and provided that the novel stimulus is not too fearsome, puppies can learn to be okay with . . . just about anything. These weeks are the time to send out the Roomba and turn up the fans, to have strangers arrive at the door and ring the bell, to roller-skate by, to play CDs of "city noise." And that is just what has begun under Amy's fostering. The radio, the birds squawking, the barks of other dogs in the background: the pups are getting nonstop exposure to these sounds—and will come to think of them as normal, not at all alarming. And I am part of that socialization: every visitor gives the puppies a chance to learn about people in a safe context. I am pleased to be a kind of Lorenz for these canid goslings. But I am trying hard not to feel too special, because to the puppies, I am just a representative bipedal, hand-using, short-nosed animal who makes odd noises and has sleeves and cuffs for exploring, quite different from their siblings. They will not follow me into the Danube. They find me smellable, bitable, scalable, and lickable, like their littermates, but while I bring distinctive odors of my home, and my own way of handling and talking to them, I am not "me" to them. For now, I'll take it.

Meanwhile, in Bryn Mawr, the three-week-old V litter is watching action movies, volume on high. A noisy, busy vacuum runs regularly, and a hoverboard hovers by them. Their socialization is a heightened variation on the theme playing out with Maize's pups: exposure to new and possibly bizarre phenomena, as well as to people of all sorts. Their foster family has three kids in the house, and they have just begun letting older and younger visitors in to meet the pups. "Anything I can find with wheels gets rolled by the pen," foster mom Alice tells me. The whelping pen is right where breakfast is served, by the kitchen, so the pups can hear, see, and smell all its goings-on. Next week they will get a visit from the Working Dog Center researchers.

Professional wag

Wander into a store in the United States catering to parents of babies and young children, and you're likely to find a child "activity gym" among the products to amuse and educate your little one. The activity gym is a mini-world for babies, who, placed on their backs, gaze not at the stars, but at the universe of material objects common to twenty-first-century American babyhood. It consists of a mat with a few plastic or wooden rods doming above it, from which hang various objects of ostensible interest to a baby: a rattle, colorful shapes or animal figures, something pullable or ringable. Versions of these apparatuses have been a part of the American baby ecosystem since at least the 1940s, when they took the form of appendages placed above cribs to engage the bright-eyed infant therein.

Designers of these gyms have in mind the early stimulation of babies, whose vision is still rudimentary, and who are still more or less trapped where they are laid, being unable for several months yet to ambulate, crawl, or even turn over. The dangling objects may be black-and-white, better to catch an eye that still notices movement more than colors. They may feature various plush animals—owls, deer, monkeys, giraffes, and other characters regularly presented to babies in toys and books—despite the fact that few babies will grow up to interact personally with any of them. There may be mirrors for looking into and rings for gripping onto. When my son, O., was a baby young enough to spend some of his day supine in a crib, he was attracted to dangling bells and rattles that he could try to kick, hit, or grab to make a pleasing racket.

What the designers of these gyms probably did not have in mind was their use by four-week-old puppies. And by "use" I mean "invasion and destruction." When O. (now ten years past crib stage) and I arrive at Amy's this week, the puppies and their new accoutrements—beds, a litter box, various pull and chew toys designed for dogs—have completely displaced the living room furniture, which is huddled along one wall. Among the pups' new possessions is an infant activity gym in the primary colors typical of early-childhood toys. Blue Camas is playing the part of the baby in the gym, except that she is not gazing at the toys with the curiosity of a baby discovering the universe outside of herself. She is knocking into them with her head and body, then moving to bite the offending dangler. A furry green caterpillar knocks her over; on the ground, she discovers she has a tail, and moves to bite it, too.

It makes sense to have an activity gym for the puppies, because this is the week that their activity mushrooms. In addition to the gym, Amy has provisioned their space with a short tunnel made of rings and nylon. Soon this is the place to look if you are counting puppies and one seems to be missing. And soon O. and I provision the space with ourselves, stepping into the pen and sitting down to be wrangled with. Six squeaks come to meet me, some underestimating their speed or our distance and running squarely into my shins. They are now the size of pretty healthy loaves of bread—only malleable and with stumpy limbs. They are toddling, walking as if wearing shoes two sizes too large. Wild Ramps lurches by, her tail radiantly wagging—the most coordinated part of her. Their tail wags are by now nearly professional dog wags. They alternate between loosely sweeping, merry oscillations and divining rods, vibrating lightly and curved, helping to hold their pudgy bodies upright. The tail-tips are tiny exclamation points at the end of their bodies. Edible ones, apparently: I regularly see a puppy reach for a nearby sibling's tail and start gnawing on it.

Maize is nearby, her ears back, her tail marking an interested but concerned beat, her belly still swollen down to her knees. The puppies continue their daily pattern of vacillating between pile-sleeping and awakedness, but that awake time is now less about finding mom's belly than about exploring the space. Or maybe it is just that they can less often find her belly, no matter how hard they look: she is no longer lying helpfully on her side, enabling breakfast, lunch, dinner, and several in-between snacks. While they are still nursing daily, Amy has begun giving the puppies a canned puppy food—the WDC puppies' trainers call it "gruel"—delivered in a circular tray so that each puppy forms a ray of the sun. It gives Maize a little time away from nursing to reflect, presumably, on her very busy past month.

I toss two long purple pull toys among the little loaves, giving each a shake as I do. The objects in the pen explicitly designed as dog toys do not seem to register with the puppies overmuch. While we look at a rope tug or squeaky ball and sense its function immediately, it is far less interesting to the puppies than the edge of the dog bed on which they lie, or a finger near their faces. With much persistence O. encourages Persimmons to grab onto the tiniest of red tennis balls—as small as you can get and still be called a tennis ball—which she finally does, cooperatively gripping it in her mouth like an old pro. Then we realize that she is frozen in place and may simply not know how to release it. O. gently removes the ball from her mouth, and she toddles on her way.

Instead of toys I have brought keys. I pull out my most janitorial key chain, holding keys for long-forgotten locks, and abruptly drop it on the floor beside me. Its clanking causes all the humans to look toward me, eyebrows questioning, but none of the puppies. A sudden novel noise disturbs them not at all: it is only the way the world is to them—noises happen, hands lift, bodies bang. Without yet any sense of how the world *should* be, their world can be anything at all.

There are other human visitors in the pen today, and we each sit cross-legged or with our legs spread in a V, both of which in puppy language are apparently invitations. We trade hosting seven or more puppies at a time. Just as their rate of chewing each other's faces and small bits has escalated, they now pile on one another more forcefully. There is regularly a puppy completely plopped over another, or a tiny head poked out from under three healthy rumps. Unusually, Amy's calico cat hops into the pen. She may be looking for the couch now crowded with puppies. She wanders among them, sniffing a few closely; Acorn opens an eye, but is not excited into action. The puppies may just be tired, but they barely pursue her. When one does extend a paw to her head, she neatly leaps up to the top of the wobbly gate lining the pen and takes her leave of them.

I have started to interpret what each puppy does as indicative of their character, though I know I am seeing only the briefest glimpse. Some are more talkative, some more bold—but this might reflect different rates of development. Distinct personalities will not truly shine through for a couple of weeks. Still, there are differences to see: behavioral habits, more than just the changes in body weight and size that we assiduously tallied in their first two weeks. Wild Ramps and Pawpaw lie in repose on their backs, little legs shot up in the air, and allow us to tickle their warm bellies. Fiddlehead wobbles over and starts gnawing Wild Ramps on the elbow. Flint has a kind of natural smile in sleep. Persimmons lets Amy plop her on her lap and trim her claws without complaint; Pumpkin arrives everywhere mouth open, looking to bite. I watch him fall asleep with his mouth completely open, mid-chomp on Chaya's face. Amid the cacophony I sit grinning widely, pleased to be in their growing world. It is an unmatched pleasure to be the subject of a four-week-old puppy's gaze, or even mouth—even though I know not to take it personally. They are equal-opportunity agreeable, including to a ten-year-old boy whose idea of how you might pick up a puppy is different from that of the fifty-year-olds in the room.

• • •

While there has been research into exactly what to try to teach or introduce puppies to at this age, the researchers could take a cue from attending to what they naturally do. Finally able to maintain their own body temperature at a canine-normal 101.5 degrees, the puppies do not have to stay huddled with one another all the time. So they are exploring, taking advantage of their rapidly improving sensorium and ambulation to introduce themselves to new things. With perception comes movement, and with movement comes contact with the world. Each week the puppies' world expands. While it is just wrong to say, as scientists used to, that puppies do not explore until four weeks of age, the ferocity of their exploration has ramped up. Two weeks ago it was still mostly restricted to the distance between the puppy pile and their mother; last week it was the far reaches of their pen; this week it is creatures coming into their pen, some of whom purr or emit a fog of smelly sounds from their mouths. This week the world includes things that are above their heads, things they can move into or grab hold of. The essence of life is movement: on a small scale, within their bodies, neural connections are forming, routines of sensation and ac-tion gelling. In human babies and in dog puppies, there is rampant generation of neurons in the first several weeks of life—even though many of those neurons will be pruned with more brain growth. And there is movement on a grand scale: their bodies' movement in space. This week the puppies were learning not just "to" but "into," "above," "through." By moving, they are learning the size and extent of their bodies, the results of their mouthing and pawing, the feel of different substances underfoot.

And these are just the things that puppies should be introduced to at this time: the pieces of their lives to be. The sounds they will hear: of nature and of human society. We all talk to the puppies, helpfully introducing them to our speech sounds—but we are also introducing them to the sounds of our movement, and the sounds of the objects we make, from radios that squawk, to chairs that screech on the floor, to vehicles whose engines roar abruptly. The animal and people smells they will smell—everything from the cleaner with which we wash the floor, to the food we will provide them, to human body odor. The feelings they will feel—including, most critically, people touching them, petting them, picking them up, grabbing their tails or paws. Having their nails trimmed is a dozen experiences at once: being held in place, on their backs, pressed up against a person; the stretch of each toe away from the other, the sharp smell and sound of the clippers, the rippling sensation radiating into their toes from the snip. Someone is squeezing their paws—likely the first time anyone has grabbed their feet—and cooing, talking, exhaling *at* them, inches from their face. After this immersion, a young pup probably needs a little nap.

With open eyes they have spent the last weeks starting to focus their gaze. Part of the reason the puppies may not have been terribly keen on the dog toys in their pen is that they are just developing depth perception, which allows them to integrate information from each eye into a three-dimensional form. Without depth perception, it is hard to grab at anything at all: the world may be rich with colors and light, but it is flat. In child development, the transformation of vision from two- to three-dimensional is tested with the "visual cliff" experiment, designed in the 1960s. In this experiment infants are placed on a specially designed glass tabletop with a checkered tablecloth directly beneath the glass—on one half of the table. But at the farther end of the tabletop the checked cloth is actually on the floor below, creating the illusion of a four-foot drop. The question posed to these young humans is whether they should cross over the apparent cliff to reach their mothers, who are standing tantalizingly on the other side of it.* The youngest infants tested crawl right over, oblivious to the seeming danger; at around eight months of age they pass the test, displaying reluctance to go over the cliff. This shows they can finally see the cliff, both eyes working together to create the perception of depth. But they also perform best on the test once they have had more than a few weeks of experience crawling: they not only need depth perception but also some time locomoting. Puppies are much speedier to get moving than babies, so they can be—and have been—tested on the visual cliff table at a much earlier age. One group of six beagle puppies spent time from their nineteenth to twenty-eighth day of life being brought to one of these tables, placed right at the edge of the cliff, and allowed to choose which side to amble across. At nineteen days old they chose randomly, cavalierly wandering over the looming cliffside. But by twenty-seven days they suddenly perceived the potential danger, and all headed for the safe side. Puppies may tremble, squeal, and back away from the edge, but few venture over to the deep end: they have excellent depth perception.

Notably, if you put *all* the puppies on the visual cliff tabletop, you would likely get either a bunch of cliff jumpers or a bunch of rump-sitters: where one pup goes, the others are likely to follow. Siblings are now one another's biggest teachers. Much of their group exploratory behavior happens because one pup sniffs this, digs that, picks up this other thing—and her siblings do what she does. This "social facilitation" enables them to find safe foods to eat and figure out what is

---

*In some more recent work, researchers have made the apparent cliff real by taking away the glass tabletop on the cliff side—with an experimenter nearby to swoop up any unconcerned cliff jumpers.

chewable, benefiting from their brother's or sister's experience. Just as their digestive systems are maturing, and they can defecate more intentionally, Amy has put a large tray, similar to a cat's litter box, by the activity pen. While many puppies walk around it, or just trounce through it heedlessly, some stop and use it. When one does, others are drawn to the scene, and sometimes use it, too. Ta-da: housebreaking, step one.

Human infants of four weeks are in a much different boat. Rather, out of the boat and on the shore: of his month-old daughter, developmental psychologist Charles Fernyhough wrote that she was "really still a beached fetus." The month-old baby still has a head that is giant relative to their body. With such a big head, gravity easily wins in a matchup with the baby's rudimentary musculature. If propped in a seated position, their head flops forward or back. By this age a baby lying on their stomach may be able to hold their chin off the floor. That's about it. To give a sense of the scale of the difference in motor development: while the pups have begun aiming in a direction and coordinating limbs and mouth to reach an object and investigate, infants have advanced from the simple suck-and-swallow newborn pattern to . . . *several* sucks before one swallow. Infants are months from being able to push themselves up, roll over, or sit up on their own—let alone ambulate across the room. Where the puppies' world is movement, the babies' world is still quite in one place. The puppies are wandering and wagging, the babies just managing their first true smile.

The pups' wagging tails are in fact a major advancement. They are using them actively for the first time: a fifth appendage, projecting backward ramrod straight as they navigate a lumpy mattress, is exceptionally useful in providing balance. Shortly, the tail wag will be a useful signal to other dogs, expressive of emotion and intent. Naturally short-tailed pups, with only six tail bones, use their tails to communicate just as the twenty-three-boned long-tailed dogs will. As for us tailless bipeds: it is hypothesized that just *seeing* a puppy tail is rewarding for humans. I know a wagging tail can change my mood. *Why don't humans have tails?* I wonder, watching a puppy's black tail, dipped in white and curling at the end, quiver as she pokes her head into my jacket pocket. A certain sign of dogs' evolution past humans.

• • •

One-month-old working dogs are developing in just the same way. The V litter, destined to be hero dogs in their future, are snoring on a soft blanket when Jenny Essler, a researcher from the Working Dog Center, arrives. She tries to rouse them: "Hi puppies! What are you doing? Pup-pup-pup-puppy!" Yellow stirs, distinguishing herself from the mass of puppy faces and rumps. Today Jenny is checking in on them before their training begins in earnest next week. She has brought what she describes as "random things for them to start climbing and to feel weird things under their feet," and catnip toys for them to try to track—the professional analog to the smelly Q-tips I brought to the puppies last week. "They are tracking it with the smell way more than with their eyes at this age," she explains.

Each puppy is awakened by being lifted out of their pen. Placed on a blanket, the pups yawn lazily as they take stock of the situation. Jenny is waving the catnip toy in front of their faces. They are slow to track it. Yellow looks blankly in its direction and stumbles toward it after a long delay. Another experienced trainer, Dana Ebbecke, brings out a camera and squeaks a toy to get the pup's attention; she is not rewarded with her attention. Blue is a little more interested in the toy, starting to grab at it . . . before losing focus. Red struggles forward, making whimper-gurgly sounds. The trainers offer a stream of reassurances and commendations—*Good girl! You're up! Look at your paws! You're down! Helooooo! Bop-bop-bop-bop-bop! Hey, good morning!* Jenny tells me that when they interview intern candidates at the WDC they ask, *Can you be silly?* because you can't be straight-faced in training dogs. The sounds and calls the trainers emit are possibly even more enthusiastic than those I aimed toward my own infant son.

Purple has especially big feet, and a tiny Shar-Pei face, which scrunches up even more as the trainers handle her paws to get her used to the sensation. Having her feet handled is the most modest of the types of situations she is likely to face in her life. As a working dog in training, she may wind up having to navigate over rubble to find human survivors after a building collapse; to pursue the scent of illegal narcotics into treacherous territory; to endure hours of being patient, waiting alone, between episodes of intense work. Many of the working dogs will be put into dangerous situations that most dogs would reasonably avoid. In a way, Jenny says, "we're training really 'stupid' dogs—in that we're training them to do things that are unsafe, that they shouldn't want to do." But they are also training them to trust the humans who bring them to those places, who will not send their dogs in to do something that they are not prepared to do. And that trust begins now, on the floor in Bryn Mawr, with Jenny on her hands and knees, gazing into a puppy face gazing back at her, and cooing.

Mouths with tails

~~~~~~

Teeth of five-week-old puppies are quite sharp. As I step into their pen, multiple puppies attack the human monster who has unexpectedly appeared in their midst by climbing on and biting all her parts. The pant leg, the snap of a jacket, the hair untucked around an ear. The end of my sleeve, the middle of my sleeve, a button on my sleeve. Toe of shoe, heel of shoe, shoelaces (a special delicacy). They bite the air around me, an invisible image of me extending two inches in all directions. No one got my nose, but that was because of many high-speed maneuvers performed under fire that kept some small portion of me unbitten.

They aim their mouths toward anything new or near, so each movement I make is a mouth-attractant. As I reach to pet Pumpkin, he nips my hand. As I lean in to coo at Persimmons, she bites at my mouth. I pretzel my legs in sitting, and Cranberry dives into that negative space and chews her way out from under my leg. Fiddlehead climbs my shirt and finds an earlobe. Thank you, Fiddlehead, for nibbling. I begin to feel defined by the parts that have been felt up by a puppy mouth.

For young dogs, as for young humans, the mouth is the first organ of exploration: the way they discover what's what, who's who, and what what's made of. For parents of toddlers, this means making their world safe for mouth-creatures: covering open outlets, putting away any objects—marbles, Lego, pennies—that could fit in a young mouth until they grow out of this stage of development. For parents of toddling puppies, this means making their world safe for mouth-creatures *forever*. They never stop being mouth creatures.

The resident cat steps into the pen with me, and I no longer am a person of interest; the puppies aim their mouths cat-ward. Watching them, I try to imagine going through life mouth first. It is alarmingly intimate. I can stand at quite a distance from a spectacle and view it through my eyes, or keep an appropriate distance from a sound as I tune my ears to hear it—but if you explore by mouth, you have to not only approach the thing, you must *put your mouth on it*. It is as if to see an object we had to run at it, eyes wide, and make unflinching contact, smushing it into our eyeballs.

The pups, of course, have no compunctions about the smush. For those of us with more reluctance about being explored by mouth, it is easy enough to proffer a tiny toy to the mouth aiming for a hand. The dog toys have reached the pups' consciousness this week. Pawpaw comes upon a ball and starts kicking it to himself. Acorn and Flint are doing their best to dismantle the activity gym by pulling on the toys until they snap. Blue Camas takes to a miniature rope pull toy, dragging it around proudly by a single thread, and then spiritedly playing tug with me. It's very doglike. When Maize appears by my shoulder and pokes her head over the side of the pen, three puppies leap toward her, licking at her mouth. One turns around and finds my mouth, too, getting in a couple of quick licks as I sputter in surprise.

In body and behavior, the puppies seem much older than a week ago. They are chunky bunnies, pushing their way through the air and anything in the air in their way. All of their tails are wagging. Everyone's ear flaps are floppy, and their eyes are transitioning out of blue. Most of their noses have gone from pink, through splotchy, to all black. The biggest pups have been caught up to, though the littlest still looks almost like a different species. Pawpaw has grown into the rolls on his face, but when Pumpkin or Cranberry lies down, you can see the extra skin just hanging off them. Acorn has a few sprouts beginning on his chin that might be "furnishings"—longer strands of hair growing around the eyebrows and muzzle. As she did last week, Blue Camas heads for me and walks into my lap, burrowing her head in the crook of my elbow. This calmness lasts for about four seconds, as Pumpkin roughly tries to rouse her into play, and she tells him off with a cat-like paw to the face.

At this age their ear canals are fully open. Finally the whispers and echoes haunting them have begun to transform into meaningful sounds. Heads turn at a distant clatter. They use sounds with one another: squeaking at the biter of their snout, the stepper on their tail. A few are working on a pretty serious bark. I brought a squeaking toy with me, a long purple tube which I bring alive with a pinch. It has the effect of bringing a moment of stillness and alert to ten puppies. All but Cranberry. She is a pretty good producer of sounds herself—indeed, the most continual vocalizer of the group, whining regularly. But it appears that she is not receiving any word back. Amy was the first to think that Cranberry might be deaf. To look at her, one might guess she would be deaf. She is fully white, her eyes still more blue than the others. As unlikely as it might seem, there is a genetic connection between her eye and fur color and her ears: the absence of the pigment-producing cells can lead to the underdevelopment or death of sensory cells in the ear.

Wild Ramps heads for the corner of the room, where she handily pushes herself through a doggy door, a small outlet cut into the house's back door with a movable flap that allows dog-size animals to push their way in or out. Outside! Just yesterday was the first day Amy let them out the back door onto a deck. Now the door flaps again and again as the puppies follow her; the whole lot exits, then enters, then exits. They are functioning as a gentle scrum, albeit one that is loosening at the edges. As they change attitudes and activities, no one is left behind; they do not notice or care about the differences in size or senses that are bubbling up. They seem bound together by invisible threads, not yet *in* the world as much as they, together, *are* their own world. In and out, active and calm, bouncing between binaries: chase a ball, then thoughtfully mouth a squeaky toy; run like mad, then curl up in a lap. An action or idea or mood that strikes one ripples among the rest. And so as Wild Ramps, while masticating a toy, tumbles into sleep, suddenly nearly all the pups follow. As though a sleeping sickness has swept the pen, within a minute nearly all are head-to-tail-to-tail in a circle on a soft bed, asleep. One final puppy, Cholla Cactus, steps into the center and relaxes his muscles into the heap. Every little bunny shakes and twitches in their dreams. Their lips curl, their cheeks puff with dream-barks. Even in dreaming, though, they are alert to the world: when a dog barks nearby or a door opens, all but one lift their heads immediately.

●   .   ●   ●

Though they are still very puppyish, at this age they have taken another step in growing out of puppyhood: they are mostly weaned off their mother's milk. Her milk production peaked last week, at about a liter a day, or a little more than a third of a cup per pup (who themselves fit *into* a cup not so long ago). Living in human households, dog moms are free to wean at this age because there is a nearby person to take over feeding. For a few weeks Amy has been diligently introducing the puppies to a highly aromatic, very soft wet food, and also giving Maize time alone, away from the puppies. Remarkably, something similar occurs among dogs not living in human households.

What we might think of as a "stray" dog, or a dog without a home, is generally considered a "free-ranging" dog if they in fact live their lives without a human home. This is not to say without humans: free-ranging dogs live around humans, usually in well-populated areas, since they rely on the resources accidentally or intentionally provided by people in the form of trash or leftovers. They live in small social groups, described as "loosely structured"—meaning individual dogs may come and go—but they do form long-term relationships. Researchers observing free-ranging mother dogs in West Bengal, India, found that after the third week of their puppies' life, lactating mothers begin to wean, and their female relations—grandmothers, aunts, and sisters—take over some of the care of the pups. These "allomothers" actually nurse the pups, as well as regurgitate food for them to eat, and generally keep an eye out that no pup wanders off or goes hungry. Some of these allomothers have their own litters, and are sharing a little of their extra milk; others seem to spontaneously produce milk. (The occasional male contributes with his own regurgitation.) Not only does this cooperation allow mothers to start to leave the dens for longer periods to search for food themselves, it helps the litters survive. Survival is not assured: in the groups observed by the researchers in India, fewer than half of the puppies in most litters survived to thirteen weeks of age. This is similar to survival rates for dogs' cousins, wolves: about 30 percent survive to a year, and it is not uncommon for none of the members of a litter to survive. Similarly, each spring, female gray wolves who have reached sexual maturity either become pregnant or may experience a pseudopregnancy, in which their body reacts as though pregnant. A pseudopregnancy can even include lactation—possibly useful in the same way that the free-ranging aunties' nursing is: to help raise community pups to maturity.

The pups who leapt at Maize's mouth, licking and mewling plaintively—these pups were instinctively requesting that she, no longer providing food from her nipples, might provide it from her mouth.

A straight line can be drawn from this puppy request for mom to re-gurgitate a snack to the adult dog jumping up and licking a human face. Once a request, later a greeting; always happy with whatever comes out. Similarly, the dog who pees when excitedly saying hello to their person has not outgrown the early connection between the ap-pearance of mom and the operation of their bladder (whose contents she initially cleaned up).

Not only does a change in diet begin to challenge their digestive systems, it provides a good primer in dog social cues. For when the puppies try to nurse now, their mother often scolds them—biting gently, growling, baring her teeth, generally telling them to skedaddle. But what a lesson! Mom is gently kicking them to the next level of maturity, using some of the same communications that they are sure to encounter as they bumble through the world of Other Dogs. Pups do learn to, in fact, skedaddle, or show submissive, appeasing behav-ior, such as licking, or rolling on their backs—or the scolding gets sharper.

Interaction with their littermates has escalated, providing constant social feedback as well. As they have grown more distant from mom, they have begun to see their siblings not just as sleep buddies but as playmates and mentors—imitating their new play moves and follow-ing them into new places and situations. The pups stalk and swoop and pounce on one another—vestiges of a predatory sequence, re-hearsed in play. Social play is the context for rapid learning about how to interact with others and discover their bodies' strengths and abilities, even one another's minds. Two puppies playing together co-operatively are executing a complex dance, rapidly matching and re-sponding to behaviors. They bite, but softly: siblings continue to be good practice for learning an inhibited bite. Pups weaned too early tend to be less skilled at this, and their siblings tell them so.

As the puppy pile evolves into a puppy scrum, and they begin to follow each other to new sights, sounds, and smells, any fear they have of this or that thing can be buoyed or diffused by the reaction of the other puppies. Faced with a scary sight—like, say, a large man with a big hat—if one puppy toddles gaily toward him, the others often follow. They do not follow any pup next to them blindly. They know who their siblings are. Five-week-olds placed in a cage with their siblings or what researchers called "alien pups" (here just meaning nonsiblings, not extraterrestrial pups) reliably approach their siblings first. With one exception: red setter pups were just exuberantly excited in all directions, and did something more like "running manically around" than "approaching puppies carefully."

Now that they are using them less often to nurse, their mouths are even freer to explore the environment. While babies are known for putting objects in their mouths, puppies are putting their mouths on objects. They are not trying to eat everything; they are trying to see everything. Perceiving an object depends not just on what it looks, smells, or feels like, but also on how one can interact with it—an idea introduced by the influential psychologist James Gibson. Since puppies interact with many objects by using their mouths, they are literally seeing objects as mouthable. Researchers put very willing dogs—including pups named Daisy, Ollie, and Truffles—in MRI scanners and showed them pictures or short video clips of objects (like a lime-green toy) that they had previously been trained either to mouth or to paw. If it was an object they had held in their mouths, a specific part of the brain that processes and identifies objects was much more active. So was the somatosensory cortex, which anticipates actions— suggesting that part of the very way dogs think about objects is, "Can I fit it in my mouth?"

Puppy brains are responding to what researchers call the "action-ability" of the object: not just what it is, but how they will interact with it. Just as humans have brain cells that map to actions of each finger and other specific parts of our body—sometimes called a "cortical homunculus"—so dogs might have a kind of "canunculus," with brain cells for paw actions, nose actions, and mouth actions.

The puppies' brains are rapidly maturing: with all their senses now up and running, connections are forged between sensory areas of the brain and areas involved in not just movements, but also emotions. Each new physical development brings secondary effects. With fully working ears, puppies can be startled by a new category of things—loud, unusual, or surprising noises—and some even develop new fears. This is the time, indeed, when phobias—or what are called "fear responses"—to a category of object, or a context, might pop up. People are one of those object categories. Puppies who do not see and interact with humans from this age through the end of the socialization period can acquire a lasting wariness of people. While not impossible to overcome later, such mistrust could be completely averted by simply having friendly and gentle humans mixing it up with them when the puppies are young. It is as though the puppies' systems are particularly raw and sensitive now: everything that happens draws a deep groove in their psyches, one that is long-lasting. Ideally, this is the age at which dogs are gradually exposed to a growing number and diversity of phenomena in order to avoid any fearful grooves.

This is exactly why the V litter trainers arrive this week and the next with a metal cookie sheet, a wet towel, and an Altoids tin half-full of pennies. The puppies attend to their arrival with excitement. They still wear their colored collars to help distinguish them, but they have also been named: Vita, Villa, Vig, Victoria, Vega, Vaz, Vara, Vauk. Taking advantage of the puppies' increasing coordination between what they see and where they go, the trainers flit a toy in front of Purple's—now Vaz's—face, reminiscent of a parent shaking a rattle in front of her baby. While the baby is being encouraged just to follow the sound with her eyes, the pups are full-on pursuing it—well, when they are awake. Vaz groggily tracks the toy, sniffing nonstop in a slow-motion pursuit. She stretches her neck as far as she can without moving her rump, but eventually gets up. She is led onto the cookie sheet, covered with a wet towel to keep her from slipping. They lead her back and forth without a hiccup. For the trainers it is a success, exposing her to a weird texture and sensation; for Vaz, it is just the way the world is.

When not being led around on cookie sheets, the puppies are mostly sleeping. Occasionally we can hear complaints from the peanut gallery, spy a tiny mouth working at the crate bars, or a little tongue darting out. Awakened for testing, all of them do enviable full-body stretches, scooching on their bellies until the tips of their front claws and back ones are maximally distant from each other. "Hello! Welcome to the day," Jenny offers. The trainers bring out each puppy in turn, showing them the pull toy and a rattly tin; every one of them is able to track the moving toy and pursue it. Some bite it, some sniff and chase it, walking gamely back and forth along the tray. Victoria (Red) shakes the toy with enough vigor that she knocks herself completely over. As she steps onto the tray in pursuit, the trainers erupt in gentle excitement. *Whoa! Puppy, that's it! You got it! Wow, good job! Yes, kill it!* One by one, the pups grow weary and curl up in a ball to have a nap. Just as with Maize's litter, when they decide on sleep they are deeply committed to it. They can be roused again, but it is clearly the time of some important growth.

The next week's testing advances the challenges the slightest bit. The trainers toss a rattle tin can at the pups, tease them with a cat toy on the end of a pole, and stick them up on a wobbly tabletop to see how they react. Jenny voices her assessments of each one. *You're a funny one . . . Not the best grip, but she's got spunk . . . She's got a good grip: you might get puppy of the day.* Vaz is wide awake this week, her tail wagging like crazy. She grabs the cat toy and shakes her head forcefully to tear it apart. *You're a little scoundrel, aren't you.*

Vauk (Green) follows the rattle can, nimbly mouths it, and walks off with it.

The trainers unfold the aluminum legs of a small table with a latticed, slippery-looking wood surface. It is just the right amount of wobbly when set up. Each pup will be placed atop it, encouraged with a handful of food. This is not training for kitchen table leaping; it is to help them get used to unstable surfaces, such as dogs might encounter working in the field. Moreover, at this point they are not training the pups at all; they are simply exposing them to new sensations. Individual differences are on display. When one pup panics, freezing in place, they simply lift her off. Vaz peers with interest off the side, and chews on the trainer's sleeves, but stands cooperatively still. When previously confronted with unsteady surfaces, Vara (Yellow) panicked, her body shaking hard enough to shake the surface; this time she sniffs the tabletop, scoots backward in a little moonwalk, then relaxes into nosing the handful of food being offered. Vauk sits right down and looks around idly, her tail wagging gently. *The bravest puppy ever! Yes, you are.*

Little bruisers

Meeting eleven six-week-old puppies is a protracted exercise in replacing your body parts with a dog toy in their mouths. Sit, and several dive for the new lap, find the hole in the crook of your arm, figure out how to unzip your jacket and burrow in. Being overtaken with puppies is like being tickled: right on the edge between delicious and terrifying. The physicality of their closeness is pleasingly unavoidable. They have no sense of personal space, no feeling that we shouldn't be in contact with each other in every possible way. The very silky coats of the young puppies have started to roughen on some, but many are still beautifully soft. They smell sharp: both mildly sour, like milk that has gone bad, and feral, like the smell you just catch in the forest of a wolf who has passed the night before. I can't help but smell them, of course, because when I sit, they are immediately in my face. They head for my mouth and nose. I have had puppies chew my curls.

This is what I expect when entering the House of Puppies. Instead, today I hear the disconcerting sound of a complete absence of puppies. It is a roar of silence—exactly like what you hear in a home you are moving out of as you look around one last time before closing the door: this is where life used to resound. Now the only sound is of my own movement and breath, my footfalls echoing brightly without the presences that made it home.

The spell is broken by a chorus of barks coming from the large meadow behind Amy's house. I hurry to the back door and see the puppies outside, in a smaller fenced area. They are milling around, poking their noses into the wind. This is the first time I have seen them all outdoors: their smallness in the natural world is surprising. Even while small, they are beautifully tubby, balled socks of puppies. Little bruisers. They have grown into their skin, and personalities are popping into their visages. Chaya has a gentle, sweet face, reminiscent of a piglet. Cranberry, who has a blue sparkle remaining in her eye, has an earnest, mole-in-the-wind look, eyes at half-mast as though blind instead of deaf. The spotted dogs are distinguishing themselves from one another: Flint has a becoming look, with a broad white flash down his forehead between his eyes, and one black eye; Pawpaw has two black eyes, giant ears, and is growing a beard. Sexual dimorphism has begun in earnest: all the girls are smaller than the boys. A dark patch of fur streaks under Persimmons's eyes—an imperfectly done but playful eye shadow application. Wild Ramps is distinctively black and white and tan and impish-looking.

I have brought both of my other family members along this time, wanting to let them in on the full puppy experience. They should have been coming with me all along, I realize: it's the type of encounter they both enjoy completely, while my approach is to slip analysis and apprehension into everything. My husband, A., is the kind of fellow who stops to talk to every dog on the sidewalk, often kneeling to vigorously pet them and let them snuffle into his face and hair. For his part, O. delights in warning A. about puppy teeth and puppy claws and puppies-all-up-in-your-face—while willingly lying down to subject himself to their attack.

A. steps into the pen first, and the promised full-puppy experience is immediate. Even as he swings his leg over the fence he is mobbed with puppies, a magnet to whom they are uncontrollably attracted.

They zoom to his ankles and clamber over one another to get to his shins and knees. As he tentatively moves forward, these iron filings move with him. When O. steps in, his own magnetism draws the closest ones over: puppies as twirling, biting iron filings, piling on one another to reach higher on his body.

Distinctive personalities are on full display now. There is the puppy who is always first to get napping, the one who cries a lot, one who pursues small flying insects, another who will hold on to the rope tug toy put in his mouth. And there are behaviors that are consistent across all puppies. None hesitates at the new feeling of dirt and grass on their soft pink toe pads—although only a few realize dirt's property of digability. Amy has put out various new objects, including a small flexible tunnel and a doghouse. These things do not register with the pups at all; they walk by them with nary a glance. But a tarp placed over a hole in the fence and flapping in the breeze draws several of the pups near and inspires a brand-new, freshly minted bark from one of them—more "bark" than bark. Movement captures their interest; peculiarly, most objects made to entertain dogs are still.

As completely enraptured as they seem to be by the flapping tarp and human magnets, when Amy pulls out what looks like a fishing rod with a squirrel dangling from it, everyone abandons us. It is a "flirt pole," just as teasing as the name suggests: a lightweight rod with a clump of synthetic fur attached by a string off one end. Amy whips the pole around neatly and begins fishing for puppies. She catches four straightaway and they hold on tight, marching with the fur in their mouths like toy soldiers.

In one corner of the yard Amy has put out another object not strictly designed for pups. It is a cube of plastic the height of a toddler (its intended audience), with stairs on one side and a slide on the other. As O. and I approach it, the puppies follow us. Though its function is clear to us, none of the puppies seems to see it as something to interact with, just an obstacle. They sniff it, run around it, pee by it. So we do what comes naturally: we point at the stairs to show these little kids how to play with their new toy. *What's that, Blue? Chaya, look at this!* Chaya looks where we point, and a few other puppies look where she looks, but no climbing ensues. Someone places Acorn on the top. Once up there he spontaneously and cooperatively slides down, nails skidding on the surface, as though he has been sliding all his life. O. lifts Persimmons to the same spot, and she freezes in place, neither sliding nor stepping off; he promptly lifts her back to the ground. She is not yet ready for the version of the visual cliff experiment where there is a slippery slide to carry you off the cliff.

At one point I stand in the middle of the yard to take in the scene. These little creatures, still so new, are exploding into the world. I see Cholla Cactus making a project of rearranging a pile of straw. I can now observe the heaviness of the doggy door as puppies pass through it: they need to push hard to move the flap with their weight. I watch as Cranberry misjudges which part of the house has the door: she throws herself first against the siding, then against the door in which the doggy door is set. When Pumpkin suddenly emerges through the door and gallops off, Cranberry watches him, puzzled, then figures it out. Fiddlehead separates herself from her siblings and is prancing along the fence with one of the Border collies, who looks desperate to herd these misbegotten sheep. Suddenly Fiddlehead whips out a play bow, the first of any of the pups; the Border collie fails to respond, but Acorn runs right up to and into her, and they begin to play.

We stay for hours, enough time to see the puppies cycle through two rounds of high activity and sudden collapse into sleep. When O. sits on the ground, six puppies beeline to him and fall asleep on his lap and one another; he must keep his arms in a wide embrace to support their heavy heads. As I approach him quietly, not wanting to disturb his lapful, I hear a low murmuring sound. Suddenly I realize the source of the sound. It is the puppies, grunting contentedly as they exhale into sleep.

In the car on departure two of us put our heads together and close our eyes, making puppy noises in sleep.

• • •

Scientists recently got interested in dogs not because of their wagging tails or sweet smell, but because of their skill at social cognition— that is, their ability to learn from others to solve problems. One of the very first studies in the field now described as "dog cognition" aimed to see what adult pet dogs would do when a nearby human pointed to an overturned cup. For fellow humans, it is obvious what to do if faced with a scenario like this: look at the cup. It is so obvious that we do not even think about it; we just look. Depending on our motivation and curiosity, we might then approach the cup, look under the cup; if there is nothing there, we get that pointing human to explain themselves. Human babies of ten months can at least do the looking, earlier than they can go over to the cup on their own: their brains work faster than the coordination of their muscles develops.

The task for the dogs in that study is to try to find a bit of hidden food. Every dog person knows that dogs can locate the tiniest crumb in a deep jacket pocket, so the question is not *if* they can find it. The question is if they can find it *our* way—by looking to others for clues. And, mostly, the dogs do: they will follow that point, knock over that cup, and gobble up whatever is underneath. In fact, at a certain age they will follow a person's guidance on which of two overturned cups has a treat underneath even over the advice of their own noses. Given how often people point at things and how seldom they encourage dogs to smell things out (or to smell at all), this makes sense: living with us, we want them to follow our cues about where and what to eat, not just hunt through the house for every fallen crumb.

It turns out that this tendency to follow a human's pointing is not just a brilliant strategy if a dog lives with humans—it comes built-in to the dog. In one study, nearly 80 percent of six-week-old puppies were already able to follow a point to find which of two cups had a hidden treat. Even more could figure it out when a person placed a special marker on one of the cups, serving as an identifying clue.

This is what dogs are now famous for in the world of comparative psychology: being excellent readers of human gestures. Pointing is a fairly abstract notion—the direction of the finger is sending information about something of interest some distance away from the finger—but one that is an early and crucial step in human development. It is through following pointing, and then pointing themselves, that babies begin to communicate with the mysterious adults in their universe, making them less mysterious to us and us less mysterious to them.

By this age, puppies in most contexts will have had at least minimal exposure to people. While there are dogs who are "pointers," dogs do not generally point. So puppies' success at reading a completely different species' gesture as a form of communication is impressive, and indicates that the ability is heritable—genetic. They get better at point-following over time and can even follow brief point gestures, finger-only points, points across the body and in other odd arrangements—demonstrating that experience helps, too.

But there is another major cognitive leap that the puppies have made this week that is folded into the pointing study. When researchers put a treat under a cup, they are banking on the notion that puppies already understand something about how the world works. One of the earliest studies to look at the development of this simple cognitive ability in puppies recruited seventy dogs, sixty-nine of whom were terriers and one who was not. Anyone who has lived with, met, or been passed on the sidewalk by a Jack Russell or Airedale terrier certainly knows that they may not represent typical behavior of all dog breeds. Their sometimes overwhelming enthusiasms, however—for life in general and for the smallest things—may have made them useful participants in these studies, which require that dogs be very much present and engaged. God help the one non-terrier.

The researchers were looking at what is called "object permanence," which is more or less what it sounds like: an understanding that objects of all sorts continue to exist even when you cannot see them. It is a useful understanding to have, living as we do in a world of objects, but it is not an ability that we seem to have when we are born. When young humans and other animals first come into the world, they experience a fluid, shifting landscape, in which objects not only disappear when they go out of sight or "out of smell," they also lack properties that will come to be familiar: three-dimensionality, some degree of solidity, and persistence through space and time.

One of Jean Piaget's significant contributions to our current knowledge of how the child's brain begins to power up was to introduce the idea that the permanence of objects is not self-evident but *learned*. Piaget suggested that infants don't grok this concept until they are eight or nine months old—and even then, they still make mistakes. By that age, they become more or less able to find, say, a toy car if you show it to them and then put it under a piece of fabric directly in front of them. A small step for baby, but a giant leap for baby's brain. But if you hide the toy again and again, then switch it up, hiding it under another piece of fabric—while the baby watches—they perseverate, and look for the car in the original hiding spot. This is called the "A-not-B" error and is very sweet to see on display. Just as the baby seems to be mastering the world, her quite incomplete appreciation of what happens to objects outside her sight comes shining through.

Some researchers claim that babies begin to understand object permanence earlier—as early as three and a half months. That's because if something is hidden and seems to disappear, they stare long and hard at where it used to be. In all events, it will be several months into their lives before baby humans know this simple fact about objects: they exist even when you no longer see them.

Six-week-old puppies? They get it. One day in those terriers' (and one non-terrier's) lives, a couple of friendly humans played with them in a very specific way: they brought out a squeaky toy, attached to a long nylon thread—just like Amy's flirt pole—and dangled it in front of the pups. Then, with one of the pair holding onto the pup, the other marched the toy right behind a box. At five weeks the pups seem to think that the toy has left this earth. They do not search for it, just show the confused-puppy look that prompts humans everywhere to utter, "Ooh, puppy!" But in their sixth week of life, they pass the test: first running for the toy as they see it disappearing behind the box, and then searching for it after it has completely disappeared. They know that things should remain where they were left—even when they cannot be seen. Henceforth, take note of where your dog buries a bone/toy/particularly good stick in a yard or on a walk: they will search for it there when you pass by the site again. At this age the human baby is just starting to focus on the bars of her crib and the bright patch of sun on the wall.

In addition to their cognitive prowess, Maize's puppies are also showing something harder to see in science, where subjects' data gets summed and averaged: the importance of individual differences. There is no "average Maize puppy"; every pup is already toddling their own path. Some like to go down slides, some do not; for some, going through a dog door is simple, while others find it challenging to even locate the door. While science looks for the characteristics dogs have in common, what may be most interesting are their differences.

Adventure pups

W e're going on an adventure!" Amy announces, recalling Christopher Robin heading out with Winnie-the-Pooh and Piglet. The puppies all tumble out of the dog door onto the deck. For the first time, the dogs are going into the Big Yard. The Big Yard is acres of rolling land, mud piles, and a pond. It is bigger than the puppies' imagination; it is the other side of the moon. We use our highest puppy voices as we lead the way out into this fourth dimension. "Pup pup pup pup! Puppy Puppp-eeeee!" Two of Amy's adult dogs run circles around us, deftly leaping over the wee ones and taking advantage of the moment I crouch to tie a shoelace to jump on or over me. Most of the pups run after us with the Pooh bravado; the one true, fearful Piglet is Chaya, who, alone among the pups, hangs back by the fence, looking out at the sea of space. The rest rush headlong into it. While now much bigger bruisers, they are quite small in this bigger world. They run in fits and starts, some alone and some in tandem, the larger dogs whipping around them. The smaller ones look admiringly at the doings of the bigger dogs, but when one runs too close, or nips at them, they are quick to dive and roll onto their backs, feet pedaling the air.

We head toward the pond, recently released from winter's grip. Its calm surface is broken by the bellies of three large adult dogs as they launch themselves from the banks. Their activities draw a few of the puppies pond-side: Acorn ventures to the bank, and then Fiddlehead toddles down it. They both look tentatively at the water, small philosophers considering the nature of this new substance. Fiddlehead sticks a paw in, quite by accident, pulls it quickly out, examines it, then places it in again, more gently. It did not do what she thought, and, looking surprised, she retreats. Pawpaw gets both paws in, as befits his name, and stands happily knee-high in pond muck. Other puppies approach the high bank (high to puppies) surrounding the pond, but beat a hasty retreat, rumps in the air and tails fully straight as if pointing their way to safety.

That the outside world comes in not just solid and air, but liquid: it is a new idea for these little brains. At seven weeks old, the workings of their rapidly developing nervous system are visible in their behavior. Their neophilia is what draws them pond-side; their increasing hesitation about new things makes the visit short. While none will jump in the pond, even the shyest will jump on one another—and now will do so not just to climb a nearby person, but for the sheer enjoyment of it. They tackle, mouth, leap, chase, bite, growl at, burrow into, and grab the tail of one another, suddenly perfect puppy players. This is play with no goal in mind, with no winner or loser; it is pure energy in the shape of dog. It is cooperative: even the smaller ones, like Acorn, can stand over a bigger one, like Pawpaw, and bite their paws repeatedly with impunity. Blue Camas makes great play overtures to other puppies—bounding approaches, sweet tiny play bows. Physically they are like oversized toddlers, their bodies too big for their little legs, their running more hurtling themselves forward than a smooth gallop. I offer Wild Ramps a stick as she ambles by me, and the great game of "see how many puppies can hold on to a foot-long twig" begins. Pumpkin usually winds up the victor in this game, while the others barely know it was competitive.

Maize is out on a long leash, her movement restricted, as she has become increasingly irritable and impatient with her growing social companions. The puppies find her leash extremely tuggable. When they tire of that, they head for her belly, and for what turns out to be the last time I watch them noisily gather in her shade and try to nurse. Only about a half dozen can fit their heads between her limbs. One can see, as they noisily and violently try to suck out any remaining milk, why Maize might be irritable.

When she starts walking she sloughs them off, and they fan out in search of other pastimes. The adult dogs are the source of new fascination. While dwarfed by them, the puppies clearly see the adults as *like* them. This week marks the blossoming of their ability to learn from the older dogs, whose every move models possible behaviors, and whose responses to them are felt deeply and personally. They investigate the pond because the big dogs did; they follow them to an old fire pit, to a gap in the fence. They jump on the dogs as they see them jumping on one another—and when scolded with a snarl, they cry out and fly toward me, tail low.

When a cluster of puppies has followed the big dogs so far that the pups have become mere tiny specks, I call out *Puppy, puppy!*, the instinctive thing to call them, though I feel somewhat ridiculous, knowing they will not perk their ears at the sound of their common name. But to my credit, I call in a high, merry voice, bringing my language close to the sounds they are already making and attuned to. One turns and heads toward me, which brings them all, ears flapping becomingly as their galloping feet hit the ground.

They have much more energy and endurance than even last week, but after an hour they start to circle the wagons. Flint heads toward me as I squat low, giving me a great sleepy wag. Fiddlehead runs to and then under me, having gotten a nip from a passing big dog. In their winding down they cycle through all their climbing and chewing tricks, like infants spiraling with energy before conking out. I get my nose nipped, my finger gnawed; my knees and ankles are as delicious as ever. Many of the puppies are pleased I chose to wear the long sweater today. Long sweaters, apparently, have lots of pullable points. Shortly, several puppies are asleep on my shoes and between my knees. Wild Ramps sits out in the field, back to me, watching the world pass by.

•   •   •

Once puppies start recognizing other dogs as "like them," they gain a great skill: the ability to learn from them. Miniature dachshund puppies as young as twenty-eight days were set up to watch a puppy nearby use a ribbon to pull a small cart with food on it to within mouth reach. While it had taken the original group of puppies many minutes to figure out how to do this, after watching the demonstration the observing puppies solved it quickly—some within five seconds. By seven or eight weeks of age, "social learning" is the multipurpose tool in their cognitive toolbox. Sure, a puppy can find out about the world through assiduous exploration, or through trial and error; but the speedier method is to watch what others are doing and try it themselves. I see this in the Big Yard, where the older dogs' mere presence draws the pups to the pond; I can see this in their play together, when an adult gently chides an over-enthusiastic puppy, or a sibling bites a biter back. They learn moves in play: play bows pop up after being play-bowed at; a chased dog learns to be the chaser. This transmission of information about how to engage with the world—about how to be a dog—can be vertical (from parents), oblique (from unrelated adults), or horizontal (from peers).

Social learning has been researched in adult dogs, and there is plenty of evidence now that dogs not only can imitate others' actions, but can understand the idea of imitation generally. Researchers in

Hungary have demonstrated that dogs can learn to "do as I do"—to repeat *any (reproducible) action* that a person demonstrates. Training might start with teaching a dog to follow simple bodily actions—lying down; touching a hand (paw) to a box—done by a person. Once the dog has the gist, the human demonstrator can then try a completely novel action, like opening a book, or pulling a wagon. Dogs who have learned to generally "do as someone has done" will come up with some way to open the book and pull the wagon themselves.

What of puppies, though, who have much less experience with others, and who are not in any sense trained? Before knowing what imitation is, they show signs of being able to imitate. One study tested the behavior of Italian and Hungarian puppies of this age on opening a "puzzle box"—simply a closed box that requires some manipulation to open. These puppies were confronted with two puzzle boxes: neither was especially challenging, to a person's eye, but neither was the sort of thing a puppy tends to open on their own. One had a lid that needed to be lifted open; the other had a lid that could be slid to the side. The motivation for figuring out this puzzle of the closed box was that each held delicious, smelly food inside. Researchers trained several adult dogs, including the pups' mother, to open each box to get to the food. One group of pups was set up so that they could watch an adult dog solve each puzzle a couple of times; another group of pups watched a person open the boxes. A control group of puppies had no demonstrations at all, just got to puzzle the problem out themselves.

In the control group the puppies went at the boxes, pawing and chewing and puzzling, but after two minutes, fewer than half had figured out how to get at the food. But in the groups that watched a dog or a person open the box, over twice as many solved the puzzle— most in less than twenty seconds.

The accomplishment of these puppies was not just getting themselves a bit of food. It was showing that, just over a month after becoming able to see at all, they could already interpret others' actions as *about* something. Far from seeing the demonstrations as a string of unrelated behaviors followed by the appearance of food, the puppies saw them as the means to the food: the way to act. And the pups could do one better: they could translate what they observed someone else doing into what they themselves needed to do. Having watched a dog push a lid with their muzzle, observing puppies were more likely to then use their own muzzle; if a demonstrator used a paw, the puppies more often used their own paw. Even if the demonstrator was a person and used a hand—a body part that dogs do not in fact have—puppies figured out the mapping from hand to paw and manipulated the lid with their own paw/hand.

To be sure, no one was asking puppies to imitate something complicated, or purposeless—dance a jig, do the splits. No one was asking a puppy to do something they were not equipped to do—sing a song, trim their own fur. At the same time, the task was not completely simple, nor was it expected that eight-week-olds could spontaneously open boxes. If they could, we would have to come up with much better methods of keeping refrigerators and sock drawers securely closed.

There was one exception to the puppies' imitative abilities: those pups who watched their mothers do the demonstration were able to open the puzzle box only as well as those pups who had not seen a demonstration at all. While a litter's mother is formative in their development not just during gestation but for several weeks after birth, when her pups are nearing two months her role is changing. At around this time lactation is over or rapidly diminishing, and with this the mother's irritability at the pups' sharp-teethed attempts to nurse is rapidly increasing. Pups now receive much more scolding from mom for nursing, for stepping close to her, for making noise. In contrast to the human model of parental involvement not just in early development but clear through their children's moving back home after college, dog moms appear to play little role in their pups' lives after two months. This may be one reason the pups do not see her as one of the kinds of demonstrators—dog or person—to watch carefully.

That said, in one research program, a group of German shepherd puppies who simply were nearby, casually observing, as their mother, a trained drug-detection dog, engaged in searching out narcotics, proved to be much better than naive puppies when later put to the task themselves. Mom is still a general model for how to act, but after a certain age, the puppies' gaze is directed much more at everyone but her.

This beginning of separation of the mother and her pups is seen most profoundly when there is no human around to swoop up the puppies and take them away. In free-ranging dog groups, parents stay with their pups for the first couple of months of their lives: dads guarding the litters from strangers of any species for six or eight weeks, and moms for up to three months. Thereafter, the dogs tend to disperse.

Owned dogs, of course, tend to disperse by being distributed to new owners. Most dogs living with humans will not see their mothers again. But this is not to say that they forget them. When two-year-old dogs, separated from their mothers at eight to twelve weeks of age, were given a choice of two towels to lie on, one of which had the odor of their mom and the other of an unknown dog, they recognized the scent of their mother, spending more time with the mom towel. Similarly, long after litters have scattered, mothers spend more time sniffing the towels impregnated with the scent of their own pups. Scent memories carry them back to those intense first weeks together.

Part of what the puppies perceive when watching other dogs' behavior is what those dogs are smelling or tasting. Dogs who watch another dog looking for food among several boxes greet the searcher by making contact with their snouts, sniffing them to see what the searcher has found. If they smell food, they go investigate the box where they observed the searcher before; if not, they don't bother. Similarly, just the sight of dogs intently sniffing an area of ground will draw nearby pups to sniff there for themselves.

Imitation would seem to be one skill that puppies and infants have in common. Famously, newborn babies imitate an adult who sticks out her tongue at them. While this looks like brilliantly early imitation (of the gesture, not of the usual sentiment behind it), it turns out that this "tongue protrusion" is one of the only expressions they can make voluntarily right after birth. It is a common response to being excited or interested in something. By the age of six weeks, babies have largely stopped imitating this gesture. Infants do not imitate others' actions in the manner that puppies do for several more months. In one study, after watching an adult handle a toy they had never seen, nine-month-olds matched their actions: closing a flap, pushing a button, or shaking an egg-shaped toy. It is only after they are a year old that they imitate reliably, though—and then they often over-imitate: repeating a demonstrated action again and again, well past its usefulness, or even imitating functionless actions, like waving a hand over a box before opening it. The puppies, by contrast, cut right to the chase.

The WDC trainers are not, strictly speaking, training the V litter yet; they are still just exposing them to various noisy and new objects, in the spirit of a generous socialization. As I watch them take every puppy through its paces, I see some of the other puppies, now tall and graceful compared to their puppy selves of just a month ago, doing something new: watching. Typically, the rest of the litter naps, or chews their feet or the bars of their pen, while a sibling is tugging the tug or rattling the rattle. This week, some pay attention to what the others are doing. Vaz spots what Villa is up to and at first jumps and paws to try to get involved; eventually she backs herself up and just sits, taking in the scene. The flirt toy is deployed here by the trainers, too: here, it is a long pole with ribbons of cloth attached to it. Jenny projects it toward Victoria, then dances it in front of her until she catches it and grabs. Victoria's interest is initially fleeting, but then she grabs it tenaciously. The next pup is more sure of what to do after watching her sister. To Vega they shake a ring of a handful of keys and toss it; she bounds after it, grabs it like a small fluttering bird, play-bows at it, then finally pins it with a paw and gnaws. She looks completely satisfied with a toy made of keys, much to the chagrin of any actual puppy-toy makers. The rattle can is now a rattle half-gallon milk bottle with coins in it. It makes a tremendous noise, but all the puppies pursue it happily. Their runs are a series of explosive leaps—a reminder that at this age, the creeping, toddling, and ambling are over; the Maize pups ran to the pond, and the V litter runs toward the trainers.

The trainers talk nonstop to their charges, but this week, less of it is baby talk. Frankly, the dogs do look less like babies. *Hello! Hello, sir!* Jenny coos at the boy, Vig. *Good morning! You're a bulldog. Hi! Hi!* Usually, Jenny says, she sees subtle differences among members of the litters she trains—one pup pulls, another wanders off, some are afraid of walking on a catwalk. Not with this litter, though. Sure, one is extra barky; another is bitey. But all are engaged with people and engage with the toys. In other words, they are perfect budding working dogs.

Your choice of models

Suddenly it is upon us. Driving north on an interstate highway in the bland brightness of a cloudy midday, I am uneasy. I am going to see the puppies, which usually provokes a wash of delight, not unease. But the puppies are eight weeks old, and it is time for them to be adopted into permanent homes.

This means that I am now tasked with turning a different eye on them: a critical eye. By the end of next week, one of the puppies will be going home with us. Instead of swilling in the wash of the energy of eleven puppies, somehow I need to say yes to one, and say no to ten others. How am I supposed to do that? And, moreover, why do I get to do that? The puppies have little choice in the matter, and no foreknowledge of what is going to happen. Over the last few weeks I have felt increasingly on edge around Maize, knowing that soon people will come and take her puppies away one by one.

As I experience with every visit to an animal shelter, I want to take them all. (Hence I visit shelters rarely.) Well, not actually all. Eleven puppies is too many dimensions of puppiness. They are exhausting—the jumping on, the freeing of sleeve and hair from teeth, the calling *pup pup puppy* into the wind. The looking out for them—subconsciously counting all the time, ensuring that there are still eleven, and that no one has found the pond or a hole in the fence.

Even if I harbor no fantasies of adopting all eleven, I hardly want to reject any. The process of adding a dog to one's family is different than birthing a child, where you get what comes out of you. Here the very fact of making a selection feels clinical: treating them as commodities rather than the living creatures they are. Go into a car dealership and you can choose among the colors, choose your model and size; visit a litter of puppies and something not dissimilar happens. I fight the urge to say that I would like a "merle," or a "small" one, or one of the "happy-go-lucky" pups—to decide based on particular features. But the features are there for the seeing, and we tend to reason our way into a choice by weighing them. Rare features—a blue eye, a particularly dark or light coat—distinguish some puppies. A few have sprouted furnishings. While it would be disturbing on an infant, I find a beard especially charming on a puppy. One has a crazed look in her eye; another has eyebrows of worry. While I see each look as a tell about their personality—good or bad—O. and A. are very even-handed about it: they like them all.

As I pull in I see one of Amy's dogs leaping back and forth over a high gate, freeing and then capturing herself. The calico cat is wandering among a small herd of sheep. From behind the house dogs appear and disappear, the larger ones followed dutifully by clusters of puppies. I let myself through the fence and accept my magnetic charge: puppies twirl and jump at me and then race away. Flint takes ahold of the hem of my coat and hangs on for dear life. There is a new cadence to their activity with my arrival: the huge thrill of a new! person! here!, then running-jumping excitement, then they get interested in one another, in tumbling play, then they veer into different sports. There are the early explorers: the archaeologists, digging into earth, examining rocks and mud and leaves with their mouths, tails beating their enthusiasms; the astrophysicists, looking out into the far reaches of their galaxy—beyond the fence, above the deck. There are adventurers, running laps on the slide, trying to scale the side of the house.

And there are the socialites, following the big dogs, curious about the cat and sheep, nudging other pups to chase them.

They have begun diverging more in looks as well: their overall shape is still best described as "roly-poly," with extra folds of skin around their faces and legs, but some are heading more toward gangly; others to pudgy. Some have bristled out of their soft puppy fur and are sporting tufts above the eyes and around the snout, like gentle quills. Their eyes have darkened from blue to a version of brown or hazel, though some retain a splinter of cerulean. Ears flop differently: perked upright; bowing deeply; cast half-mast. If we were to look very closely, we could even see each dog's identifying "noseprint" is distinct, with its own pattern of ovoid shapes fitted together like puzzle pieces. Only their tails are all cut from the same mold: each one half the length of the puppy, ending with a question-mark curl.

I have noticed personality differences, too. Chaya is always a bit shy, less likely to be caught up in the contagion of puppies! running! after! something! we! don't! know! what! Cranberry, so vocal in the first weeks, is now thoughtful, sitting and observing (between gallops). Fiddlehead is an independent player, ready to pace the fence with the big dogs on the other side. Blue Camas wants to squeeze into the barely-there crook between arm and body.

Each thing a puppy does, every wily glance or playful bark, feels extra indicative of who they are. There's the way one stops running to step gingerly around a patch of mud. Another bounds toward me when I call him, only to lose his train of thought mid-bound and race after a leaf floating by. A third runs with abandon to one of the big dogs, a Border collie, and is roundly smacked by her; she slinks away. And today, one disappears.

Counting the puppies out in the Big Yard, we reach ten. The eleventh, Blue Camas, is inexplicably missing. We cross the broad field, looking at the fence with suspicion—does this bit under the deck push aside? Is that hole large enough for a small body to squeeze through? I worry that we have lost her, let eight pounds of guileless toddler wander out of human gaze and firmly into the gaze of predatory animals and racing headlights outside the fence.

As we search, I remember when Pumpernickel, the first great dog love of my life, went missing. One night, returning home late, I found the front door wide open, light pouring out of the house into the darkness. The radio, which I had left on as audio company, still chattered on guilelessly. But Pump was not in the house. Even as I panicked, I began compiling a list of all the things I would need to do: walk and drive the routes we usually take, calling her name; visit the parks and beaches she knows; find a characteristic photo and put up posters with her face on light posts and telephone poles; call the local shelters and vets to ask about found dogs. Ultimately, I knew that these measures would be insufficient: they were but small shouts in the wind, unlikely to bring her back to me. She was, most likely, gone.

In fact, Pump did return, that very night: I phoned friends who owned a local pet food store, asking them to come stay at the house while I began my futile walking-and-calling for her. On their arrival I saw Pump sitting calmly in the back seat. My friends had driven by their store en route to my home, and saw her waiting there, patiently, for the store to open.

Even without knowing—or owning—Blue, I got that same panic, that feeling of duty unmet. The excitement of bringing a puppy home is streaked through with the realization of the responsibility for another life I am taking on.

We find Blue. At some point, when all her siblings were traveling the far reaches of the yard, she turned around, maneuvered indoors, and found her way to her bed, where she promptly fell asleep. The relief of locating puppy eleven is matched by my surprise at how, in a moment of uncertainty, she raced toward the comfort of a crate with a soft padding. Amy has begun putting them into crates at night, separating them from one another. She began by crating them in pairs, then gave each their own place to sleep at night, ignoring their protests. This crate-training is meant to bridge them into the ultimate separation: into human homes, where there is no warm puppy pile to sleep in. By two weeks in, the puppies have adapted to this new reality—one more than the others.

I bend down and get a puppy in the face: Cranberry. I hear myself talking to her—*What are you doing? Ow! You're a silly goose. A bitey goose*—even knowing she does not hear me back. I am mournful to leave her. More than choosing "the best" or "my favorite" pup, a description I could apply to any of them, I am struggling with knowing that in choosing one, I am saying a possibly permanent goodbye to the others. My choice feels extra freighted, too: I find myself believing that it is up to me to pick the *right* puppy for us—the one who can bear the attentions of a ten-year-old and the scrutiny of a dog scientist. Who can live in a city apartment or run around in the country. Who will be gentle with two older dogs and not eat the cat. Who will, in other words, fit fully into our family.

I look at each puppy, wondering: *Are you the one?*

• • •

It has long been suggested that people have a soft spot for infantile features, such as bulging cheeks and an over-large head—features that prompt us to take care of this presumed underdeveloped young thing. That soft spot is an evolutionary necessity with human infants, who are completely unable to take care of themselves. We had better be drawn to them, because they are hopelessly needy. But the allure of the human baby might also explain our preference for certain nonhuman babies, even though most of them do not need our care. People prefer dogs with bigger eyes, smaller jowls, and a largish space between the eyes—all features that eight-week-old puppies have in spades.

Indeed, it is the time that they are at their cutest. By asking undergraduates to rate the attractiveness of photos taken of Jack Russell, Cane Corso, and white shepherd puppies every week from their first to their twenty-eighth, one research study tried to identify puppies' "peak cuteness quotient." While all the puppies were seen as at least somewhat cute, the one-week-old sweet potatoes were rated as relatively uncute. Their superpower to cause spontaneous cooing behavior from humans increased weekly, until peaking at the impossibly cute form of eight-week-olds. Coincidentally this is also the time that most breeders and researchers think it is best to place a puppy in a human home. With their mothers' involvement waning, their bodies and brains maturing, they will leave their place of birth and be born anew.

At this age the puppies are also at a second transition point. Not only are they about to be thrust into another living situation, they are also going through a secondary socialization period—a developmental moment when they are maximally social and not yet too fearful of new things, people, sounds, and smells. At eight weeks there is a convergence where fearfulness is on the upswing and attraction to strangers is on the downswing. The startle response they began showing a few weeks earlier is spreading not just to actually startling things, but to novel things—things like a crash of thunder, certainly (reasonably startling to all ages), but also a talking stuffed animal, a wobbly stair step, or a spent balloon bopping across a lawn. If you have seen a dog crouch down warily, freeze in place, or tremble and bark or whine when approaching a (to us) perfectly benign-looking puddle, that's the fear response showing its face. Tread gently, for the fear can overwhelm, or it can be approached gingerly and dispelled. Breeds differ in the time at which these fears might take hold: dogs bred to look more infant-like, "paedomorphic"—like Cavalier King Charles spaniels, bred to have small heads and big eyes—only begin to show fear responses at eight weeks. Dogs with longer noses and more wolfy features, like German shepherd dogs, startle to novel and surprising objects at five or six weeks—as the V litter and Maize's pups did. The spaniels' breeding actually slows their rate of development generally. This time of hypersensitivity to novel situations, which has long-term effects, might be part of why pet-store puppies at this age have more fear and anxiety than those raised properly by breeders or fosters: they are especially vulnerable, lacking the controlled socialization other puppies receive.

The flip side of the fear response is the development of attachment. If the world is scary, find a safe person, and hold on, tight. By this age puppies show just the kind of behavior we see in young children who have formed a secure attachment to an adult: if exposed to a new place or person, then separated from their mother, the pups become distressed. They try to get back to her, they cry; if they could furrow their brows, their brows would be furrowed. But they are flexible, and brought into a family of humans, they redirect that attention and bond toward one of us.

All puppies are still approaching new people and dogs with confidence and a wagging tail—and that is why researchers believe this is the best time to place a pup into a human home. Mom has completed weaning and is probably highly irritated with her pups; they are getting more aggressive in their play with one another. They are cognitively quite advanced from their abilities two months ago. Recordings of the electrical activity of the puppy brain, done with electroencephalography (EEG), in which a handful of electrodes is placed on the scalp, shows that brain activity is already adult-like, organized completely differently than when they were neonates. They are now pretty good at inhibitory control: stopping themselves, say, from impulsively lunging at a large, transparent plastic canister if they can see a tempting piece of food inside it. Instead, most pups can figure out to search around the canister for the opening—frontal lobe activity mediating their behavior. If they watch us put something on top of an overturned cup, they can reason that there might be something interesting under that cup, not under another one with no marker on it. They are seeing our intent, our attempt to communicate with them with the tools we use with one another. Their memory span is getting longer, and they no longer have forgotten completely about the toy you took from their mouths and "hid" behind your back; thirty seconds later they may look at you expectantly, or just go find it themselves. In short, they have started to be skilled at navigating the world without their mother's guidance, and at figuring out the funny hairless, bipedal creatures who keep coming around to rub and coo at them. They can leave the nest.

Everyone has a tale of finding their dog, and most have an air of inevitability: "When we saw her, we just knew she was the one." Scientists have looked at puppy selection, too. I know my own choice is based on emotion as much as knowledge: I am drawn to certain dogs by how they look, for the behaviors they show. I trace my choice of Pumpernickel to her sitting on my sneakered feet, looking up at my face; of Finnegan for the affecting way he leaned against me when we met; of Upton for his winning tail thump on seeing me approach his cage. Certainly how a dog is acting at the moment is relevant—a puppy who uses barking to communicate now is likely to continue to bark in the future; a dog who shies away from people at eight weeks will have more trouble overcoming that fear later. Research backs me up: a dog's appearance and actions in the shelter are adopters' top reasons for choosing one over another—even if the behavior is simply "she came right up to me" or "he lay down near me." In one study, dogs who lay down by the potential adopter were fourteen times more likely to be adopted than those who did not; dogs who did not respond to a request to play were the least likely to be adopted. Given that people spend approximately *eight* minutes with a dog before deciding whether to adopt them or not, the process is not entirely rational.

It turns out that we are matched by the puppies in our irrationality. Puppies are not in a position to choose their people, but they can and do make choices—if sometimes odd ones. Researchers giving eight-week-old puppies choices between two quantities of food—one piece of kibble, or four—found that they chose a single piece just as often as they took more. Adult dogs, as all people who live with dogs know, have no such compunction. They may be better at counting; they may be better at maximizing their choices—or simply better at seeing when there is a choice to be made. Most likely, puppies do not yet realize that they exist in a world of options, of which they can select some and discard others.

They are much more advanced than their human analogs, though. At two months the human puppy is not ready for a second birth—starting again with a new family (let alone species). Far from running around, imitating others, exploring water and earth, the human infant at eight weeks is starting to master holding their own head up. I think back to the just-born puppies who struggled with that. They got it by the following week. Two-month-old infants are just beginning to be able to look at something voluntarily. While this skill is developing, infants will sometimes stay staring at something right in front of them—say, their parent's delighted face. This way of looking is called "sticky fixation": it feels as if they are gazing directly into your soul, but the explanation is really that they are not yet able to look away. Perhaps the one thing the two-month-old puppy and infant have in common is that we adults are ready to see each of them as *seeing us*: the gaze of the child or the approach of the puppy is meaningful to us— even if it is not clear that it has any meaning to them. Not yet.

Calm before the storm

Actually, there is already a storm outside. A westerly wind turns the hanging bird feeder nearly sideways. The wind chimes frantically chime; on our walk, Finnegan's ear is a ship's sail. Rain is blowing in, dashing small new blossoms off the maple and dogwood.

Inside, the house is relatively peaceful. The woodstove warms the room, and the cat takes up residence on the back of the couch, the nearest soft surface. The dogs are in repose: Upton on the couch proper, after a bout of play; Finnegan settled on a dog bed, tracking us with his eyebrows as we cross the room.

The room is in its usual state of active use. Objects have been left on the floor willy-nilly: shoes, several bags, bongos, towels, a leash. There are several pillows tumbled from chairs, a dozen books with their spines splayed mid-read, kindling by the stove. Tomorrow, I think, suddenly noticing the extension cords and the wire dangling from a lamp, this room will need to change.

For tomorrow we will return to this room with a puppy in our arms.

We have entered preparation mode. We need to get the stuff, learn the training, man the battle stations. Roll up our sleeves, gird our loins. We are quiet about our plans to our dogs, who eye us warily. But the three humans in the home are all getting ready, each in our own way. Ever the scientist, I regale A. and O. with puppy facts, with reminders of how puppies learn, with how we should behave. They listen and nod, and then do their own thing: A. constructs a small fenced area by the house for early morning outings; O. simply lies on the couch, staring at the ceiling, grinning mightily.

Our first joint action is deciding on a name. While all of the puppies have been provisionally named, we will rename the one who is coming home with us. To give a puppy a name is to begin their life with us—to start them on the track of being part of our family. Our family confers a significance on coming up with a name that is usually reserved for landmark life events—weddings, graduations, christenings. While we will forgo any ceremony, we retain the attendant single-mindedness. We spend long walks with the dogs lobbing suggestions to each other, lolling some words around in our mouths, rejecting others out of hand.

On the evening before we drive to pick up the puppy we sit down on the floor to decide. We have eighteen candidates. I scrawl each name on a small tear of paper. We have animal names (Otter), weather phenomena (Zephyr), old-fashioned human names (Eudora, Sigrid, Steig), even punctuation (Tilde). We invent a convoluted decision game on the spot: beginning with our list of eighteen, each of us chooses six top names, and can eliminate one. Then we repeat with the remaining names, choosing five, eliminating one; and so on. "Eudora," never a great candidate, disappears quickly. Down go "Sid" and "Sigrid." Along the way one person's favorite is inevitably nixed by someone else, so when we are down to two apiece we are granted the right to bring one of our eliminated favorites back into the game. O. brings back "Squall," which, like another of his candidates, "Silveny," turns out to be the name of a pet in a book he is reading; A. resuscitates "Em dash," a joining punctuation which felt like a way to add a third dog to a two-dog family.

Inevitably, these names reflect us: ardent readers (O.); worker with words (A.). Isn't naming essentially an extension of oneself onto an unknown other? We name our children—and our pets—in order to start them off with a part of us in them. Their names are rarely arbitrary: they're named after relatives; admired or beloved people; authors and hockey stars and favorite book characters. Sure, a dog is more likely to be named Peanut or Bear than a child is, but the intent is not so different. The name must suit them, whether it matches who they seem to be now, or who we hope they will become.

Our final round has Em dash, Squall, and Quid—another of O.'s suggestions. We have one last vote apiece. A. and I converge on a name, and Em dash wins. The moment of the choice, I look at them both with anticipation: Did we just begin to meet our puppy? We agree to sleep on it.

In the morning we list the pros and cons of each name, and bring back any names that might have haunted our dreams with their aptness. This is a word we are going to be saying thousands of times, I remind us—maybe a thousand times in the first week alone. We ought to make it something we are happy to say out loud. A lot. On this reckoning Quid wins—with Quiddity as the full name. The word means the essence of a thing: a thing's thingness. The common element of all the puppies is how perfectly "puppy" they all are. This time, we all nod agreement. It's Quid.

The click of the name into place makes it real: a puppy named Quid is about to come home. A name feels like the first step in making her a good, happy dog: circumscribing the kind of dog she can be. At the same time, I know this is a conceit, the notion that by naming them we somehow command who they will be. Puppies are a force of nature, like thunderstorms, uncontrollable, only observable from a safe (or unsafe) distance. I know this—but I need to put away this understanding for just long enough to bring the puppy home.

Now, we just need to get her. Quid does not even know we're coming.

In fact, we do not get a choice of eleven. As their caretaker, Amy was charged with trying to match puppy to person. In the last week or two, she has predetermined which of them she thinks would fit with our family, based on the personalities she saw blossoming in the pups and the potential adopters clamoring at her door. She offered us a few candidates, then let us choose among them. I suggest one to my family—the female among them, given the strong male energy currently in our home—and they agree enthusiastically. Still, I want to think about it one more night, to be sure. Finnegan, listening to us talking, looks at me with mournful eyes; I glance at Upton, who lifts his front leg for a consoling chest rub.

On my final visit I looked at each of the puppies and realized how little prepared I was to decide against one. At home I sit down in front of my computer, wondering if I could make the right choice by just typing rapidly and seeing what came out—by sending my subconscious mind into my fingers before my conscious brain interferes. Instead, I sit with the cursor tapping patiently on a blank page, waiting me out. I close my eyes and start typing. In the morning, I wake up to see this, written in my sleep:

i went o see both of them. well, i got 11. they alllooked good. nnn cn

PART 2

Second Birth

Arrival of the storm

We've got her.

Before dawn on an overcast morning my mind wakes me up with a litany of thoughts—*Oh, we need a sling for carrying her while we walk the dogs; do we have another water bowl? What about nail trimmers?* I look over at the dogs on the bed. Finn's feet are padding through a dream; Upton yawns lazily. They don't know what is about to happen.

Because of the pandemic we haven't gotten to a store, nor have store deliveries come to us, so we don't have a puppy gate. Instead, we find an old privacy screen in the garage that belonged to my grandmother. She used to dress behind it; it is dotted with mirrored, colorful spangles. She would be surprised to see it put to use to create two walls lining a puppy-safe space in the living room.

By noon we are home with a puppy. Three hours later and she is sleeping on a soft bed in a soft-sided carrier, like a pro. So much has happened in just three hours—more activity than in most of our days. In moments of repose I look at her and wonder how she is processing this entire series of events: she has gone from being among all her siblings, to her first car ride, to wearing a harness and leash, to meeting two big dogs, a *cat!*, an entirely new space with smaller spaces within it, balls filled with kibble, toys filled with treats.

Several hours ago she was lying under a tent on the other side of a

fence, flanked by eight of her siblings, when we pull into Amy's driveway. Two puppies, Persimmons and Chaya, were already off to their
new homes. Maize was inside, out of sight.

All the pups rise as we approach, disentangling themselves from
one another. Whimpers and yelps and excited tail wags fill the space.
Wild Ramps is first at the fence to greet us; various noses and tongues
and claws touch my hand through the chain link. Amy steps out of the
house, looking cheery. She neatly picks up Wild Ramps and heads into
the house. Five minutes later, they return, Wild Ramps in a towel, a
bath having transformed her into a wee mouse. Amy is still rubbing
her dry as she hands her to me. She is dense and warm and delivers
impressively soft licks to my face. I hand her to O., who can hardly
contain himself. For the first time, we meet Quiddity.

Amy takes a photo of our new family, pressing the button just as
the puppy's tongue reaches my face. Later I will see photos of the other
families who arrived today. The puppies are dispersing, dandelion
seeds on the wind to New Jersey, upstate New York, Rhode Island,
Massachusetts. Each photo is a variation on the theme of "happy family cradling wet puppy who's just kissed the person holding her." There
is a poignancy to seeing the puppies, still more part of the litter than
they are their own persons, going off into their separate lives.

In the back seat of the car we plop Quiddity in a cat bed in the
center seat; she is cat-sized, and can easily curl her body into a comma.
O. and I sit on either side of her. I take a new look at this puppy coming home with us. She is stuffed-animal cute, mostly black with perfectly placed drops of paint: two round rust-colored eyebrows; the tip
of her snout, tail, and each of her paws dipped in white. Her eyes are
small and searching; her ears, large and soft, folded in the middle
under their own weight. White whiskers ring her muzzle, and the tiniest streak of pink is visible on her lips. She is trembling, but calmly
searches the space with her eyes and nose. It is a lot to take in. Bath

(new), people (new), car (new). Smells of car (new), moving car (new). She takes turns sitting on the bed and moving between us. I slip a harness on her without her noticing, though later she looks suspiciously at this thing she has found around her midriff (harness: new). Although it is new as well, quite soon she is settled on O.'s lap, her head becomingly on his knee. New but perfect. Halfway through the drive home I take over driving so A. can meet her in the back seat, but it is too late: she has already committed to O.'s lap for the ride.

At home I run inside to get the dogs. *Something very exciting!* I tell them, bringing them to the small fenced-in area behind the house for the puppy. The puppy comes into view, on leash, led by O. She is sniffing and peeing and agreeably following, wagging heartily. I could not have predicted what they would do on meeting. The dogs are interested but calm; they give her a perfunctory sniff and then go on their way, as though they meet a new puppy by their house every day. Quid, though, is quite alarmed at the sight of these dogs, and immediately tucks her tail between her legs. She looks perfectly miserable. Though she has been around Big Dogs for her entire life, these are New Big Dogs—about the twentieth new thing in the last hour—and she ducks her head into the crook of A.'s arm. O. skips around the enclosure with the dogs, calling her name a hundred times, giggling with pleasure.

As with just about everything thus far, though, she just needs a little time: even as we pause, deciding what to do, she becomes bolder. As A. puts her down on the ground, she musters the courage to reach her nose out toward the dogs from the safety of his feet, stretching as far as she can without moving her rump.

It is raining lightly, and so we head for New Thing number 21: inside. I see immediately that the pleasure and comfort I feel at stepping into my warm home, out of the rain, is precisely the opposite of her experience. She enters this unknown space with hesitation. We go about the business of taking off our shoes, and getting the dogs a treat, and she is without her bearings. We sit down with her as the cat rises to greet us. "Greet," or "confront": she gives a fiery look, new to this occasion, and stalks over to examine this alien creature. Their colors—black, brown, white—are identical, only painted differently. They do not seem to appreciate this commonality, and the puppy turns her head away as the cat sneezes and prances off.

While we are ready to sit still for a bit, the puppy is just getting started. So we begin some gentle training, giving her a treat if she looks at us, or if she sits down. She is either ravenous or a good learner, for in ten minutes she has received three dozen treats. O. instructs us all on the routine he has learned: show her a handful of treats, hold that hand by your belly button, and expect that the puppy will jump. When the puppy jumps, ignore her. When she finally sits and looks at you, quickly crouch a bit and place a small reward in her mouth. The child-puppy team demonstrate ably, as though they have been practicing for months.

With a puppy this young, unlike what I remember with Upton, adopted at over three years old, the strategy of "waiting until she does a behavior that you like and then rewarding her for it" works beautifully—because she is always trying out new behaviors. Her life involves moving between twelve behaviors in ten seconds, and it is just up to us to catch the ones we like as they flit by. She may be biting my hand now, but the next moment she is carrying a rope toy proudly, and then running after a moth wandering by. There is no idling for puppies: they are chasing the next moment before it happens.

Two hours pass, and O. remembers that it is time to take her outside to pee again. Puppies cannot be expected to hold their bladders, or even know that they are not holding their bladders, so by taking her out every two hours we let her be that puppy without ruining the carpets. And so we head to the penned area where she first met the dogs.

She seems quite uncertain what is to happen there. A ladder lies on the ground, and she does some fine footwork through the rungs; she mouths some inedibles—rock, an acorn; she zoomies around the perimeter. A crow caws, and she stops, gazing out beyond the fence, then tries to jump through the fence. But she does not pee, so we head back inside.

The pace of our day becomes: inside, outside, inside; hesitation, action, hesitation. And, finally, epic naps. I recognize at once the resemblance to the cadence of days with a toddler: alternate whirlwind and slumber. As the sun sets, she begins tearing around the house madly, as though trying to outrun her own tail. Her enthusiasms match those of a ravenous three-year-old with a bag of candy. Just as a storm precedes calm in children, she runs until she conks out, literally on her feet. While some people think (perhaps unadvisedly) that getting a dog will prepare them for the responsibilities of parenthood, I wonder if having raised a son has prepared me, partially, for having a puppy.

She naps for two and a half hours. We were tiptoeing around the house but now are making normal amounts of noise; nothing rouses her. When the dogs finish dinner they come over and poke their noses over the wall to her corner of the living room, sniffing. The cat, who has been running around chasing the sounds of squirrels on the roof, suddenly becomes very suspicious of who is on the soft bed in the corner of the room, and pigeon-bobs from a safe distance until she can go in and check her out. I am waiting for the day when she curls up with her, but it is not today.

The day is long, and we take her out and in a dozen times, gently trying to show her how the leash is attached to both her and us. She fails to see the connection, pulling ahead, across, between our legs in comically intricate fashion. I start calling her "the puppy," as contrasted with "the dogs," as she seems like an entirely different *species*.

For one thing, she is a light bulb burning bright. When she is on, you can't not notice her: she is chewing, running, peeing, scratching, whining—doing. One forgets, or does not realize, that "adding a puppy" to the family is completely unlike how it sounds. As though she would fit smoothly into the pace of our family just as easily as she fit into the car. With her addition, the air inside the house is charged, full of potential energy.

O., after one hour with the puppy: *The thing about puppies is that they can be chaotic and high energy at one point and then they can be sleepy and sweet and low energy.*

O. at bedtime, after nine hours with the puppy: *I love her so much.*

At night she falls asleep in a canvas crate, in her dressing screen–walled room in a new house, in a new city, without any of her siblings. We all sneak into our beds and whisper memories of the many things that have happened that day. Several hours into the night I hear some whining. I would say it was a yodel, almost a bark, then many yodels—not something I would like to hear in the middle of the night. Oh, wait . . . it *is* the middle of the night . . .

I am up late, in the dressing screen–walled room in my house, with a new puppy. A. promises to take over the early morning shift.

The rest of the week is a blur. The puppy I had met in her litter is being quickly replaced by this new creature. Before bringing a puppy home we imagined our future with this dog: the snuggles, long naps on her bed, brief bursts of playing with us and the dogs. After bringing a puppy home that potential dog vanishes, and is replaced by an actual biting, running, peeing, whining dog in our home every hour of every day. She bites the cat in the face and bothers the dogs, who have taken, rightfully, to just turning away in disdain. Upton has a new growl, and Finn is grumpy all the time. Quid's mouth has been on most surfaces in the home, including: couch, chair, table, grandmother's screen. She has gnawed on dog toys, but also fingers, sticks, pencils, books, the wall, and the cat's ears. At the same time, she is impossibly cute. Her smallness is pleasing. It is satisfying to pick up a small, warm bundle of puppy. Along the length of her nose a line of hairs stands erect, a mohawk of the nose: we christen it her nohawk. When she is uncertain she pulls her ears back against her head, morphing into a little fox mouse.

We take her for several short runs in nearby parks: when she is off the leash, she is a steam engine, barreling away. She attends, and dozes through, her first Zoom meeting. She eats a stalk of broccoli. She tries to leap up the single step from the yard to the deck, as tall as she is. She makes it. She pees outside. And inside. And going from inside to outside. She does not sleep through the night.

She is a baby, but she appears more like an adult fully packed into a small dog's body. She can leap and bite and run like the wind: she is not a baby. But she is untethered to society in the way a baby is. She does not know what matters (to us), what is happening next (to her), what to expect and do. We didn't just adopt a dog; we took on her education into everything human.

•   •   •

Bookstore shelves sag under the weight of instructional books for this key moment when a new dog enters the house for the first time. The best of them stress that it's not going to be a part-time gig: "Make time for exercise and fun activities and . . . gentle activity . . . and establish . . . a schedule for eating, toileting and event/crate time and play . . . plenty of naps . . . nail trimming, baths, vet/groomer visits," one trainer advises. Like the inventory of supplies for your newborn child, the list of "vital supplies" you must have for your puppy has gotten ever longer over the years. It now likely includes at least the following: crate, dog bed, baby gates for every opening, a variety of toys, different puppy foods, plentiful treats, treat bag, leash, collar, dog brush, nail trimmers, toothbrush . . . more things than one packs for children for summer camp. New dog people dutifully shop their way to being prepared, since these books are the only operating manuals provided on how to navigate this new situation.

This advice is not wrong. But to think that is like saying that if you have diapers, a crib, and a bassinet, you're ready for your new baby. With the baby, at least we are given ten months to prepare ourselves psychologically for the life change. A new dog can be bought at a pet store on impulse; even the most arduous process of approval by a shelter or placement by a breeder will take only a few days. While a checklist can be helpful, what is unstated in each of those books is the struggle that so many people have with their new pups. The struggle is real. And it is due to the collision of dog and human worlds that is apparent from the first hours of bringing home a new dog. Especially for those who have never lived with dogs, the experience can be shocking. This might account for the number of people who return their dogs to the shelter or breeder within months of acquiring them, usually for reasons of being a dog: barking, being excitable, not knowing where to pee, damaging the house, difficulty making friends with other pets, not understanding the rules of the house. All are called "misbehavior" on the intake forms, but what they are is "normal puppy behavior." Dogs don't know how to live in our homes, don't respect the pronouns we put on items—*that's my bed*—don't have a clue about the identities we give to objects: *that's a shoe, not a chew toy!* Despite the social appearance of dogs as (more or less) cooperatively walking alongside their people in public, sitting peaceably at our feet at sidewalk restaurants, taking their seat in our cars (nose peeking out the window), dogs don't naturally come to these behaviors. Walking with us is awkward: we are not at the dog's pace. Dogs are sprinters, not long-distance walkers. Moreover, they don't want to go in a straight line, keeping an even gait. They zigzag, stop and sniff, run off to chase unseen moving creatures in the grass. They turn around, go sideways, stop entirely. They wait for other dogs, they pull for other dogs. They smell a spot on the ground intently for minutes. Sitting with us is agreeable enough—unless there is *anything at all* happening nearby, in which case they must bark, lunge, investigate, jump, or retreat. Cars are doubly strange places to occupy: the first experience most dogs will have of their bodies moving at high speeds without their control, a world of smells racing by outside the window.

Research into dog behavior might give the impression that they are born ready to live in a human world. Well, they are, as compared to non-domesticated canids, like wolves and coyotes, who have a natural wariness of people. Dogs have a natural interest in people. From the very first weeks that they can see, they look at any available people; they approach people; they lick at people, run with people, and, as every puppy in Maize's litter has done, occupy any available human laps. They follow our gaze and pointing, as we have seen. This is a good start. But "following a point" is a far cry from understanding the byzantine rules of social interaction, human homes, and behavior outside with new people and dogs.

Recent research that has demonstrated dogs' propensity to look at humans does come with a caveat. When confronted with a task that is impossible to solve—such as how to get to a treat that is locked inside a plastic container—adult dogs make an effort to break into the container, but soon look to their person for assistance (which we mostly deliver). Puppies make that effort, too—but with a slight difference: they don't yet look to us to open the container. Dogs need to learn with experience that we are going to solve the puzzles of the world for them—how to get the treats, but also how to behave with us. Imagine needing to learn not just how to be a dog, but how to be a dog among humans. It is no wonder that the first weeks of life with a puppy are challenging: while we spend our lives trying to learn how to be good humans, we now are tasked with teaching another species how to do so, too.

To add to the species divide, by the time a puppy is old enough to leave her mom and come live with us, she is the developmental equivalent of a preteen. She is also at the tail end of her socialization period, learning about the world. All the exposures to dogs, cats, radios, cars, people, and the occasional low-flying helicopter that she experienced along with her litter need to continue: until she is twelve to fourteen weeks old, she is especially receptive to new things. But even after that age socialization needs to be kept up, or those "misbehaviors" are likely to be a dog's response to something new later in their life. Moreover, just as one doesn't teach "come" only once and then expect the lesson to stick for a lifetime, one can't expose a dog to one child and assume that they will be delightful around all future children. In our own puppy's case, her world just expanded, whether she was ready for it or not, to include an already complete family of three species.

How that tween will behave depends on us more than we would like to think. Oh, sure, some of it arises from the equipment she comes with—the keen nose, the alert ears, the flexibility to see people as family. The brain she has, the body she wears, her parents' genes. Her way of acting on the world: with a mouth, not a hand; in close proximity, not at human-handshake distance. But in these several critical weeks of early development, she wields those tools to engage with the environment she is exposed to: they help her organize what she hears, feels, sees, and smells. So much of what we see her doing in her first week in a new home is starting that project. We are witnessing the unity of mind and body as she takes in this bright new world and learns to act in it. The world becomes divided into things that she can engage with and those she can't; friendly and unfriendly; prey and predator, friend and family; things that can be mouthed, licked, jumped on, jumped over, scaled—and things that can't. She is forming categories, just as the young human learns "doggy," generalizes it to any four-legged furry creature, then refines it to just *Canis familiaris*. The more we can help her see that, to us, fingers are not "things that can be mouthed," while sticks may be, the better equipped she will be among people.

We are so completely familiar with our worlds, and especially with the world inside our home, that we can forget that this new creature will experience it differently. It is not a "dog bed" to her; it is something soft, marked by its proximity to (or distance from) other people and dogs, maybe smelling of a dog who used it before. Exploration by mouth happens at mouth level, so the book and the dog toy on the floor get the same treatment.

We're bringing home a dog. We all think we are doing something as simple as that phrase: just adding them to our already intact home. The great surprise is that they change our home. As soon as she crossed the threshold into our house, Quid changed the space inside. She changed how we use the spaces, how we think of the furniture. People seats become puppy seats. Table legs and bookcases are chew toys. More often than not we all wind up on the floor, crammed into the Quid-designated space, while the rest of the furniture huddles together, recovering from the inexhaustible puppy.

Nicknames used with the puppy
in her first week with us:

Quid

QuidQuid

Quiddle

Quidnunc (when she's acting pleasingly naughty)

Quidsome

Q

Beastie

Gremlin

Ears (Finn is Nose; Upton is Mouth)

Puppy-do

Pupper

Pest

Peanut

Peanut sauce

Little one

(Im)perfect puppy

It's three-fifteen in the morning. Quiddity is howling. Actually, she started with crying, which morphed into a kind of yowl, and now, a half hour on, she is doing her best coyote impression in our living room to an audience of one. It is her third performance this night. Somehow I am the only one awakened, and I am completely awake, staring at the ceiling in the dark, waiting for her to settle. I stay perfectly still, willing her voice still. If she quiets for even a minute I will go down and lie down by her crate, hoping some company will calm her. That is what one of us has done every night for the last several nights. I am sleep-deprived and grumpy.

She does not stop, and eventually I go down anyway, grumbling as I go. I might have said "I hate her" under my breath. At night all my concerns are amplified, as though they feed off darkness. The little worries that have bubbled up in her first week with us are now giant billboards: we have made a mistake. She is the wrong dog; the wrong breed of dog. She is too demanding. I don't like the commotion, the constant supervision; I don't like having to be on top of everything, anticipating the next need to pee or object that will be chewed. I am worried about the stress she is placing on the dogs: Finn is constantly sending me accusatory glances; I feel sure that he has got new gray hairs on his muzzle. Upton has stopped playing with us altogether, and often just up and leaves a room when we enter (puppy at our heels). She is over-needy and underfoot. I lack the energy required to maintain the encouraging, enthusiastic tone of voice needed to get her attention, to egg her on to climb that step, to follow me, to stay off, down, there. I am needed and I do not want to be needed. I churn with irritation and impatience.

Even worse, I am impatient at my impatience. I know better. *Be patient* is the first thing I say to people who, fearing they have made a terrible mistake, come to me for advice about their new puppy. *This too shall pass*, I say, looking at my calm, professional dogs, who are models of restraint and charm. And it does pass—and, if they hold tight, they get through early puppyhood before they know it, and form the bond they thought they were signing up for. My puppy regrets, even my moments of aversion, are expected. Yet in those moments they are tangible.

I know that sleep deprivation fogs the brain—familiar, surely, to any parents with a newborn human. There are various schools of thought about how to deal with a crying infant at night. There is the "cry it out" school, which treats the cry as an instinctive behavior that will resolve itself, not a desperate communication from your otherwise incommunicative baby. We were practitioners of another school, the "Go comfort your crying baby, for goodness' sake" school. I found a crying infant to be viscerally distressing: my concern was what might be wrong; my only option was to try to solve the problem. The puppy's cries are also communication, but now I know what the problem is. She is alone. She is crying because she is alone. I know how to fix it, but there are only so many dogs who can fit on our bed. We had introduced her to a lovely soft crate, filled with soft bedding, just as she had had at Amy's house. At the start of the night she toddles in peaceably. In the middle of the night she wants to be anywhere else. In my brain fog I turn the concern into "Will this be her personality forever?" My answer is yes; my conclusion is, "We made a mistake."

In the morning A. reassures me that he can handle the fingernails-on-chalkboard that her vocalizing is to me at night. He is sure, he says, that I will be good at something else with the puppy. I wonder what that would be.

Then he reminds me that, several weeks into living with Finn, I told him, "You know, he's very cute, but I just don't think I'll fall in love with him." And we both remember crying with anxiety after adopting Upton, unschooled in leashes or relaxation. Now I look at disgruntled, sweet, ever-earnest Finn, and the goofy, good-natured Upton, and love them so much.

A. takes the puppy to his office for the day while I work. He reports that she sleeps happily at his feet. Well, no wonder, she was up all night. "I sure as hell am glad we didn't foster a whole litter," he confesses.

There is a concordance of the new season's frustratingly slow appearance with her own development from chick to maturity. Spring is reluctant to arrive this year; a May snowstorm causes the daffodils to hang their heads. Quiddity stands in the doorway, looking out at the snow, with a hesitation warranted by the spectacle of the sky opening. Then she throws herself outside and headlong into it.

Her general-purpose exuberance can be contagious, even when I am feeling sleepy and frosty toward her. I find myself grinning widely later when, snow-tired, she plops onto my lap. Her nohawk is blossoming nicely, and now is matched by great tufts of hair growing out on either side of her chin. Feathering is sprouting on the backs of her legs, like the grasses pushing up through the cold earth. Her ears are growing faster than the rest of her tiny head: giant triangular rockets headed straight to the moon. But I soften most when she pulls them back and flat against her head. One morning we find that her ears have dropped, folding in half to flop when she trots along. It is cute, but disconcerting. Tomorrow will her tail start shortening?

After three weeks of mostly ignoring her, the dogs suddenly, after dinner, turn to look at Quid in a new way: as a possible playmate. She is beyond excited, her tail wagging her entire body. Upton looks gigantic, comically so, next to her: given her outsized presence, it is a shock to see how little she is among the dogs. He stays mostly lying on the ground, letting her hop back and forth over him, gently pursuing her with a wide-open mouth. Finn tag-teams, nibbling her flank as though eating corn on the cob. Quid pulls out all of her play moves. She rolls over, nips and tucks, licks each dog's mouth, and somersaults repeatedly, sometimes to hide under my feet or the couch. But she keeps coming out. A five-minute all-out session turns into hours of off-and-on play. I am cheered to see the dogs acknowledge her positively. Their mutual game makes it seem pre-considered, as though they have been plotting the best way to deal with this new creature.

Soon, every night after dinner, the red carpet in the center of the living room turns into a kind of stage for dog play—and we sit on the sofas surrounding it, giddy spectators. Quid snuffles, a piglet eating quickly, as she bites the folds of skin on Upton: his jowls, the loose skin around his neck. A few times she has gotten her head in his mouth, somehow, and he gags as she holds on to his tongue. Half the time he seems to love it, his tail curving over his back with pleasure, his mouth whale-trawling through the air. Then he growls severely. Quid knows what that means. He is communicating simply and effectively, and she lies down, ears pressed flat against her head.

Unlike Upton, I need to bring out my enthusiastic, high-pitched voice and a willingness to do a little jump and run to communicate with Quid. I put away this voice at home when O. aged out of infancy.

But it is worth reviving: she picks things up with surprising ease when she knows we are talking to her. Why don't we all get puppies at this young age? I wonder aloud. Yesterday she learned to stop what she is doing and look at me when I call her. Frankly, this is better than what our dogs, with whom we have lived for a dozen years, will do. And she began to walk on leash, going along with our cadence, not bothered by—or biting—the dangling thing by her side. She steps into her harness, with the encouragement of a few of the tiniest pieces of kibble you ever did see. Amazingly she is now peeing outside in the same place, after we did nothing but bring her there.

We take her to a nearby pathway fenced on both sides to practice her "recall," coming when called. I drop her leash and run away from her; she chases me happily—and quickly catches up, looking at me to see what's next. Two hundred yards back, A. and O. turn and run in the other direction, then call her name. She tears toward them, a furry bullet. And then after the small celebration for catching them, I call her back to me—and then they to them, and on and on.

I see that, despite my misgivings, she is trainable. And she is busily training us, too. O. starts a game of chase by rolling a ball across the room for her. As she picks it up and brings it back, he squeaks another and rolls it, causing her to drop the first one and chase the second. Or, from her perspective, she drops a ball to cause him to roll the second so she can chase it. She is wagging, and O. is laughing. She has trained us to take her outside with a particular searching look, performed dramatically on the first stair of the staircase leading to our bedroom. It took us only one instance of her peeing on a thick pile carpet before we learned the meaning of that look. She has trained us to pick up all the objects on the floor, even the obviously-not-chewable ones. Although, who am I kidding? Everything is chewable—sure, library books and shoes, but also every pen and pencil, a yoga mat, gardening gloves, the mail, the kindling, the fireplace poker. Per her training, we replace them with toys that bring us to the carpet to toss or tug with her.

The next week is all water. Just as some of the goldfinches have brightened to a startling bright yellow, spring turns south. We awaken to rain and violent winds, and Quid trembles as we open the door. She refuses to go out, but gazes with great interest at the dogs, who, with their superpowers, ably survive the attacking air and the wet ground. She rallies for breakfast and in her enthusiasm steps completely into her bowl of water. She pulls out her feet with what can only be described as a look of horror—followed by a reproachful look at me, the person clearly responsible for all of this. Within an hour we have three napping dogs; it is only nine in the morning. They are themselves liquid, spreading on the couches to fill all the available space.

The following day we bundle everyone in the car to go for a longer walk, releasing some of the energy stored up yesterday. We all step cautiously out onto a pier projected over a pond; the dogs peer over the side at actual frogs sitting on actual lily pads. Quid does not step cautiously: she reaches for one of the frogs, and she, the frog, and the lily pad all go under.

I have never lived with a dog who has not fallen into a body of water once. Nor have I lived with a dog who has fallen in a second time. Quid is determined to defy this trend. Later in the week we visit a friend with an in-ground pool, surrounded by glorious meadow for running in—which O. and Quid are. Fifteen seconds after our friend says *Don't let her fall into the pool*, she . . . slips into the pool.

Each time, I find myself thinking two thoughts at once: *Oh no!* (followed by my racing to the edge of the body of water) and *Dog paddle is well named* (as she ably transforms from landbound mammal to swimming mammal, her front paws churning the water in front of her, but keeping her head above the surface). She is surprisingly good at it, given that these are her initiations into bodies of water. Even fully mobile humans would be in dire straits in similar situations if they had never learned to swim. I scoop her into my arms, reining in the many scrabbling claws working in all directions. She is more saturated than it feels possible: her fur is doused; her ears droop, her tail is leaden. On land and on her feet again, she takes herself right off them, rolling frantically in the grasses, then takes off, as though she can outrun the sensation of her body. Later, when she is fully dried, her fur is extra scruffy; even her scruff has scruff.

Back at home, a dryish puppy at my feet, the cat, Edsel, is staring me down. Quid has overcome her initial concern and is now treating Edsel as a conspecific—as another dog, a playmate. As such, she assumes it is perfectly okay to, say, bite the cat's face. And, when Edsel hisses and swats at her, to bark and chase her under the couch. Quid meets and re-meets the cat a dozen times a day, each time seeming to be as excited as the first time. Her reflexive response is undiminished by exposure. We followed an episode of cat chasing with a session of rewarding Quid with food for sitting and looking at me, doing nothing cat-directed, when the cat is nearby. Edsel looks irked, but sticks around.

One reason the cat's around is that the arrival of Quid has brought new sleeping arrangements and eating opportunities. Finn has perked up considerably since we suddenly always carry smelly dog treats on our walks. Our pockets hold great promise. Edsel, too, the only one not deterred by the walls of the puppy's corner, comes in at dinnertime and demonstrates her command of food puzzle balls. Quid watches her and tries to dart in when the food topples out, but Edsel gobbles it up—eating quite a bit faster than she consumes her own dinner.

By now the small dog bed we bought for Quid is usually occupied by Edsel. Quid tries to fit in there with her, and Edsel discourages her in no uncertain terms. Quid keeps trying. She sniffs at her earnestly, play-bows at her excitedly. Edsel hisses back with a seriousness of purpose it is hard to mistake. I have never seen Edsel's whiskers so flared: a bearded dragon's worth. They are each communicating well, but not with their audience in mind. Edsel cannot translate the play bow; Quid misinterprets the swat. In what looks to me like a gesture of peace, Edsel approaches a resting Quid and licks her right on the nose. Quid growls, and Edsel saunters off. Their miscommunications are not so unlike our own, as we struggle with telling Quid what we need, or with giving her what she seems to. I gaze at Edsel with what I hope she reads as a shared sense of beleaguerment. Finn gives me his best long-suffering look, his head resting on the arm of the sofa, which is no longer exclusively *his* sofa.

But I sympathize with the puppy, too. She has lost her puppy companions—the bodies, matching hers, which show her where to go, what to do, whom to bite, what to pick up, when to run, when to rest. Now there are none. She must be missing the warmth and closeness of them. For the great majority of their lives, they were in bodily contact with one another: woven together in a sleeping pile, jostling in play, tumbling over each other as they climbed a person. They would run in parallel, stop running almost in unison, fall asleep in a scrum. That has all disappeared in a flash. So Edsel looks like a good candidate for such camaraderie, perhaps. Both dogs have by now indulged Quid's habit of lying in the crook of their bodies: she is a body-crook locator. And she has made the move to nap with her head fully resting on Upton—Upton willing—or on one of our feet, or on a stuffed toy. She is piling with the only pileable items available.

When I remember this, we bring her sleeping crate into O.'s bedroom, setting it by his bed. If not *on* a body, *near* one. We visit her before bed ourselves, and hear her suckling in her sleep. A full moon, bright, keeps me up, listening for the slightest yowl. The next morning I write in my notebook, in all caps: *SLEEPS THROUGH THE NIGHT!*

Maybe I don't hate her. But I don't love her. Yet.

•   •   •

The television personality Cesar Millan wrote a book titled *How to Raise the Perfect Dog*. In his mind, it involves applying (mistaken) notions of dominance to your puppy to achieve perfection. The skillful trainer Sophia Yin wrote *Perfect Puppy in 7 Days*. Should the proximity of "perfect" to "puppy" appeal to you in your book title, might I interest you in *Perfect Puppy Training*, *DIY Perfect Puppy Training*, *Perfect Response Training*, *Everything You Need to Know to Raise the Perfect Dog*, *50 Tips for Raising the Perfect Dog*, *Raising and Training Perfect Puppies*, *Raising the Perfect Pet*, *How to Pick the Perfect Puppy*, or, simply *The Perfect Puppy*?

I find the language of "perfection" in regard to puppies to be both hilarious and tragic. The hilarity is that, of course, they are perfect straightaway. They are soft bundles of pleasure who let you pet them and who gaze into your eyes! Perfect! The tragedy is the notion that the goal of training should be perfect behavior, or perfect enactment of several "commands": a flawed notion, though very common. One of the pleasures of dogs is that they are full of messy behaviors: this is why we do not adopt robots.

I wish there were training books for new dog people entitled *Perfect Person in 7 Days*. All you need to do to be a perfect person for your dog is to keep an open mind about who our dogs are, and how they should be acting in this new environment. Oh, and to learn to be consistent in how you talk to dogs—and to learn how they are talking to us.

We are working on that curriculum at home. For us, learning Quid's signs—the way she is talking already—involves an intensive lesson in observation. We are watching her constantly, trying to see what look precedes what action, what she notices and what she responds to. And one must not arrive with preconceptions. We are already in the remedial class here, because four hours into living with Quid we were already describing her personality: who she was, why she was acting the way she was. Ninety minutes of that time she was asleep.

This is typically human of us. People don't enter into human relationships thinking we know everything about another person, or that there are a handful of behaviors they need to perform for that relationship to work. We get to know people by seeing what they do and listening to what they say. With dogs, somehow, we work backward: we talk about how and who our dogs are from the moment we meet them. Despite the fact that no one can get into anyone else's mind in a lifetime, let alone a week, it would be the rare dog person who does not make any claims about what their new dog wants, desires, or even thinks within a week of knowing them. We speak for our dogs, talking about what they like and dislike, and explain their behavior as caused by fears, thoughts, and passions. Some researchers have kept tabs on the kinds of statements we make: "He just loved Christmas," a woman said about her new puppy. "Somehow he figured out which were his presents under the tree and he happily opened them all himself. . . . He loved the tree. He thought we had brought it in from the outside just for him."

Watching our own dogs deal with the newcomer is a master class in attending and communicating. Both mother and siblings were the puppy's first lessons in how to dog—not just what to sniff and where to pee, but, importantly, how to interact with one another. Visit a dog park in any city and you will see rules for dogness being followed, flouted, and enforced—and I do not mean by the dog people (who often step in and mess things up). Upton's growl at Quid was his way of telling her that she had stepped over the line; her response was immediate and deflected any further upset.

This is not to say that a person, too, should growl—or yell, or shout—at a puppy when she does something undesired. Upton's growl works because that growl means something specific—and is perfectly timed. To a puppy our yelling can mean many things, and may or may not happen when the unhappy-making action did, leaving a puppy thinking that whatever they *just* did (like coming over to you when you called) prompted the yelling. As important, because we are the ones who are controlling where the puppy can be, can sit, can eat, can pee, can sleep, and how and when they are allowed to do perfectly natural dog behaviors like "biting" and "running," we as yellers are also in quite a different position toward the puppy than dogs as growlers.

For pups it is a tricky business transitioning from living among dogs—in a society maintained by dog rules, communicated by dogs to dogs—to living among people. Part of the Perfect Person curriculum is imagining what that might be like for them: translating what we want to what they can hear, and translating what they are doing to what they mean. It is remembering what Quid's first weeks were like—the close contact and puppy pile that she grew up in—in designing a space at our home where she can thrive.

And it is remembering that a puppy's enthusiasm takes shape as energy: not just moving limbs in space, tails a-tocking, but also sound energy. As soon as the puppy is projected into our world she begins making noises: we might call those noises whimpers or cries, but they are all just early expressions of the energy that is bottled in her. That bottle will not run dry for years, but over the first year it is especially explosive, gusting out prodigiously. We have had some glimpses of this in Quid's nighttime noisemaking. The reason is simple: whines and yelps worked to get her mother's attention; now they are transforming into other vocalizations that mean more or less the same thing. The bark heard round the city—the "alone" bark, high in pitch and frequency—evolves straight out of those early pup squeaks.

What all the perfect-puppy books are selling really has nothing to do with perfection: it has to do with training a dog to be more like what we, in today's culture, assume dogs *should* be like.

Happily, the method of training currently in vogue is based on positive reinforcement. What all training is intended to do is to get dogs to learn things of value to us—and to learn which of their behaviors we approve of, and which we do not. This form of learning is called "operant conditioning," described by B. F. Skinner as he put innumerable pigeons and rats in boxes and trained them to perform specific actions, like pushing a button or a lever. Using this method he trained pigeons to play ping-pong—even to pilot a guided missile designed (but never deployed) for use in World War II. Operant conditioning is based on the notion that pigeons and rats—and dogs and people and everyone else—learn effectively by connecting what we do to the consequences of what we do. As we wander around the world behaving, we find that certain actions are followed by delightful consequences; others by nasty ones. Whether we do that action again, or don't, depends on whether the result was something we wanted. Training, then, is creating a context in which a dog can naturally learn these associations.

Positive reinforcement training is the good guy of learning. I get to realize that something I do, intentional or not, leads to something super: a reinforcement, or reward. Imagine that I come across a vending machine with bananas inside and levers on the outside. I pull a lever, and a banana is released from its housing and drops down where I can take it. I quickly learn that lever-pulling is an excellent way to get bananas. That is positive reinforcement. I like bananas. I will doubtless try that lever again.

That is simple enough. To train a dog this way, you need to wait until they do a behavior you like, though—and catch them in the act, as it were, so that you can deliver a perfectly timed reward for that specific behavior. Every person you see congratulating their puppy for peeing on a patch of grass outside is doing this form of training: showing the dog that *peeing here* yields a reward (if not as persuasive a reward as a handful of freeze-dried salmon might be). Online you can watch video of Skinner training a pigeon in a minute flat to turn in a counterclockwise circle—simply by using positive reinforcement to shape each step along the way. It is not the only form of operant conditioning, though. If instead, when I pull a lever I get a shock, you can be sure I will be reluctant to do it again. That is called "positive punishment": "positive" because something new happened—the shock—and "punishment" because it was, well, shocking, and done to reduce my rate of lever-pulling.

Positive punishment, though it sounds like something beneficial, is what most people mean when they say "punishment": spanking, yelling, hitting. It is not positive-feeling, but it indicates an addition (plus, thus "positive") of something to the dog's world. There is also a method called "negative punishment," which is taking away (minus, thus "negative") something that is liked. If I am touching all the levers, getting all the bananas, and you don't want me to, then you rig the machines so they no longer yield bananas. I will probably stop pulling the levers (eventually).

Rounding out the quartet is "negative reinforcement learning," where you increase the rate of a behavior by taking away something bad. If the banana machine is buzzing loudly and I can fix it by banging on its side, I have learned by negative reinforcement that machine-banging miraculously makes things better. This form of learning is used quite a bit in horse training: by pulling on the reins to try to get a horse to slow down, the horse may learn that if they slow when they feel this unpleasant pressure on their face, the pressure will stop (if the rein-pulling is done right).

We—and dogs—learn from all of these methods in our ordinary lives. Stick your finger in a bottle and get it stuck (or, for dogs, your nose in a hole in the ground and get it bit), and you are less likely to do that again (positive punishment). Scream—or bark—and everyone comes running over to you to see what you need, and you are more likely to do that again (positive reinforcement). A dog who is able to chew through her crate to escape confinement becomes a crate chewer (negative reinforcement); one who finds that you put the tennis ball away when she brings it to you becomes less likely to bring it to you (negative punishment).

The great debate among trainers and in psychology concerns which is the most effective learning method. In terms of longevity of learn-ing, training via positive reinforcement wins. Positive punishment—yelling "No!" at a child or puppy—can be effective in stopping a behavior, but it comes with lots of side effects: the punishment needs to be timed perfectly, or it is unclear what behavior to stop; its use can lead to the recipient becoming generally fearful, angry, or aggressive; and it gives no clue to what behavior would be good instead. Thus it can lead to learned helplessness, or feeling unable to act at all.

Learning via the good guy means that if your puppy is barking in another room in the middle of the night (say), you do not go in there and yell at her. Instead, when she is quiet, you sneak in and reward her with your presence. There, the behavior being reinforced is actually "not barking." Since it can take some serious patience to wait until "not barking" occurs, the positive punishment move—yelling—is a common mistake. No one feels better after that—and the pup may still bark.

While positive-reinforcement training is popular now, it is not the only form of training used by dog trainers. In point of fact, negative punishment—ignoring a dog doing something you dislike—is quite often used with it. It is fairly benign. But if a trainer recommends an e-collar, which delivers a shock or stimulation, that is classic (positive) punishment. And in the past, methods using this form of punishment were much more common. Nineteenth- and early-twentieth-century training manuals were likely to use the word "correction," and to talk about "cuffs on the nose" as part of the tool kit of the trainer— although it was classic positive punishment, through and through. When a dog makes a "mistake," Blanche Saunders wrote in 1946, in *Training You to Train Your Dog*, "Take the puppy firmly by the collar to the spot where he has erred. Point to the place and shame him, saying 'Did you do that? Bad dog.' Give him a sharp cuff on his rump." Her solution to stopping a dog from barking when left alone at night— or what she describes as "feeling very sorry for himself"? She "crept inside the kennel with a BB gun," on the other side of the door from the dog. "[W]hen he decided it was time to begin again I pulled the trigger." The explosive sound of the pellet hitting the door led to "perfect silence" for the rest of the night, she wrote. You better believe that the dog didn't have a good night's sleep, though.

Early training was also more likely to use hands-on methods for "shaping" a behavior. Instead of waiting around for a dog to sit, then rewarding them, trainers advised people, "Take hold of the skin under his throat with one hand and push down on his hindquarters with the other." This is not a learning method at all; it is how you sculpt a bust of clay, but not how you encourage sitting. To stop a dog from barking, trainers advocated "holding his jaws together" (while shouting "no"); a handler of a working dog may "strike his dog in the windpipe with his hand or grasp it by the throat and apply pressure until the dog stops trying to make noise." Then "as soon as the dog is quiet it should be praised." Many of these antiquated manuals celebrated this perplexing mix of punishment and reward. "If he exhibit[s] symptoms of being refractory," an 1814 manual on training hunting dogs to track and retrieve advised "*showing* him the whip, i.e., let it fall lightly over him"—but cautioned, "but no flogging." This kind of training was sometimes called "breaking," and no wonder. The "crack of the whip" is more than once wielded, as is the spiked collar, "a leathern strap, through which are inserted a dozen or more small nails" attached to a cord and used to rein in, say, a dog's tendency to run away.

Not all training manuals were so dystopian in their treatment of dogs. Any dog can "learn all that it is necessary for him to know without a single blow being struck or a single harsh word being spoken," Stephen Hammond wrote in 1882 in *Practical Dog Training*. "Do not fail to abundantly caress him and speak kindly words, and never under any circumstances, no matter what the provocation, allow yourself to scold or strike him." His was not the prevailing view, to be sure, at a time when dogs were barely considered chattel.

The earliest training manuals focused on training for sport—as hunting companions. These trainers were not teaching "sit" or "shake." But with the rise of purebred dog breeding and the increase in dog-keeping in the late nineteenth century, many more fanciful ideas about what a dog might be trained to do popped up. Dog shows and dogs in circuses were becoming popular: dogs as spectacle. Fittingly, this is when people began training dogs to lie down, beg, and leap on command. These have endured, sufficiently so that nearly any contemporary training guide will have a method for teaching one or more of these behaviors. Happily, some fell out of fashion, such as walking on stilts, dancing on hind legs, standing on their heads, jumping rope. Of another trick, having a dog grab his tail in his mouth, one doctor and trainer wrote, in 1881, "This trick is exceedingly funny, and is always hailed with roars of laughter." He added, "To attain success at teaching this trick the dog must be gifted with a good deal of tail."

I think training is mis-pitched: it should be called "teaching." It is not about tricks; it is about a worldview. We encourage—even expect—some kind of teaching of children, and for a good reason: so that they can understand the world into which they have been born and the civilization in which they are going to be a participant. So, too, for dogs: teaching should be about what they need to know to live in the world of humans, and what they need to learn in order to more fully enjoy life. The behaviors taught today are a mash-up of those important for safety, important for the sanity of the human, totally unimportant for any reason, possibly offensive, and actually fun for dog and person. What I want to teach Quid, most of all, is how to be a dog in this family in this place in this time—while still letting her be her unruly self. Maybe that last part is something I have to learn.

Some things the puppy has eaten/chewed that are not for eating/chewing: an observational study

rocks

deer poop

stick bits

bit of fluff from my pocket

pants

cat's ears

fingernails

my finger

human hair

her own paw

woodchuck (no woodchucks were harmed)

wall

windowsills

window handle

insect walking across the floor

moths

pencil tips

pencil erasers

black rollerball pens

dried leaves (after shredding them into a thousand
slivery pieces first)

dirt

sofa arms

pillow

rug

dog crate

dog bed

her own leash

icicles

carrot ends, celery ends, asparagus ends, kale stalks,
strawberry tops

string

flashlight

compass

dryer balls

vacuum hose

cover of paperback book

first thirty-one pages of book

bookmark in book

bottom edge of book

book

Ghosts

I'm typing w left hand as rt hand is unfer pup cannot be bothterred to ck ctyps.

I am extracted from captivity by the puppy when someone opens a door downstairs; she beelines to see who. Three months old, Quid has slid neatly into the family. She has places she likes sleeping (head on our hands, head on our feet, head on dog rumps) and has routines with the dogs (evening play bouts); in the mornings she hops on the bed and counts each of us with her nose. We are now hers.

As she has relaxed into this space, her particular spirit is bubbling up. On a walk today she neatly leaps from the paved path onto the horizontal rail of the fence lining the path. It is like a bird alighting: without preamble, she just takes flight. Back on ground she finds a stick as wide as she is long and carries it neatly, head held high. With the stick in her mouth she whines continually, working through some inner conflict opaque to us. Once in a while she veers off-path, per-haps looking for a place to bury it, or chew it—then thinks better of her choice and continues to whine-carry it.

These glimpses of an inexplicable character are charming: we are seeing more of who she is. And at the same time, as with all young things, who she is is changing. Physically, she is bigger: still only twelve pounds, but her paws have begun looking pleasingly large compared to her body. Her ears continue skyward, and each day

brings the game of Up or Down? as we chart their development into
perked or folded. Today one is up and one is down. O. and A. find
each variation cute; for me, a switch is turned when they are up (cute
response off) or down (cute response on). She is overly cute, almost—
like a stuffed toy that veers, uncanny valley–like, into the unsettling.
Or maybe I am just wary of handing my heart to this young thing. I
am waiting for the falling-in-love part to kick in.

After we adopted her, Amy began a Facebook group so that the
siblings' families could keep up with one another. I am not on
Facebook—but Quid is. We spend evenings scrolling through the photos of her siblings, marveling at their increasingly visible differences
and their notable similarities. The biggest males are a full 50 percent
larger than Quid—how is there so much more of them already?—and
we can see a division growing between the scruffy dogs and the
smooth-coated, between the up-ears and down-ears. Some live in
multi-dog families; others are singletons. Photos show a few suited up
for hiking expeditions, or among horses or in lakes; others are mostly
photographed lying in a curl on the couch or on their backs, legs in the
air. People compare notes on the minutiae of new-dog-ness: what are
they feeding, where did you get that harness, what are people doing
about car sickness. They admire each new trick or look or curl. I find
it comforting to see all of the puppies, even as they grow out of the
familiar dumplings they were to me—and to glimpse inside the homes
of their people. As millions of people who adopted a dog while quar-
antined from humanity are surely feeling, there is a surprising loneli-
ness to raising a puppy in isolation. This is ironic in the extreme, as
"companionship" is one of the primary reasons given *for* adopting a
new dog.

But typically, life with a puppy is two-pronged: private and public.
The struggles and pleasures of raising a wild animal—er, young dog—
are mostly the former. Outside the house, though, being appended to

a puppy is, in normal times, surprisingly transformative. For that private struggle is obliterated when that smol cute thing is sitting, puzzled, on the sidewalk. Puppies, like babies, are attractants: strangers pause at seeing them, veer to your side, coo and squeal. They want to touch, talk to, and know everything about the puppy. They comment on her beauty; they smile at the two of you. In just the way that strangers do not typically do with one another on the street, they provide affirmation of what a great choice you have made. Your puppy's cuteness is an endorsement of your good judgment—maybe even evidence of *your* cuteness. It is affirmation of us by extension—and confirmation, that one is a participant in life.

In a pandemic this public dynamic is lost. No one approaches anyone within touching distance. Sequestered in a house a half mile from our nearest neighbors, we could go days without seeing anyone at all. On our first trip to the vet, I was startled to be greeted by a technician who said, clearly, "OOOOOOHH!" when she saw me. At first I was confused, forgetting that the puppy in my arms was so distinctive, a duckling appearing among ducks. For the moment, I reveled in the adulation and cooing that the staff showered on Quid. It was a reminder that, in addition to being a nonstop new presence in our house—a whirling biting machine, a thorn in the side of our dogs, a sleep-stealer—she is also a "cute puppy."

At home, cute puppy is being put through a rigmarole of "exposures" while still in her socialization period. Each day, of course, she is exposed to new things not of our design: the thunderstorm transforming the air, the chipmunk racing by her feet, a visiting raccoon. She has been serenaded by gunshots in the distance, crashes in the kitchen, slamming doors, cars driving by, high winds, high wind chimes, and heavy rain. She has sauntered by tractors, faced down vacuums, heard a couple of sirens, a circular saw, an electric drill. She has taken it all in stride. So we add our own odd sensations to her sensorium: setting her on the sisal cat scratcher, or a sheet of aluminum foil, to feel that underfoot. We present a large box on its side; the dog bed, inverted; a yoga ball. When she touches any of them, we reward her, and soon she is touching the foil and box and bed and ball purposefully, looking at us for her medal. When we leave this household obstacle course in place, lo and behold, she finds herself walking over and into and through it all, making all sorts of ruckus. We reward her for that, too.

Outside, A. concocts a seesaw by nailing a plank to a stump on its side. We lure her close. Before I can encourage her onto it, she walks right up the down side unflinchingly. Flinches are for surprises; to the puppy, this is just the way the world is. Her easygoing nature allows her to take it in stride. She was less sanguine about the hammock, but with a treat she is soon the sphinx in netted canvas, being rocked by her minions. We check off items from trainer Sophia Yin's list of ways one should gently handle a pup to acclimate her: we touch her feet and ears, pinch and poke her skin, tap her nose, turn her on her back, pull her to our laps; we turn her momentarily upside down. While we can't expose her to a city's worth of new people, we bring her out to visit any delivery people delivering. And we make ourselves into new people, pulling out hats, sunglasses, and a fake mustache to try to appear like strange strangers. We ride by on our bikes, don helmets and hoodies, carry umbrellas unnecessarily.

She steps into every new situation with the same confidence as her first step in the morning: complete. It is only when we bring out the ghosts that we get a hint of a new Quiddity.

The idea of exposing her to ghosts comes from a Swedish working dog community. They regularly gather to test their dogs' reactions to novel stimuli, like gunshots, rapidly moving objects, and unknown people. Somewhere along the way, it must have been decided that a good test of the dogs' composure and responsiveness would be to expose them to ghosts. Not real ghosts, but ghostlike figures, as imagined by a low-budget Halloween costumer of yore: people dressed in sheets covering their bodies and plastic buckets with holes for eyes over their heads, emerging slowly from hiding places.

O. gets to play the ghost. He dresses in a drapey hooded caftan, and we prepare by watching a video of professional dog-ghosting behavior. First the "ghost" walks slowly toward a dog, stops four meters from them, then turns around. Throughout this performance, the dog's reaction is gauged. Part two is the big reveal: the dog's handler marches right up to the ghost, chats with him like they are old friends, and helps the ghost remove his costume. The dog's reaction to this turn of events is gauged again.

The Swedish Working Dog Association has ideas about what behavior they hope their dogs will show in response to this surreal theater. I am less sure. I try to imagine what I would want Quid to do should a ghost emerge from our forest: Do I want her to simply accept the appearance of this apparition, and calmly walk away? Should she instead chase and tackle this obviously bonkers (or, to keep an open mind, deceased) person? Should she look at me dubiously?

She doesn't do any of those things. Before we leave the house, O. walks into the forest, hides behind a tree, and waits for me to get into position with Quid. At my signal, he creeps out slowly, arms partially raised in front of him, half-zombie—a spontaneous flourish. Quid is fixated on some nearby squirrels quarreling with each other; it takes her a moment to notice him. Her body tenses; she peers toward the forest, her ears tuned to the slightest rustle. When he creeps his next ghost-zombie creep, she is sure of what to do: bark like mad. While she had quietly accepted approaching vacuums, licking cats, and suddenly appearing motorcycles, she is *not* prepared to accept ghosts.

Per the playbook I approach the ghost directly, and we begin talking. Quid barks nonstop, a completely new development for her. Then

I help O. disrobe, so that it is clear to everyone, Quid included, who this ghost is. He is there to be seen, heard, and smelled. Quid is unconvinced, despite having spent dozens of hours in full-body contact with O. We walk back to the house; she barks the whole way. Inside, once she has run out of barks, she spends the rest of the day looking at him out of the side of her eyes.

Though our efforts at teaching Quid anything are scattered at best, she is spontaneously learning much that is useful in organizing our life together. She has learned to go to doors, and sit or scratch, to tell us she needs to be on the other side of the door. She is responsive to "Come!" even with some distractions. And, thrillingly, she has picked up "Wait": around here it means being the polite one pausing at the open door to let someone else go through first. Many *people* I know have not picked up "Wait." She will sit down to be let into the house—which I consider an incredible feat of self-control. How one connects "Put your rump down" with "because then you will get to move" is beyond me. Conversely, "Stop barking"—another negative—is trickier to teach; we are positive-reinforcing the hell out of "being quiet," but I sense that something else is being learned, like "That person often has snacks in her pocket." Some people teach "Quiet," or even teach "Speak," trying to route the bark to be on cue. For now, we are distracting her, trying to get her to do a behavior that is impossible to do while barking, like holding a toy or eating a treat.

Quid's training of us, on the other hand, is going fantastically well. I have learned to fill my pockets with peanut butter treats. I can be coaxed into rubbing her face merely by her looking at me beseechingly, ears laid back against her head. She has begun telling me when she sees something terrifying or exciting—like a person appearing suddenly—by simply turning to me, anticipating a treat (which she gets). She has taught me to speak in an exceedingly high tone if I actually want her to come. She has trained O. to play with her by nosing him and nibbling his toes, and she has trained A. to collect good-looking sticks (diameter greater than an inch; length between one foot and three) for her. Upton she prompts into play by jumping at him, kissing his mouth; Finnegan will engage her if she stalks him on our walks.

The dogs are the best teachers of all. One evening I am walking back to the house and see the three of them—two dogs, one puppy—lined up at different windows of the porch, all sniffing outward with anticipation. It makes me wonder who this puppy would be if there had not been Finn and Upton in her life. They are her guides to dog-hood in our house: how the house runs, what the pace of the day is, where we wander—and what is allowed, expected, gotten away with, and appreciated. Upton, with very few words, has taught her to calm herself when her enthusiasms about *Life! Running! That beetle on the floor!* run too rampant. I see her follow each one's nose into a patch of grass, follow them to pee where they pee, to bark when they bark. When we drop her leash she uses her freedom to follow the dogs, the lot of them returning to us like a shot when we call. Yesterday she was scolded by Finn, which sent her ears back and her tail under her belly, and yet later they created a spontaneous running race, with back-handed moves (biting legs, rump) allowed. Each of the dogs deals with her differently, per their different natures; both of them are models of how to be: her mother goose.

* * *

This month could be described as a protracted exercise in "impulse control": so much of what it is about is squeezing her id into the weird shape that we call being "polite" or "responsive." Just when she discovers squirrels, a puppy is also told *not* to chase that squirrel; as soon as she learns she can reach my mouth by jumping, she is told *not* to jump. Outside is full of important things to pursue, but *no*, we say, *don't dart out the door.* And now that she lives in a land of bagels, for some reason she is not allowed to grab that bagel I am holding so tantalizingly close to her.

In child development, researchers talk about self-control in various terms: one learns "willpower," or has the ability to "delay gratification," or has "executive function" skills. The most widely known measure of willpower and delay of gratification was developed by the psychologist Walter Mischel: the marshmallow test. One version goes like this: a preschool-age child is seated at a table directly in front of a single marshmallow (or pretzel, for those more moved by savory treats). The experimenter tells the child that they will be left alone in the room for a spell, and that if they refrain from calling her back in the meantime, they will get to eat the marshmallow (or pretzel, if that was their preference). If they do summon her back, they only get to eat whichever treat they liked less.

Mischel was interested in how children's performance on this task related to their own self-control—and test success—later in their lives. But let's imagine the puppy marshmallow test. Inevitably, any puppy left alone would grab at it at once. Now let's imagine what "the marshmallow" is for puppies. It is: the bone, that bit of food, that squirrel, the finger in front of them, the moth, the cat, the bird, another dog—it's the entire world. Much of what we are asking the puppy to do all day, every day, is to *not eat the marshmallow*—to not go at the world.

It is worth noting that in Mischel's study, four-year-old children could not bear to wait even half a minute. The marshmallow in front of them was so tempting that they soon called the experimenter back in—and were rewarded with the lowly pretzel.

No wonder young children have trouble managing that temptation: their brains are still immature. Executive function, important for self-control, involves the frontal cortex, which continues to develop through their adolescence. Puppies, by contrast, grow a fairly mature brain by four months old. Not just their gray matter—the neurons—of the brain, but also the later-developing white matter, the myelin, is more or less adult-like. These young pups show big-dog electrical activity in their brains. While a four-year-old child is miles away from being able to resist temptation, our puppies are tasked with being adults. Come, sit, wait, calm yourself. It is a wonder they can do any of it at all.

While we are contorting ourselves to try to get the puppy on board with living with us, without even trying the dogs are natural teachers. They teach by scolding, at times, but also just by *being*, by modeling behavior. Dogs are drawn to where other dogs are, or to what they are doing—what is called "stimulus enhancement" or "local enhancement" in psychology literature. It is not quite the same as teaching, but it affords the chance for learning: the presence of one dog lets the second one notice that there is something or somewhere worth interacting with—like a smell in the grass, or a treat on a table. One study on this phenomenon set up a room so that subject dogs could peek in on other dogs while they searched for food in various boxes. When all the dogs were reunited, the observing dogs made "snout contact" with the dogs they had watched; if the dog had found food, the observers raced to the place they had seen them searching. The opportunities for this kind of social learning in a multi-dog household are constant. Not everything learned is what we would hope, though. A non-barker can learn to bark by exposure to barkers; a cat's litter box can be discovered by following an experienced litter box visitor to the source. If one dog is allowed to get away with being on the bed, good luck keeping a second dog off it. There is a kind of stimulus enhancement from puppy to person, too, we have found. Thus we learn to follow the puppy when she quietly disappears from sight (usually followed by miscreance), and to never open the door without first looking out for the birds or chipmunks that she is in search of.

Quid has also made us aware of how we talk to her—the words that get through to her, and those that are not heard. The meaningfulness of language, to humans, gets in the way of our seeing its arbitrariness. Of course "come" is an arbitrary assignment of sounds to mean something like "move your body over here." There is nothing about it that compels someone to move; nothing that models any part of movement. But when we use the word, we assume that a dog will get it. It takes great effort not to use full sentences with the puppy: *Not now— we'll go out later, after dinner*; *Why are you looking at me like that?* Even knowing that we are just talking to ourselves, we still use those sentences. But I think that deep down we are a little surprised or put off when they do not understand.

In the last decade there have been a few well-publicized examples of highly trained dogs, such as Chaser, a Border collie, who could respond to over a thousand words: mostly names of toys, and verbs for what she might do with those toys (*take, paw, nose*). And people report that their dogs know, on average, between twenty and seventy words and expressions. While seventy words do not a language make, research has shown that dogs have a dedicated "voice area" in their brain: neurons that are responsive specifically to sounds from other dogs, just as we have for sounds from other humans. And dogs, unlike us, appear to be more responsive to sounds from non-dog sources (like humans) than we are. Humans are pretty dismal at even telling their different barks apart, but dogs are at least putting in the effort to understand what we are barking at them. Adult dogs get so good at recognizing their names that they experience what in human psychology is called the "cocktail-party effect": they can hear their name when spoken by a stranger across a room full of noisy talking. Bring your dog to your next cocktail party and try it.

Of course I am talking nonstop to Quid. *Hi, little one*, I catch myself saying in the morning. *Scooch! Okay! Let's go pee!* When she pulls ahead, straining to free her body from this cloth coil of the harness and beeline for the squirrel, my way of communicating to her my displeasure is to say *You're not helping*. It is not that I am completely oblivious to her noncomprehension; I feel certain that we simply narrate our lives out loud with our dogs. But this habit does leave a lot of communication unfulfilled. By assuming that there is any bit of meaning conveyed, we miss the chance to actually talk to her in a way she will understand: through our behavior.

We have got one thing right, at least. Almost automatically, when we talk to dogs, we use higher-pitched tones than when we are talking to humans. Puppy-directed speech is highest of all. The best trainers I have met work their voices into eye-poppingly high pitches to call them—the *pup pup pup puppy!* of the Working Dog Center trainers, or even just *beep beep beep beep beep!* to get a dog's attention. And it turns out that puppies, more than adult dogs, are really responsive to this kind of speech: they react more reliably and faster, and approach the speaker more often, than if the same request is given in normal human-directed tones. We also slow down the speed of our speech when talking to dogs; we articulate our vowels more—similar to the "motherese" that naturally comes out of mothers (and fathers) when talking to their babies. O. has gone one step further, and begun calling Quid with the high *hoo-hoo hoo-hoooo* of the local barred owls. She is the only one he talks to in owl language. It works.

As the puppy grows ever more into herself, I find myself musing overmuch about her appearance. Just as we assiduously noted the puppies' weight in the first weeks of their lives, each new sprout of hair, tail feather, or coy look of Quid's is noted and recorded. It is as though we are reassuring ourselves that she is still cute. A study of dogs and their people in Australia found that people who have a strong relationship with their dogs also see them as cuter; and strangers assume that cuter dogs have more-desirable personality traits. In other words, just as we unfairly do with people, we rate dogs by their cover.

Fifty things you should
notice about your puppy

1. how she looks at you
2. how you look at her
3. the precise day she learns to associate the crinkle of a plastic bag with food
4. the evolution of her nose from pink to black
5. the evolution of her eyes from blue to whatever-they-become
6. the ratio of black whiskers to white whiskers
7. when her incisors come in
8. which side she likes to lie on (Quid: left-leaning)
9. where she likes to rest in a room, vis-à-vis you and any other humans and dogs; whether it is in the sun or on the hard floor or by the door
10. the progression of toe pads from pink to dark (today: one pink on front right foot, two on back right foot)
11. what punctuation mark the tail most resembles
12. where she likes to be tickled

13. where she doesn't like to be tickled

14. when she realizes that her tail is following her

15. when she barks; what you do when she barks; whether she continues to bark nonetheless

16. which paw she uses first to descend the stairs; which paw she uses to ask you for something; which paw she uses to pin down a squeaky toy to begin its evisceration

17. when she coordinates the rear legs and front legs

18. non-barking, non-growling sounds she makes (as of this week: *arooo*, snuffling in play, whimper-sigh when settling down to rest, whimper-cry when holding on to a precious ball or stick)

19. the warmth of her belly

20. how the room sounds when she is in it with you

21. the sound of her running up the stairs to attack you on the bed in the morning

22. the precise number and names of all the colors of her fur

23. eyebrows: their existence

24. her noseprint: the unique shape of the front of her nose

25. how her head smells

26. how the pads of her feet smell

27. the tiniest eyelashes

28. the sweetness of sleep

29. how she corners (skidding, slowly, rump glancing the ground)

30. whom she looks to when she needs something

31. how she tells you she needs something

32. how she can scooch forward with limbs extended out front and behind
33. what makes her happy
34. what scares her
35. how high she can jump; how much higher that is than she is
36. the ways of her ears
37. when she overtakes you in land running speed
38. her opinion about her own shadow: friend or foe?
39. the staccato exhales as she relaxes into sleep
40. how her ears can move independently
41. when she realizes birds can fly, and squirrels can go up trees
42. the part of the house she doesn't yet know exists
43. when she notices the puppy in the mirror
44. different ways to sit: sphinx, George Booth dog, rump barely on floor
45. how she looks without a collar
46. how she looks when she's wet
47. which thing you don't want her to eat that she's most interested in eating
48. sleep-suckling
49. sleep-barking
50. how happy she is you're back

Puppy's point of view

~~~~~~

Shelter in place!" O. yells, as we dive for his bed and pull the blanket over our heads. Quick on our heels we hear the distinctive rapid *tick-tick-tick-tick* of small-dog toenails on wood floors. And then she is upon us, hurdling onto the bed and snuffling us out under the covers.

Mornings alternate between bodily attack and a restrained, ears-back greeting, accompanied by audible sniffing of me as I reach over to tickle her face. Both dogs come down and play with her, everyone feeling good and up for some open-mouthed wrestling. Watching them play is somehow barely different than playing myself, as though through observation I am transported into their acrobatic mayhem—as though I were so frolicsome and free. I feel my facial muscles tiring and find that I have a huge smile on my face.

We are all affected by the sybaritic pleasure of late spring: of being able to be outside without coats and hats, of a breeze on bare arms and legs. I tentatively pull out my shorts, wondering if they will still fit, only to find I am still exactly the same size as the time I put them away. Quid has gained a few inches in height, and her body is filling out into more "sausage" than "dumpling." But she is impressively little among the dogs. Her scruffy fur is emerging weed-like, everywhere and often. It is coming out of her eyebrows, it is in the crook of her ears, it is popping out from between the tiny pink pads of her feet. All the cute internet dog words apply to her: smol blep mlem boop.

This is the week we put the GoPro on her. Having spent my career trying to understand the dog's point of view, it is only a matter of time before the dogs in my household get the GoPro treatment. Pitched as an "action" camera, the tiny GoPro is typically used by skiers, cyclists, skydivers, sea divers—or anyone who wants to document their travels through space without holding a camera (often because they cannot hold it in their hands while skiing, cycling, or sky- or sea-diving). Soon enough, people realized that it could also be useful to document the vantage of that other hands-free traveler in their home—the furry, quadrupedal one. While it does not pass for mind reading, a good first step in understanding someone's worldview is to simply get to their height and go at their pace.

Just as she only noticed her first harness after I had attached it, in her enthusiasm to be outside, Quid barely flinches as we attach the tiny camera to the back of her harness. It sits atop her shoulder blades, giving us a view of the white blaze on the back of her neck and her giant ink-black ears, mightily working to stay erect. The wide-angle view is not enough to rival the dog's 240- to 270-degree visual field (and indeed the camera is hidden in the only 90 degrees out of her vision), but it feels extravagantly large for a camera image.

As soon as the camera is on, A. runs out into the forest, prompting our little person-herder to charge after him. O. and I watch on my phone, connected to the camera, as the back of his legs and shoes come into sight and disappear as she catches and passes him quickly. Viewed from the house she looks to be running smoothly, but the camera gives us a dizzying view of arrhythmically bouncing ears as the world wobbles by at high speeds, punctuated by pauses when she turns her gaze to the ground, to her feet, to the sky, as though attempting to collect every detail of her surroundings. There are long montages amid tall grasses. We call her back to us; as she gears up for another run we can nearly *feel* her full head shake: ten complete cycles in a second and a half, from left ear to the sky to right ear to the sky.

We can see how her attention flits, drawn by a chipmunk chirp, a stirring in the fallen leaves, or something imperceptible to us. More startling, perhaps, is to realize, via the camera, how often we are at the center of her gaze. Towering figures, we are gesturing and smiling and making mouth noises. Sometimes our arms extend suddenly and touch her head or curl a finger around her collar. When we start moving away, she is nearly compelled to follow. We have begun to be her sun.

This peek into her perspective makes it easier to imagine what she is experiencing as we walk with her. I put my nose in the direction of the breeze that hits us; I keep my eye on the stone wall where we saw chipmunks that one time; I take note of all the acorns on the ground that she might mouth. My friendly scratch of her ears startles her; yet she fails to notice as a small flock of deer in the meadow starts to rise from rest. The wind stirs last fall's leaves on the ground, and each leaf dances for her, flirtingly darting out of her reach. I am under no illusion that I know what it is like to be her, but I have started seeing into her world.

As we imagine into her point of view, I wonder if Quid has a sense of who she is, and where she comes from. It is time to try to visit a sibling. I message Annie, who adopted Acorn—still named Acorn—and who lives less than an hour away. Ordinarily this would be a straightforward visit, but we are knee-deep in the pandemic, sure of nothing except that other people are potential carriers of a horrifying virus. Our family has been in proximity with very few other people, and then only when masked and at an impolite distance. "Outdoors" is starting to feel relatively safe, though, when masked/distanced, and so we agree to meet in a little park not far from where she lives.

Quid, O., and I arrive just as Annie is approaching the park on foot with Acorn. If Quid has stuffed-animal good looks, Acorn is the original model for the stuffed creatures. He is about her size, tan, with the same white paint on his tail, legs, and snout—and completely scruffy. He has a full beard, quite distinguished for a four-month-old puppy. His ears are folded upon themselves, giving him a charmingly rumpled look, as though he has put on linen ears right out of the dryer. We hop out of the car, and Quid barks a hello, causing Acorn to turn and head toward us.

Their noses meet, and their bodies tense with excitement. They have lived apart as long as they lived together. I am alert for any sign that they recognize each other—a knowing look, a delight at reunion. I see . . . nothing. Not, at least, before they run off into the field and begin playing together. They quickly start a game of chasing-fleeing-tackling-biting-somersaulting, alternating roles. Watching Acorn makes me see Quid better, in noting their differences. She is a practitioner of the bite-scruff-jump-on style of play; he is more of a self-take-down kind of guy, pushing his head into the ground and flinging his body down after it. Her run is done with serious intent, whereas he teeter-totters, enjoying the moment. He knows about "holding on to other dogs' leashes"; she knows how to spin her way out of a jam. But mostly they look like variations on a theme, despite their little differences. And I finally see their recognition of each other: it is in the ease with which they began to play at all. With barely a preamble they just took up where they had left off two months ago when one morning brought a series of cars and a diminishment of siblings.

•　　•　　•

Parents are the only continual witnesses to their children's first years: the children themselves are not, it is now thought, witnesses to their own lives—at least not witnesses who can later report what happened. While the first three years are full of memorable events—learning how to walk; where mommy usually is; how to say *dog* and *baby dog* and *I want to touch baby dog*—people typically cannot later remember back to that time. The memory systems are still in development, and though we can later recall the *how*—to walk, to talk—the lived experience of that learning is lost. (Although some people feel confident that their memories of these years are real, "infantile amnesia"—described by psychologists as "one of the most robust findings in the memory literature"—has been proven time and again: at least in Western cultures, seeming memories of these years are by and large memories formed later, from other people's accounts of that time.)

One wonders whether it is the same for puppies. To say that children, or puppies, do not have memories of their early years or months is not to say that those memories are not present, or that this time does not affect them later. It is only to say that they do not have a sense of their early selves as themselves, whose story runs continually from that time through to whoever they are today. When Quiddity sees her brother, they likely do not share reminiscences about their early weeks on the towel with mom. That said, their behavior toward each other is different from that toward an entirely unknown dog: the littermates seem to recognize each other on some level, in a way perhaps not consciously available to them.

"Kin recognition," the unsexy name for knowing whom you are related to, makes evolutionary sense. Even without consciously being aware if someone is a family member or not, most animals have a way to avoid inbreeding with a relative. For dogs, that is likely by smell. In fact, one study found that even when presented with the odor of their siblings (collected from the towel on which they lay at night) without their siblings actually being present, pups who now lived with other, unrelated dogs could recognize their relatives. Another study, which let dogs sniff the urine of their siblings and of unrelated dogs, found that they still could distinguish their siblings—even if they had not sniffed these siblings for eighteen months. Male dogs were particularly adept at that, spending more time with the odor of unrelated female dogs.

Eventually this skill translates to recognition of their people, too. Dogs who are separated from their person for up to three years preferred to spend time with a tug toy or towel with their person's scent—the scent left by their hand—than with one a stranger of the same sex had held.

By four months puppies are thinking of people as "their" people. They show classic attachment behaviors—distress at separation, delight at reunion. Dogs have evolved to, perhaps, show more attachment to the people who adopt them than to the mother who birthed them. Even wolves make less effort to find and stay with their mothers after six or eight weeks old, and by four months, they show more attachment to their entire pack than to their mothers. Domestication may have extended this family pack to include these bipedal pack members. Dogs attach to us—and quickly: adult dogs in a shelter who receive three ten-minute visits from a person start showing signs of attachment behavior.

Without our noticing it, Quid has slipped into the next stage of her young life. While we tend to call any dog under the arbitrary age of one year a "puppy," strictly speaking they have matured out of puppiness at about twelve weeks. Now she is a few weeks into the "juvenile period," which starts where the socialization period left off and lasts until puberty, several months away. It is still a wildly formative time in their lives: their brains are still quite plastic, changing in response to their experiences. Weirdly, though, dogs of this age have not been widely studied. Anecdotally we know that events during the juvenile period can affect their behavior into adulthood—in other species, it is clear that certain abilities are set during this time and become inflexible—but scientifically, they are basically off the map.

What research there is has focused on the continued importance of socialization, even outside the socialization period. If those early exposures were the vaccines, these weeks are their booster. In one study a group of guide dogs in training were socialized to humans until they left the litter at twelve weeks old. Then, for the next several weeks, half of them went to kennels, where they saw very few people; the other half were placed in homes. When tested later on whether they had the skills to graduate to be guide dogs, the kenneled dogs more often failed—and more failed with each extra week in the kennel. Many failed because they were frightened of people and new things, thus not suited to the life of a guide dog, who must constantly be among new people.

While most dogs do not need to pass guide-dog tests to be terrific companions, this finding attests that even good training can be undone by time in an impoverished environment—say, being left alone in a kennel, or in an understaffed shelter without enrichment programs. Another study found that dogs who spent their juvenile period living in a kennel, garage, barn, or shed were more likely to be aggressive toward unfamiliar people, and avoidant of new situations, than those who lived in a person's home. Similarly, dogs who spent this time in a busy urban environment were the least aggressive or avoidant.

Their cousins, wolves, are much the same. Captive wolf cubs who have been socialized to humans in the first six months of their lives grow up unafraid of humans, but those whose exposure to humans lasted only three months lose the benefit of that after the next three months without people.

While "puppy classes"—where many pups are given a chance to socialize—are often recommended during this time, it is not clear that these, rather than other factors in the dogs' lives, have any particular positive effect on the dogs' future behavior. Nor is there any evidence that they are harmful; but given how different these classes are from place to place, it is clear that they ought not to be used as a substitute for regular exposures to new things, animals, and people.

At the Working Dog Center this period of time is a chance to try some of those novel exposures with the pups, who are no longer living with Pinto and the rest of the litter. They are each fostered in a separate home and come to the Penn campus for testing; there, Dana Ebbecke graduates them to a more rigorous protocol, the next step on the way to being trained to find odors. The pups are taller and lankier than when I saw them last. Vara (previously Yellow) is the first dog out of the gate, and arrives with a gaily wagging tail. She conquers the flirt pole—now flirted over a slick surface—like a professional fisherman. The rattle can has graduated into an even bigger milk jug with coins in it. It is tossed across the room and as Vara bounds after it, Dana drops a two-by-four to the ground, making me jump in my seat. Dana laughs: that is the idea—to see if that startling sound dissuades Vara from her pursuit of the exciting milk jug. It does not: she does not even wince. She merrily carries the jug by the handle, head held high, her body curved to support the heft of the thing, which probably is a quarter of her own weight. She throws it down, drops herself after it, and begins gnawing, her tail explosively happy. Finally Dana jingles a set of keys and drops them in a wheeled metal cart, which looks as if it is suited to moving boxes in a warehouse. Vara jumps into the cart without a pause, like a professional cart-jumper-upper. *You got it! My goodness! Good girllll!* Dana coos in a descending arpeggio. Vara is ready for the next set of tests that she and all the pups will take outside over the next months, exposing her to a greater variety of odd sounds, places, and people—mimicking what working dogs might encounter in their lives.

At this age, incidentally, children are a month into holding their heads up. They can raise their arms to try to reach a toy dangled in front of them. But they are not so great at reaching it. I can't help but admire the puppies: not only holding their heads erect, but holding them erect while reaching, grabbing, and pulling a toy, and jumping into a cart taller than they are.

In and up

~~~~~~

The grasses in the meadow have grown faster than she has; they now tower over her. In the wind they undulate as a continual sea, spraying us with the bright smell of a spring morning. From her vantage, though, she is facing a verdant wall, and refuses to enter it— or perhaps does not see that there is any way "in." Upton forges through, and the grasses bow in his wake, obsequious flora. I follow him. My legs up past my knee are washed with the cool dew that lines each blade. Upton wears a slightly crazy-eyed expression as he smells into the distance, tilting his head. He dives shoulder-first into the ground, rolling deliriously.

She not only doesn't get "in," she doesn't get "up." A new preoccupation is tearing after squirrels minding their business outside our house. The squirrels, used to our respectful older dogs' benign attention, are a little slow to react. But then they head for the safety of trees. At this, Quid is completely perplexed. Even after tracking them right up to the foot of a tree, when they go up, they essentially disappear from her universe.

Despite the heights she can jump, in the house we can still disappear from her world entirely—and give the dogs a reprieve from puppy attentions—by going upstairs. Each of the eleven steps to the second floor is eight inches high, but may as well be a mountain. She looks after us for a moment, but then walks resignedly away. We are just on the moon. Will be back later.

Quid finally takes the plunge into the grasses, mustering the biggest leap she can: Full Puppy Intensity is necessary to get in there. Soon she is stotting through the fields, neatly beheading dandelions with her mouth as she goes. Each descent, as she dips under the green horizon, her ears are the last part of her to disappear. On emergence she smells of mint, and I wonder for a moment what has happened to my nose, or to her breath, before I see the mint plants ravenously growing up amid the grasses.

Those ears. We are still monitoring her ears every day, with the obsessive attention of a dieter to the number on the scale. Daughter of an Australian cattle dog mix, she may have giant, erect ears in her DNA; we can't tell yet, though, since each day they tell a different tale. They may figure out "up" before she does, though. Today both ears are erect and gently folded over at the tips—though one pops up when the last of the food is being scraped off the dinner plate. Her ears stand in for the changeability of self, each day a chance for expression of a new shape. We gather a surprising expertise in the flag-language of ears. There are the half-mast ears, which rise up—only to fold back on themselves; asymmetrical—one up and one down; full mast, completely pricked; the rose ear, half-mast and pinned back; button ears, totally flopped. We can't make sense of their development. One day they salute; the next they bow under their own weighty effort. We scrutinize the photos of her siblings for their ear-fates. Each of the pups of the litter has differently directed ears, compass signs to varying life paths.

As invested as we all are in the minutiae of her life, my friend D. laughs at me, gently mocking, when I describe "how it's going with the puppy" and start off by saying I don't love her yet, and wind up having to defend myself against the accusation that I am coldhearted.

But I do like her, I say. I just do not know her well enough yet, I say. Sure, she is cute, I say—but love is more than acknowledging her cuteness. D. listens with skeptical eyebrows. *Heartless.*

Harsh. But even as I list reasons for my guardedness, I realize that in some ways they have nothing to do with her at all. They have to do with her predecessors. For most of my life I was a serial monogamist with dogs, adopting one only after another's death. When we met Upton, we had a two-dog household for the first time. It was nothing like the math would predict. One dog plus one dog does not equal a simple doubling of affection, play, and joy. It changes the nature of the family altogether. With Quid, we did not just adopt a puppy, we completely disrupted everyone's lives in the house, including those of the other animals. My relationship with Finn, with Upton, the dogs' relationship with each other—everyone's relationship with everyone else—is changed by this addition. And every moment of all of our days is changed. If the math of one dog plus one dog was complicated, two dogs plus one puppy equals some kind of irrational number. It throws the entire number line out of whack.

Getting a puppy changes us. The infusion of her young self into this environment brings out new or latent elements of our selves. O. has a brand-new smile: an ingenuous, big-toothed smile. I am vigilant: under-slept, worried about the future ramifications of a growl here, an urge to run there. A., already unflappable, now epitomizes the phrase "taking things in stride."

For the animals Quid's arrival has consolidated some of their most endearing traits and birthed some new ones. Finn wears the face he had as a puppy, with a steady, earnest excitement that surprises me. (It doesn't hurt that our pockets are suddenly full of treats.) For the first time ever he jumps out of bed in the morning and heads down the treacherously steep stairs before me—in order to see/growl at Quid. Upton oversees great open-mouthed play bouts where he is the friendly teacher looming over his young student. Finn nibbles her back, air-humping and growl-barking. Ever a goofy-looking dog, with his large body and rolling gait, Upton looks so much more dignified in comparison to the two of them. Edsel's early feline overtures were met with such predatory gusto that she now sits on the highest perches in the house, guardedly watching the puppy. Both she and Upton have ways of looking away from an overexcited puppy disdainfully that are quite effective.

You know, O. says one morning, *having a puppy is awesome, but it really makes you appreciate your time with the other animals.* The dogs' pace is familiar, pleasant—under control. On a morning outing they sniff the air, then move to wander toward the changes from the night before. Quid runs headlong into the day, hurtling her body into the new space (and/or leaf piles). By providing a constant contrast, living with the puppy allows us to see the other animals better. This might be the thing I do already love about Quid: her arrival changed the scene before us. Everyone's individuality is heightened. "One is unable to notice something," Wittgenstein wrote, "because it is always before one's eyes." Finn looks much older—by comparison, surely, but I notice as he teeters, loses his footing, as he hadn't before. He is always surveying the room, seeing where we are, what the puppy's gotten up to, where the cat is prowling. Upton's goofiness is tempered by a stoicism as he lies still, even with a puppy jumping desperately over him.

The puppy, by contrast, was completely unfamiliar, so all of her actions are highly conspicuous. Living with a new dog is a reminder of how much of what we think about dogs is speculation, inklings, glimpses, and innuendo—not based on the plain reality of you and a dog alone together in a room, looking at each other.

To counter this we have been playing a game developed by the trainer Kathy Sdao. As visible as the puppy's difficult behaviors are, every moment between them is filled with pretty desirable behaviors. Sdao's idea is to bother to look for these behaviors, and reward them, in the classic positive reinforcement way (with a happy *Yes!* and a tasty treat). Do it fifty times in a day, and you are forced to see all the good behaviors she is already doing—and encourage them. "Start with any behavior that is simply not annoying," Sdao says, helpfully. I look at Quid at my feet, asleep. I kind of love that. She is partially on my foot. That's nice, too. *Yes!* I wake her up, and offer a little treat. She looks puzzled, but I feel better already. She notices the goldfinches outside fluttering around a bird feeder, and does not bark, or run at them, or do anything but look and sniff. *Yes!* She wags and cocks her head. *Yes!* Bemused, she waits a bit, then eyes the couch, occupied by Finn, and wanders over to curl up in a dog bed instead. *Yes!*

For me the end result of this kind of activity is to suddenly feel much better, noticing all her non-annoyingness. I am reminded of the hopefulness of getting a puppy during the pandemic: the assumption that we will get to grow together as a family. That, more broadly, something like our Before Life will eventually resume; that there are things to look forward to, plan for, hope for. What a lot of hopes to put on a little puppy.

It is about this time that I realize that, because of the pandemic, our dogs are the only dogs she has interacted with for more than a few minutes since we adopted her. Even knowing the importance of exposing her to new dogs, we have mostly not. Our outings to a local park, famous for dog walking, have been our concession—but even there most people do not want to get close enough to meet a puppy on a leash, worried about breathing the same air, or about dogs transmitting the virus to their dog, or to themselves. Quid has met a sweet pit bull, a couple of other young puppies, a pair of lovely drooly bloodhounds. Maybe a half dozen more. Most only for a few minutes. Nothing near what a life in that hopeful future will bring, dog-wise.

So we go to meet a dog. Caine is a very large, sweet Tigger in the shape of an eight-year-old boxer. His greeting leap, begun at a modest gallop, will knock me down. Caine's people, our friends, invite us to walk with them in the meadows outside their home: they are happily game to try to forge a canine friendship between the two.

On arrival at her first ever playdate, we learn that Quid has hackles: fully down her back to her tail. They appear promptly after Caine approaches us with his usual enthusiasms. Quid hides under me—if you can get "under" a standing biped. She growls a little, barks, and ignores the treats offered to her. By contrast, Caine seems delighted to have a puppy on the premises and is romping in circles around us, politely not crowding her, just keeping an interested eye in our direction. We all stand around talking, as people do, while Quid stands around growling, her eyes fixed on Caine.

Ten minutes into this I finally suggest we begin walking along the wide mowed path of their meadow. I drop Quid's leash so she can move at her own pace. And at that moment the entire dynamic is changed. At once she is chasing and being chased by Caine, jumping on him and letting him bound over her. They race ahead of us, disappear over the hill, and return running in parallel. Their relationship has gone from "lightly hostile" to "best friends" in sixty seconds. And so goes the next half hour. Along the way she hops into the meadow after some scurrying thing, unwisely sticks her nose down various large excavations made by a ground-dwelling animal, and is completely fine with both the presence of another dog and these two new, masked people.

And that is how I was reminded that it is easier to meet a dog while moving. Our normal human social encounter has us stopping and facing one another (for now, a social distance away). For dogs, this may simply be too much. Quid's approach is more as if we met someone new and just started running madly along with them, occasionally tagging them and racing away screaming. A game which, I think to myself, she wouldn't be unhappy if we played with her ourselves.

．　．　．

With our eyes on her ears, we have missed being witness to the biggest growth happening in front of us: the transition of her body out of puppyshape and closer to adultshape. She will continue to gain muscles for the next few years, but by fourteen weeks or so, her body shape is halfway to full dogness.

Dogs' bodies mature in what is called a "cranio-caudal" direction, meaning head to rump. The puppy head starts out quite large—part of what makes them look cute, with their heads out of proportion to their bodies, like those of toddlers. After early puppyhood most dogs' heads don't grow much, while the rest of their body catches up. Their head becomes a smaller proportion of their body mass, and its length is less of the overall body length. Maturing dogs go from plump to longer and slimmer.

Their legs, or what some biologists call "three-segmented limbs arranged in a zig-zag configuration," develop at different rates, too. Just as the head beats the rump, the front legs mature faster than the back legs. This gives puppies their appealing, bounding gait—one that is also likely tiring, so they may need to suddenly rest in the middle of a walk. And the top segment of the leg, the kind of "upper arm," grows faster than the lower segment. The most stable adult dog body has an even length of each of the three segments, once the forearm grows out. This proportion can be all out of whack in dogs who have been bred to have very short or very long legs.

As she grows, the puppy has to adjust to a world that feels as if it is changing size, too. The cat bed she fit in during her first week with us, she no longer fits in. But she is still trying to squeeze into it. Similarly for laps and safe spots under the couch. Despite their rapid growth, though, dogs adapt spectacularly well to their changeable environment. In our lab's own research, we found that dogs trying to get through a doorway whose height we repeatedly lower have a good sense of what they can fit through, given the size of their bodies. They might try to fit through too small a space, but rarely attempt it more than once or twice before trying another method. The ratio of their shoulder—"withers"—height and the doorway size at which they began to adjust was nearly the same across all sizes of dogs, from Yorkshire terrier and Chihuahua to Airedale terrier and German shepherd. Most dogs use a similar series of adjustments to squeeze through an increasingly small doorway: first ducking their heads, then bending their elbows, and finally, if necessary, corkscrewing their bodies to the side.

So maybe their insistence on sitting on your lap when they are grown, and no longer lap-sized, is due not so much to a lack of awareness of their own size. They know how large they are. It has simply to do with their love of your lap.

Knowing their own size, incidentally, does not mean that they appreciate the size of objects they carry, as we saw in our study with a subgroup of dog participants who carried a stick while trying to make their way through the doorway. We provided the "three bears" of sticks: too long, much shorter, and just long enough. The dogs not only picked indiscriminately, they more often than not plowed ahead with their too-long sticks, banging both sides of the doorway. Oh, they eventually get through—but not by reasoning out the solution. Instead, they just brute-force it, trying again and again at different angles until it works. Dogs can limbo under a fence beautifully, but if you want to momentarily trap them, just give them a stick wider than the gate they are passing through.

As she grows in stature and her body grows more proportional, we start seeing the parabolic growth curve in the height Quid can jump—and also the full spread of gaits that are seen in most adult dogs. From her very first steps with us, she was doing the classic dog walk— the slow gait in which each side's rear limb chases the forelimb: rear right, front right, rear left, front left. Three feet are always on the ground. With puppies, though, movement escalates into a run pretty quickly; the run is called a gallop if they achieve full flight for a moment, all legs off the ground. Due to her shorter back legs, Quid's gallop is half bunny hop: front right, front left, back two at once. It is part of what gives her that stotting appearance in the tall grass, and contributes to puppies' toddle. As a small dog, walking on leash alongside one of us, she trots: the opposite legs move together—front right with rear left. On each side, the step of the rear leg more or less hits the same spot as the front leg does (more so in coyotes and wolves, who have clean, tight gaits; dogs are a little more "sloppy," in the tracker's vernacular).

We are used to this now—to her gallopy, leaping ways. It is worth comparing what she is doing to the development of the species studying her. By five to six months old, when puppies are barreling through grass fields, infants are just sitting up on their own. Well, striving to sit up, and often succeeding. Their balance is not great, though, so they steady themselves on their arms, like a tripod—which often leads to their toppling forward completely when they try to reach for something. (And missing what they are reaching for, too.) Once on the ground, five-month-olds might be accomplished enough to accidentally roll themselves from their stomach to their back—something they have been working on for months. When it happens, researchers describe their "extreme surprise" at having so reoriented themselves. This tripod posture can evolve into "frogging," a stage among twenty-three stages in the progression from lying still to walking. At five months, they still have sixteen stages to go.

As our puppy matures, we are getting more of a hint of what effect a global pandemic might have on her, and dogs like her. Through our only consistent connection with others—online—we began hearing about this new phenomenon: *pandemic pets*, the media began to call them, as though they themselves were a rampant virus. Our society was suddenly connected by the shared experiences of those now dealing for the first time with a companion animal. In fact, though, nearly 330,000 fewer animals were adopted in 2020 than in the previous year, a 17 percent drop. This defies the impression many people had that their local shelters were "empty": indeed, many did clear their available dogs—but either more did not come in, or this count did not include dogs whom people did not want to adopt. But rates of dog *purchases* may have increased. (Sales numbers are not tracked in the same way.) A very real phenomenon for all these pets, though, is the unusual glimpse that they are getting of human society. Early development is a time when a puppy can learn how the human world works—only it is not really working now. It is limping along, as we try to figure out what is happening, how to behave, and whether there is a way out. What is visible to dogs is the experience of the pandemic that we wear: we are wearing masks, and we are wearing our anxiety.

It is not long into the widespread acceptance of mask wearing when I begin to be asked if dogs can recognize us while we are masked. While I have been surprised to not recognize a few familiar people with their masks on, I am more surprised at how many I *can* recognize. Apparently I know more about my friends' hairstyles, foreheads, and clothing choices than I thought. And I don't even have the dogs' superpower: they know our smell. In a recent study from our lab, we presented dogs with the smell of their persons—absent the presence of the person—to see if they could distinguish it from other people's smells. To gather the "person smell," we asked one person in a two-person dog household to wear a new cotton T-shirt for two nights without washing it, washing themselves, or using any fragrances—including soap and lotion. Our shirts capture the very normal odor that humans effuse all the time, which is detectable to our nose but that we do not consciously take in (except, perhaps, with our family members, on the one hand, and strangers on the subway, on the other). Dutifully following our instructions, the T-shirt wearers then stuffed the shirt in a large Ziploc bag, sealed it, and gave it to us. When the second person in the household came to our lab with their dog, we presented the dogs with the stinky T-shirts—as well as with a T-shirt from a stranger who had performed the same routine. By timing how long they sniffed each one, we found that the dogs had no trouble distinguishing their person's odor from a stranger's.

If a dog knows who you are without your even being present, your having a mask on is not terribly confusing to them. That said, to identify us by smell, they must be relatively close to us—or we have to be extra stinky and have a breeze at our backs. Dogs are much better readers of our bodies than we are of theirs (or of ourselves); we tend to focus on people's heads overmuch. Dogs do rely on our faces, too. A recent rush of studies on how dogs perceive human emotions found that they are good at distinguishing happy faces from blank expressions and happy from angry faces (preferring the former, of course), can match a photo of an angry or happy face with a vocalization in the same emotional valence, and can use the happy or disgusted face of a person opening a box to choose wisely which box to approach themselves. And they can identify these expressions even when presented with a photo of only the top half of the face—in other words, with the part that they can still see when we are masked. They are just as good with top-half faces as with full faces.

The only downside of our wearing masks that I can see for dogs is that we are providing less lovely food-breath odor for them to sniff. I do wonder about human infants born during this time, though. Might they grow up thinking that their parents are the only ones with full faces?

Even as we are building a relationship with the puppy, training her to be good with other dogs, other people, with the noises of the world, I feel unsure what we are preparing her *for*. As with our children, it is not obvious what the future holds: perhaps we will not return to the social world that we inhabited before. It puts to a point the very question of what it means to be a dog in the human world: What does it mean to be a dog in this pandemic-stricken world?

For now, being young is her reality, and the condition at hand. Perhaps the best we can do is see her as she is now. I gently pull my foot out from under a sleeping puppy's head and turn off the computer to go to bed.

Height Puppy Can Jump: An Alarming Growth Curve

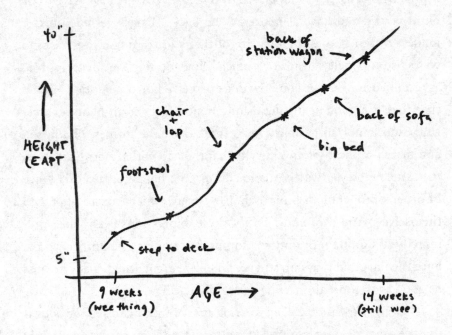

The troubles

She is running in a distant field, ears levitating with each step. She is already a more mature dog, longer of limb and firmer of body. Five months old, she has lived longer with us than she did with her litter. O. has become tall and gangly, too, right before my eyes. While Quid's white whiskers are turning black—reverse aging—Finn's black muzzle is streaked with white hairs, the backs of his legs now woven with gray.

Time has folded onto itself: the isolation induced by the pandemic colors each day similarly, and, without clear markers for the days, we have lost our sense of the date. Every now and then we realize that another month has passed, as though we have been in a deep sleep. And so we wake up each day surprised to see a slightly different puppy. Early photos of her are already unrecognizable—she was supremely tiny, a puddle of warmth and light, in contrast to the leggy, swaggering dog in front of us now, her hips rotating extra much to pull her long legs forward. She is replacing herself continually.

Her development feels as if it is defying time: it is out of time. Living with her is one of the few things that gives texture to the day. Each day is punctuated only by how long it has been since the puppy was out; when she last ate; the last time we threw a ball for her or hid some treats for a treasure hunt. While we all swim in this new reality, her daily needs and weekly development give us our bearings. Still, the protracted feel of the ten weeks of early puppyhood, when so much was happening, contrast with the ten weeks she has been with us: every day an eerie variation of the previous.

The variations are concerning. Quid's days are not taxed with worrying about the future. But I have begun to worry. Her behavior is mercurial—it is as if she could become a new puppy each morning. One day she is brave and confident, charging through a fence to greet a dog on the other side; another she is shy and unsure, hiding between my legs when a woman comes to say hello. She alerts, hackles up, at a man in the far distance walking along but then also wags and licks at the face of another who holds out a finger for her to sniff. It is as though her sense of categories is in flux: Is this friend or foe? Something alarming or ordinary? Should I bark or should I hide?

Recently, she has elected to bark. At three months she began barking at unknown dogs and people—and at anything notable at all. I remember back to her youngest days: the house where she was born was filled with barking. All the puppies learned to bark before they were scattered into different families, different homes. But with us Quid's bark had been quiescent; she was choosing her voice carefully. Now it's out. She barks when she plays, when she runs, when she hears a car pass. When a bird lands on the bird feeder; when a plane flies overhead. On the particularly full-moon evening, she barks at the moon.

Too, she has become what I would describe as *fixated* on little furry things. Her fondness for chasing squirrels has extended to chipmunks. And mice. And voles, and woodchucks, and rats, and any other furry, scurrying thing. Also not furry or scurry: hopping birds, snakes, moths, and swallows darting through the grasses. She cries piteously when I leash her; ignores me as I try to entice her with a treat, or a run. Once she has spotted someone, she must chase.

Her enthusiasms in the house have grown in scale. She has begun play-biting—a lot. And hard. At times she looks at O. and growls. In a mood to have some attention, she will grab my leg and mount it, staring at my face. If we pay her no heed, she goes and finds the cat and incites her.

It's troubling.

It is not undoglike, of course. What is troubling is that the literature suggests that single events in this period can change how puppies respond to whole classes of stimuli. My first-love dog, Pumpernickel, was accidentally outside in a thunderstorm one day; until she blissfully lost some of her hearing in her dotage, she was terrified of incoming storms. The puppy who receives an overly sharp nip from an annoyed adult dog may be reluctant to approach another dog for years. With Quid, I have no concern about her being afraid. Her world has thus far been friendly and safe. She and all of her siblings had gentle handling by people since they were out of Maize's body. They met patient sheep and cats and birds. The constant din of people talking on the radio, of cars driving by, of nearby farm equipment and construction, have acclimated her to the noises of humans. One day a military helicopter flew low over Amy's backyard; I stared at it constantly, covering my ears. The puppies were completely unmoved.

So the trouble is not whether she will do okay. It is whether she is ready for this world—and the world for her, for that matter. I am concerned for the small dog who reminds her of a squirrel—to say nothing of the squirrel; the child innocently going by on a bike; the over-friendly neighbor who reaches to pet *such a cute little head*. Quid is set on "high," and the rest of us are running at medium-low.

I realize what we need to do. We need to re-up her socialization, to further expand her universe. We need to take her into Town, capital T.

We start with a small t: a nearby upstate town, Hudson, New York, whose main street is usually lined with strolling pedestrians popping in and out of its coffee shops, gourmet cheese shops, and antique furniture stores. In the warm early evening of a summer's day, we drive there. We have not visited for many months—nor have most of its usual strollers. While the pandemic has loosened its grip on us somewhat, we see on approach that the sidewalks are fairly empty. With our windows down I hear little but our own car; I feel as if we are visiting the Ghost of Hudson Past. All the better to take things slow with Quid—for whom this sleepy version of a city will be the first version of any sort.

While we find the town to be decidedly one-horse, Quid is agog. I listen more carefully, and there are lots of sounds she has never experienced: a mailbox clanking as it swallows a letter; a walk sign ticking down the seconds; an unmufflered car cruising by; another's engine idling; a squeaking door. The train along the river, a mile away, hoots its arrival. A thick smell of heat radiating off the asphalt colors the air. Every nook has a smell, and the shop entrances, set in from the sidewalk, present new inlets for exploration every twenty feet. Every minute or so someone appears ahead on the sidewalk, which begins a little routine: I see the person, I see Quid see the person; she prepares to go on high alert. That is when I ply her with a stream of tiny treats, and we continue on, my hand near her mouth, until the person is blissfully past. Ten minutes of this and she is exhausted—as am I. It is effortful to notice everything. She naps all the way home.

The next day we try Great Barrington, a town of similar size—and similarly ghost-towny compared to its usual activity. Quid leaps from the car with a look of anticipation, scanning the scene as though looking for a person, squirrel—anything—to bark at. There is no one. The walk seems disappointingly free of Quid-exciters, but then we hit the gold mine: the hardware store. Its doors are propped open; inside are two or three customers strolling its capacious aisles, and three young clerks. They light up at the sight of her. They approach. Quid freezes. I freeze. They make the sounds of people seeing a cute puppy. I ply

cute puppy with treats, which she takes from the side of her mouth
while staring down the approaching clerks. They are three young
women, and they walk toward us in the very nonthreatening way that
three young women do: in a meandering route, as directed toward one
another as to their destination. This kind of indirect approach works
perfectly. They murmur at her; Quid cocks her head. I could not have
designed better new-people-to-meet. Quid lets them close, they get
some petting in, and she gets a metric ton of treats over the course of
three minutes. She is now looking to us when she feels wary—and
expecting a treat. We oblige.

This small victory emboldens me. It is time, I decide, to go to the
Big City.

"Oh, it's not the usual city; what a shame," my friend K. says of
New York City, a few months into its social-isolation turn. She means
that we cannot expect its usual shoulder-to-shoulder sidewalk density,
the unending construction noise, the reliable runways of dogs being
walked from apartment house to park and back. But I am optimistic.
We have to imagine it from Quid's point of view. To her, *everything* is
new and incredibly surprising. She has never seen high-rise buildings.
Elevators. Miles of sidewalks. Sidewalks with people, sidewalks with
people and dogs and pigeons and trash cans. The sheer numbers of
people on even a quiet street. The sounds—the backing-up truck; a
door slamming; a metal gate being raised or lowered. And the smells!
The condensed stew of smells from all the life-forms that have passed,
and the considerable odors (and objects with odor—be it poo or a tis-
sue) they drop. (It was Upton who made me aware of some of these,
through his ravenous interest.)

Driving into the city, I look at Quid in the back seat, her body
curled into a round dog bed, and wonder if it will be too much. While
she is an agent of chaos and energy in our house, this is New York! I
promise her sleeping form that we will leave if it is overwhelming.

As we reach the outskirts of the city, I smile at the dearth of car traffic. Otherwise, from an outsider's perspective, the city looks much as it always does. It is a fine early summer afternoon in the middle of the week, and there are incredible densities of people everywhere: by the river, along the streets, going in and out of shops. I see more people in five minutes than I have in the last five months. After parking I take a final look at Quid before I put a leash on her and introduce her to the city where we live. She looks ready.

And then she encounters all the things. There is person after person—some appearing suddenly from between cars, from buildings, or from surprising metal portals to the underground. Some have hats, canes, are in motorized wheelchairs, are very small people who run directly at her and try to pick her up. Some are loud. Some have wheels on their shoes, or sail on loud rolling boards. Faces mostly have masks, and some have hair flowing down their chins. Some smell quite profoundly strong, even to the person on the other end of the leash. There are things on the sidewalk: Paper bag? Check. Fast food wrapper? Check. Plastic bag lofting gently in the breeze? Check. There is birdseed and birds on the wing and birds on the air conditioners. Birds are also frequently on the ground, which is very exciting, except they disappear as we approach and she looks in vain after them. Pigeons are a new kind of giant bird that are nearly her size. There are very daring squirrels who stare her down and saunter off only one Quid-snout-length from us. The ground itself is a kind of permanently tough grass that holds all its secrets in layers on top, not buried deep down so that one has to snuffle long and hard to find them. Then there is a different kind of grass, hotter to the toes, bearing giant noisy animals that roll and lack the usual animal smell. They make a vaguely threatening rumble. Some emit melodious tunes; some make repeated persistent flatulent sounds; some sing a loud repetitive tune that rolls up and down. Other animals get out of the way for that one. Sometimes a person is *disgorged* from one of these creatures and comes toward us cooing like the doves at home.

There are rocks to climb, trees to sniff, running people who she assumes want to be chased, right? She gets no encouragement from me. She tries anyway.

There are other dogs—so many dogs. We meet: Puddles, Milo. Stella. Poe. Layla, Luna, Bernie, Ziggy, Gio, Echo. We meet giant dogs, fluffy dogs, doodles, more doodles; geriatric dogs; toy dogs, barky toy dogs. Dogs in baby strollers; twin dachshunds; three-legged dogs; blind dogs; dogs who are "bad with dogs"; dogs who "love people"; shy dogs; dogs who "hate kids." We meet an inordinate number of wide-eyed puppies—and dog people with various degrees of wide-eyedness themselves.

Even over the course of a few days, my own perception is changed to notice the things she might be alarmed by. I, like her, take notice of each person in the distance; the very large or small kid on a scooter, scootering wildly, or with an especially big helmet; the cyclist, the bell-dinging cyclist; the rumble of train underground and the heaving weight of the buses cruising by us; people with limps; people with walkers. I register all the types of ways a young child can be unexpected: they head straight for you; they teeter, they fall over; they grab at you; they yell, they scream, they cry; they shake things, throw things, drop things. I fixate myself on stimuli I have learned, from living in the city for years, to ignore: motorcycles; a screaming man raging down the street; a larger-than-expected rat. I fixate on things I have learned to deftly step past: wafting plastic bags; puddles; out-of-control grocery carts; moving men walking blindly behind dollies stacked high; delivery people launching off their bikes on the sidewalk. I know that at seven o'clock people will lean out their windows to clap, to ring cowbells, to shout their gratitude for first responders; Quid does not, and on hearing the clamor, looks at me expectantly.

And then I see that she is turning to me at other times, too, which is basically telling me that she is noticing something that she feels unsure about—and so I find whatever is unnerving her and we bravely walk past it together.

Quid's smallness—combined with her big ears—turns a lot of heads. As people reach down a hand or want to pat her head, she ducks and weaves out of the way. At the same time, she tries her own form of reaching-down and patting, as she is curious to approach and close-sniff each person. (Some of them veer out of the way, too.) And I learn that she has conquered the leash to the point where she is now ignoring it completely. The force that comes out of that puppy's enthusiasm, translated through her harness and along the leash, impresses me. And is another area of trouble. The best moment this morning was before nine a.m., when dogs are permitted off-leash in the city parks. I drop her leash and she flies toward a handful of dogs at play on a park hill. For all her isolation, Quid shows no hesitation with these brand-new dogs and is soon caught up in a zoomy run with a smiling yellow lab and a small black puppy. For a moment I relax. She is just a good pup.

Then on the way home, as the crowds clear the park, she sees a single person in the distance and barks a single shrill bark. Then looks at me expectantly for a treat.

•   •   •

Barks are considered "noisy" in the language of audio, where "noisy" means there is a lot of broadband sound—full of different frequencies but without a clear tone or note. To amateur ears, they are just noise. But "noisy" does not mean meaningless. Barking is communication, and our reaction to this noise—to shush it or punish it—is more or less like slapping a child for talking unbidden.

What are dogs talking about? Barks convey a lot of emotional information—there are barks to induce play and barks barked when alone; there are barks to announce a stranger and barks used as a request—and also have information about the age and sex of the barker, for anyone listening carefully. Indeed, while most people are unenthusiastic about any barks their pups make, it is notable that barking is right smack in the frequency range of human speech—and may be an attempt to talk with us in a way we could understand. Wolves, dogs' nearest relatives, rarely bark. Dog barks are certainly pitched to get our attention. Some authors see a homology between baby crying and some kinds of high-pitched barking: both are considered "annoying" and trigger a response from people; especially afflicted are young adults of childbearing age.

The dog person's concern—*will she bark all the time?*—is a real one, given the societal view on barking. And yet that quiet puppy in the other room: watch out. With a puppy, as with a baby, silence is desired and yet disquieting. One of Quid's early lesson plans for us had her being perfectly quiet. After ten minutes we realized that we could neither hear nor see the puppy. We found her in O.'s room, methodically disemboweling a Sharpie. Often, quietness indicates miscreance.

Many people's instinct when a dog barks loudly is to yell, delivering a stern *No!* or *Stop it!* But when we do this, we are responding with a kind of bark right back at the dog. It is funny, and a little sad, that we do this, since their barks are not angry yells, but messages with content. Now, the *No!* might work for a moment (*what is she barking about?* their cocked heads seem to say), but this is not a long-term way of getting a dog not to bark. The dog's behavior indicates that they do not understand "no" as meaning "no barking, please," but rather take it as general opprobrium. In the face of barking, the truly savvy keep quiet.

This is not to say that dogs do not have a sense of what "no" means;

any dog who has been on the receiving end of a human's angry nega-
tion surely does. They understand the anger of it—if not exactly which
thing they are doing we might be angry about. And it is nonobvious
even to humans: it is eight or so months before a child understands the
word "no"; a puppy raised among humans will have picked up the tone
of it five months earlier. A comparison of child and puppy language
comprehension in their first year is informative—about what we assume "comprehension" involves in each case. Babies appear to begin to
recognize their own names by four and a half months; Quiddity knew
both her name and her most common nickname within, conservatively,
two days of hearing them. I should clarify what researchers mean by
"recognize" or "know." Those four-and-a-half-month-old children
turned and listened longer to their own names than to those of others—
e.g., a child called Emily listened three to four seconds (about 25 percent) longer to the sound of her own name than to someone saying the
names Christopher, Marissa, or Samantha. When I say Quid "knows"
her name, I mean: she looks at me when I say it, stops moving when I
say it, and (a big ask) comes closer to me when I say it. And she fails to
look at all when I say "Samantha."

While dogs will never become fluent language users, we weirdly
downplay their own communications. Children, it is widely touted,
have a few words in their arsenal—in addition to the early *mama* or
dada—by twelve months; Quid, at five months, will never say *mama*
to me, but she has different whines and barks for needing to go outside,
wanting attention, disturbance at the cat's taking her bed, and requesting more tickling-of-ears; she knows the spatiotemporal difference between "wait" and "stay"; she knows not just her name but the names
of Finn and Upton. She lies "down" when I ask her to get "down off
the bed"—not so much a misunderstanding, I would say, as a wry
commentary on the equivocation inherent in our requests to dogs.

When a researcher (or parent) gushes over the creativity of a two-year-old child's ability to put together words in a novel way, to express a new meaning—*water* plus *bird* for a duck, say—I smile, nod my head agreeably, and remember the moment that Quid put together two actions—walking over to the stairs to our bedroom, and looking at us—to express a new meaning: *I need to pee.* I'm just sayin'.

Vara, aka Yellow, has a different experience with barking: when she does come out with her shrill, insistent bark, the trainers at the Working Dog Center shower her with praise. Amritha Mallikarjun sends me videos of each member of the V litter in their sixth month. There is surprising overlap between the enthusiasms of each V and our Q: I see them whining to begin a game; nearly outrunning their own legs with their energy. But their life courses have otherwise diverged dramatically. Long and lanky, Vara is clambering over wooden pallets, lightly navigating a pile of cement rubble. She gallops by a school bus with its hood open in a rakish manner and stop sign permanently out, then trots back and starts nosing around various large pipes. She halts at one and starts barking repetitively, her tail curling flamboyantly with each broad wag. Surprisingly, a person pops out from behind a barrier and shrieks her praise, while also proffering a rope to tug. This is the "live-person search," in which the dogs are asked to find the survivors in a pile of rubble intended to mimic a disaster scene—and Vara has found her live person.

All the dogs of the V litter have been in "odor training" now for weeks. Odor training is not training to notice odors; all dogs do that naturally. It is training them to think about that one odor that *we* care about—and to tell us when they have found it. The working-dogs-in-training are first imprinted on a novel scent: "universal detector calibrant," or UDC. In large quantities UDC smells to the human nose like "sawdust and cleaning supplies," according to Amritha's human nose. The compound was designed to be unlike odors one typically comes across in daily life, as well as being stable at different temperatures, safe to handle, and volatile (enabling detection by nose). Using this odor allows the trainers to teach the dogs to search before they are committed to their "career" odor, be it narcotics, missing persons, or the smell of disease.

The dogs first meet the smell when taken to a specially designed room. It is empty but for a few elbow pipes set on the floor; other pipes are set into a plywood wall like portholes. In one of these pipes a very small amount of UDC is hidden. Harnessing the power of puppy curiosity, trainers simply let the dogs explore the room. When a pup happens, after a few seconds or many minutes, to poke their nose near the UDC-smelling pipe, the trainer sounds a clicker and, thrillingly, a dog treat is spontaneously tossed onto the floor near them. The dog is led away after eating the treat, and then released again—so of course they go looking for more treats. When they happen across the odor again, *click-treat*. Their recognition of the game being played here is almost visible on their faces: soon they strategize, trying the same *place*, the same *behavior* . . . until they get it—the same *smell*.

From this first exposure the V litter has graduated into practicing finding an odor in larger rooms and on a custom-designed scent wheel—a merry-go-round with odor-containing glass jars where the cars would be. And now they are in training outside, too, searching for other smells, like one likely to be found in the world—person smell—but unlikely in the environment of a pile of rubble, or a big field. When they detect the scent, they are encouraged to bark as their way of notifying their handlers that they have found whatever-the-thing-is-to-be-found. Not to bark once, or a few times, but a dozen times. Two dozen wouldn't be worse. The V litter dogs are larger than Quid, but their barks are surprisingly similar: piercing. The audio manifestation of excitement verging on desperation. To a dog, they excel at the bark alert.

In a parallel universe, where everything is identical but for our urgent need of a skilled locator of and alerter to squirrels, small dogs, and passing cars, Quid would be a hero. I feel a little sympathy for her that she, so clearly a master bark-alerter, was destined to live in a family where that skill would not be celebrated.

Barks, whines, and growls aside, most of dogs' talk is with actions. None of these action words has been taught to her. A paw on my hand: a request to keep petting her. Turning her head away: a refusal, expression of distaste or disgust. Head resting on my lap: somewhere between possession and affection.

There are canid-sapiens overlaps in language learning, too, though. Dogs have the same problems with reference that children learning language do. Imagine a child walking with her parents, who, spotting a bird in the distance, direct her attention to it: "Look at that bird!"— or even, "Look at that woodpecker!" Assuming that the child has not already learned about birds, this is a significantly confusing statement. There are any number of things that might be meant by "bird": the trees, leaves, sky, clouds, something between the tree and the parent's gaze, or the bird itself. It could be the redness on the bird, the fact of flight, the small thing, the big thing. It could be the heat on their face, the brightness of the light, the smell of summer.

Eventually, kids do get it. We have all eventually gotten it "within the first few years of life," one paper exults. "How do [we] accomplish this task?" It is indeed quite a feat of cognition—but the caveat here is important for us to remember. It takes *years of life* for a species being explicitly taught, talked to near constantly, and already genetically predisposed to learn languages, to understand references like "Look at that bird." And yet with puppies, we say "no" to their barks and expect that they will understand our meaning out of the gate.

To sleep, perchance

~~~~~~

Right now a puppy naps beside me. Quid is melted onto a cushion, her legs and tail outstretched in a kind of supine flight. Her top ear lies inside out. She twitches her toes, and her tail thumps a beat on the cushion. No doubt she is dreaming of the hike.

We have had a five-mile hike with my friend G. and her terrier mix, Jaxx. The two dogs probably covered twice that distance. Regularly Jaxx disappeared from view, his long limbs quickly carrying him into the dark woods and out of our sight. G. was unworried, only occasionally stopping to inquire after his whereabouts with a piercing whistle. On meeting Jaxx, Quid brought out her hackles and her piercing bark, but Jaxx's particular nonchalance seemed to calm her. She settled into complete idolization. Where Jaxx sniffed, she sniffed. Where Jaxx peed, she peed. And each time Jaxx bounded off, Quid tore after him—but then, to my surprise, stopped, looked into the distance, and turned back to me. I doled out her entire breakfast kibble by kibble this way, calling her back to me dozens of times. She turned on a pin at my call: it was amazing, a dog I did not know she was.

She is nearly six months old. Spring has turned into deep summer. The bright, distinct leaves of springtime trees have blurred into a green darkness that shades from a powerful sun. On the porch together, she hops up to sit on my lap as I write, watching the tiny twitches of my pencil until her ears alert her to a distant dog bark, a barred owl hoot.

Her attentive gaze—eyes, ears, and nose—tracks a woodpecker's metronome in a tree, then a quarrel with a nuthatch. The top of her head smells like the air above a river, that fresh, clean smell of water and energy. She *is* that energy, a rush of river and air made flesh.

She is homing in on her style. It includes the dreaded barking—at a passing runner, or trotting dog, or kids with water pistols. I see passersby pausing, gauging the threat attached to my leash. Despite her shrill greeting, she plays well with others; she seems happy to play with puppies; with tall, large dogs; with old dogs; with dogs with three legs (she likes to walk under them). Her repertoire is not closed, though. She learns that squirrels disappear into trees, bringing her awareness to a whole nother dimension: up. She jumps after their disappearing tails, surprising herself, and one day she discovers that she can launch herself up the stairs in explosive bunny hops. Our upstairs hideout is rendered useless. *Down* is another thing entirely: to go down she tumbles, letting her legs scatter forth, marbles let loose down the stairs. For the dogs we have placed carpets as traction on each landing, concession to their aging limbs. The stairs remind us all of our bodies.

Finn lies aside me, shooting me occasional looks. He has been my dearest companion for so long, I can read his tenseness at this trespasser. Once in a while he stalks her on the path to the house and swipes at her with his mouth as she tries to run by. *That's fair*, I think. He has been slowing down precipitously, though. His back legs are uncoordinating; he exhausts more quickly. Sometimes he stumbles; sometimes I find him marooned, standing with his back feet together, a tripod. He is easily knocked down by an over-enthusiastic puppy. His face has gotten leaner, and his eyes have lost their luster. Even as Quid's tail is winding up, Finn's has lost its vibrancy.

Each dog reflects a part of me, I think: I see in Finn the responsible one, always the good student, following rules; in Upton the clownish character, a pleasure in being silly. I don't see Quid in me, yet. Must I? Is that part of coming to love her?

I do love her *asleep*. I know the science says that petting a dog lowers blood pressure, but just gazing at a sleeping dog is my relaxant—just like finally getting the baby to sleep was. Oh, the many satisfactions and ways she sleeps! On O.'s lap in the car on the way back from walks; on my lap in the evening after the final play zoomabouts with the dogs; on, by, or under a dog or cat. Last night Finn, Edsel, and Quid all piled into bed with O., each a puzzle piece fitted to the others. Earlier, after a run, she conked out on my feet as I stood at the sink washing dishes.

Some evenings, while she dozes, we open the computer and check in again on the other puppies via their people's social media posts over the previous days. Even as we have monitored Quid's every change, her siblings' changes are all the more surprising for appearing in bursts. Now one of them is an ardent swimmer; another has a new dog sibling. There are more smooth-coated than scruffy pups, but five have furnishings like Quid—the beard; unkempt eyebrows and nohawks; furry toes. The scruffiest also look the most mischievous and wizened, with a sometimes unsettling gaze. The smooth-coated pups look sweeter, more like the big babies they all are. Four pups still have at least a glint of gem-blue in an eye. This week I see, across pups, the full display of ear postures: two floppy (four pups); two half-mast (two pups); one floppy, one half-mast (four pups); and one pup whose ears are giant satellite dishes, saluting brightly but for the tiniest bend at each tip. It is gloriously anticipatory, the flower just on the edge of explosive blooming. We nearly reach through the computer screen to unbend them.

· · ·

Being charitable, I could say that my fondness for seeing a sleeping puppy comes from knowing about the cognitive growth that happens in sleep. "A reversible state of immobility with greatly reduced responsiveness" is how sleep is defined in scientific papers, but that is only what an outside observer can see: that the puppy is relatively still and quiet (but can be roused). Despite the seeming lack of activity, there is a firestorm happening in the brain during sleep. In humans it is a time of memory and learning consolidation, as the jargon goes—meaning: memories are strengthened; things learned during the day are solidified. Getting REM, the dreamy rapid eye movement sleep, is important for emotional regulation and interpretation, as well as for creativity. The rest of the body benefits, too: sleep helps maintain a healthy immune system, normal metabolism, and even cardiovascular fitness.

Dogs' ancestors, wolves, are for the most part nocturnal, active at night. Under the cover of night is a good time to hunt (and evade predators), and with keen noses and great night vision, wolves have no need for daylight to make their way. Dogs have adjusted—or been adjusted, through domestication—to our non-nocturnal human schedule, and are mostly active during the daytime. This is not to say that they never sleep during the day, as anyone home from work during the pandemic witnessed. Adult dogs might sleep for up to a quarter of the daylight hours (and three-quarters of nighttime hours)—more, if they are given nothing to do during the day. Young puppies, and even six-month-old puppies, sleep much longer during the day than they will as young adults.

It is not a coincidence that most of Quid's sleep is on or near us. In one survey of dog sleeping behavior, researchers found that if allowed to, 87 percent of dogs choose to sleep close to a person. (Well over half of people forbid their dogs to sleep near them, though.) For us, letting Quid sleep in O.'s bedroom allowed her—and us—to sleep through the night; one wonders how many similarly simple "fixes" of behavior could be enabled by just changing the rules around where a dog sleeps.

On the other hand, all that healthy brain- and body-developing sleep not only gives full rein to her proper development, it permits her more difficult behaviors to thrive. Ah, well, a risk we have to take.

Exactly how sleep helps learning in dogs has not been as well researched as it has with people. In 2020, the researchers in my lab and I took advantage of all the people at home full-time with their pups and recruited subjects for an experiment to test this. We asked volunteers to teach their dogs to "touch"—to touch their nose to their person's open palm on cue. The clever trainer Victoria Stilwell, who provided our human subjects with a step-by-step training video, uses touch as a way to scaffold more-complicated requests. Once you have a dog moving to get their nose to your palm, for instance, your palm becomes an attractant, and you can move your dog around—off the bed, onto a perch—by just asking them to touch it.

Our canine subjects were divided into two groups: one learned "touch" in the evening; one in the morning. Then each group of people tested their dog's performance twelve hours later—after a night of sleep, or a day of (mostly) awakedness. Every pup learned the trick, and both subject groups performed pretty well when tested again. But the pups who had slept before their test were both faster and better at the task than the daytime group. Of the daytime group, those who napped more during the day were better than the light nappers. As with most of the science from our lab, what we find translates into an immediate change in how I think about the dogs in my home. After learning this, we have shifted what training we do to the evening—to be followed by a long night's sleep. And I now monitor my sleeping pup not only for suckling and running in her dreams, but for dream nose-bumping.

It turns out that Quid is actually the biggest sleeper of her litter. At half a year old, I was curious to hear more of the pups' stories behind their Facebook posts. I have seen that the eleven Maize puppies have developed their own ear, nohawk, and eye styles, but what about their personalities? There is no science that links the genes for scruffiness to mischievousness per se. (As it turns out, there is one gene that, when dominant, leads not only to the furnishings—beard hair, crazy-man eyebrows, willy-nilly longer hair—but also to coarse and low-shedding hair.) But much is made of the influence of dogs' genes on their personalities: breed standards for purebred dogs are founded on the idea that, given a known set of parents, their young will be in many ways predictable not just in their appearance, but also in their temperament: bold, friendly, fearless, and so on.

I send everyone a survey asking about their habits, their pup's behaviors—and also asking for three words they think best describe their puppy's personality. For Quid I list *rambunctious, playful, clever* (sometimes too clever by half). Several other pups are also described as smart; a number of others as "energetic"—if not of the rambuncting variety. "Affectionate" or "loving"—even "all-loving"—appear in several responses, as well as "cuddly" (definitely not Quid). One pup is "thoughtful," another "kind," and another "gentle." These are not *full* siblings, surely . . .

Other answers swing similarly spot-on or way off. Few of the other puppies' people describe any problems with barking—although, to be fair, most of them did say that their dogs bark at delivery persons, or new people and dogs. They just do not see it as a problem. Two dogs— presumably the kind and thoughtful ones—*never bark*. I stare at those answers a long time, envying them. On the other side, five pups are described as shy or fearful when meeting new people or dogs, and whine or hide behind their person—now unimaginable, for Quid. She has company in her devotion to chasing small creatures: ten of eleven pups love to chase birds and squirrels. A handful chase their tails. All but Quid, apparently, are described by their people as snugglers.

As a completely isolated new-dog person, I find the most edifying section to be everyone's response to the biggest problem they have encountered with their dog. The answers are a testament to the ways that even genetically similar dogs can grow up differently, despite a very similar first nine weeks—and to what people prioritize, worry, or care about. Car sickness, over-stimulation, digging in the yard, whining. Difficulty staying in their crates, wariness with people. Biting. Barking at kids. Most satisfying, though, are what people say are their favorite things about these problem-filled dogs. "Everything," one person replies. Another: "I wouldn't change a thing."

The biggest tell of the pups' relatedness—or of their pandemic lifestyle—comes with the question, "Does your dog generally follow you from room to room?" Unanimity. Eleven pups, scattered out in different parts of the northeast United States, dutifully keeping at the heels of their person from kitchen to bathroom to bed.

PART 3

Quid Years

Longing

~~~~~~

I sit on the living room floor with my legs out, my book resting on my lap while I watch her. All four animals are in various postures of repose. The air is late-summer hot; my water glass beads with cool moisture. The dogs lie on their sides, legs extended mid-trot on an invisible wall. Quid rises and moves to the soft dog bed in the corner. She curls in its curve, stays twenty seconds, and rises again. She tries lying right at Finnegan's rump, her head resting over his back feet. Nope. Up again, to the dog bed, which is really Finnegan's. A short stay. She approaches me and plops down perpendicular to me, close enough to rest her head on my knee. That's it, I think. That's perfect.

Nope. She moves her head astride my leg, fails to find the perfect place, then gets up again, and hops on the couch where my son is reading. Not quite. Finally, she heads under the dining room table and flops on her side, squeezing herself between the table legs. That's the one.

The puppy is in heat. Finnegan is the one to tell us about it. One day, well into my third Zoom meeting of the day, it occurs to me that he has been playing with her incessantly. That is odd: their play is occasional at best—and usually after dinner, when their leftover excitement about a good meal is redirected toward each other. The next day Finn is her shadow, regularly gnawing on her back in his corncobby way; the next, he has several episodes of attempting mounting. It is nice to see him rejuvenated, but it is clearly her smell doing the rejuvenating. Though he was neutered when we met him fourteen years ago, a neutered dog can still smell—and desire—sex. Quid is more interested in her own nether regions than usual, too, I notice. There is no blood, no obvious signs of menses, so I just keep a close eye (and leash) on her. In New York City two days later, we meet a calm, perfectly coiffed mutt with white eyelashes named Glinda who shows a strong interest in Quid. "Oh, let me guess, is yours a young male?" the person at the other end of Glinda's leash asks, explaining that she is only ever interested in male dogs. I watch Glinda, and see her teeth chattering. She is flehmening, the spectacular, often grotesque facial expression that animals use to bring hormones—pheromones—to the specialized vomeronasal organ under their nose and above the roof of their mouth for sniffing.* The hormones of ovulation would be wafting off Quid—and would be fascinating to a dog of either sex, given how rare an intact dog is in the city. Glinda is smelling her, confirming Finnegan's diagnosis. Quid has become a lady.

Given the science showing the importance of gonadal hormones in early bone, brain, and muscle growth, Quiddity will go through a heat cycle or two before being spayed. Our vet is on board; Dr. Cindy Otto, director of the Working Dog Center, tells me they do not spay their females until fourteen months; renowned vet Dr. Karen Becker advocates waiting until three to four years for a routine spay—but, short of that, recommends simply waiting "as long as possible . . . every month adds beneficial hormone secretions that will serve her well, later." All we have to do is keep her from any unneutered males, which is completely doable with some attention (and a leash). Happily, Quid is mostly on leash already, because of her over-enthusiastic interest in

---

*The most familiar flehmen response may be the horse's: a teeth-baring upper- (and sometimes lower-) lip withdrawal that is halfway between a surprised grimace and "Look at my brand-new teeth!"

squirrels, so there is no change there. We avoid the dog parks. And we get her some diapers specially designed for dogs once we see tiny blots of blood around the house. One day as she is keeping me company while I make the bed (read: lying unmoved on the sheets I need to use), I cannot resist the urge give her "the talk." I will never have a daughter; seems a shame to let all my years of knowledge of womanhood go to waste. I try to tell her about what she might be feeling, and how male dogs might act around her. She stares at me wide-eyed for several minutes, then rests her head on her front leg with a sigh. Mother-daughter talk accomplished.

With the diapers on, Quid is suddenly a terrifically pleasant, calm dog, who jumps into my lap for comfort and rests peacefully for hours at a time. She is subdued, perfectly mannered, and quiet. Take them off and she is her usual impish self, straining at the leash after every chipmunk in the tri-state area, and willfully oblivious to us. We start calling the diapers "behavior diapers," and goggle at the change in her disposition with just a cloth wrapped around her rump. It reminds me of the effect of a raincoat on dogs: dogs who do not like them freeze in place. They stop being *themselves* a little bit in this new fashion. Happily for Quid, she will wear the diapers for a week or three at most. Happily for us, they serve as a reminder that she can be calm— and a reminder for her, too, that calm is as accessible as frenetic. In the same way, training her to "sit" when we ask her to is not about her "sitting" per se; it is about her learning that she can do more than one activity: she can be running around, and she can be still. And that we value that stillness now and then.

Her heat lasts three weeks. I mark its length by how keen the dogs are on her in the morning and evening. Evenings are a big riot, with Finn and, more recently, Upton nibbling her and angling to mount her. Neither is a successful mounter—no wonder, with a lifetime of zero sexual experience—though Finn can briefly grasp her body with his paws. She is perfectly okay with it all—even instigating. I see her long-ing to scratch this itch that, despite our bedside talk, is an inexplicable new part of her. Showing a new and surprising flexibility, she torques her tail to the left to enable access. She sidles by both dogs provoca-tively. Their flailing attempts and her general energy every night make for a spectacle. Watching the two boys pursue her relentlessly, and her dodging between them and under them, I tell O. that this is a preview of his life in a couple of years, with some boys skulking around trying to get some girl's attention, and her going hot and cold with the boys. It does feel recognizably teenagerish.

• • •

We don't know Maize's life history, but we do know that about sixty days before she arrived in upstate New York she had an encounter with a boy dog.

As domesticated animals, dogs have been subject to our interfer-ence in their sex lives for many, many millennia, but only in the last century have scientists studied dog sex in earnest. One of the pioneers of this nascent field was Frank A. Beach, who got into it innocently enough, through studying the effects of hormones on behavior. He wound up eavesdropping on the sex life of a large colony of beagles at a facility in the Berkeley hills above the university's campus, later to be home to a colony of spotted hyenas (whose reproduction was also surveilled). The site had an indoor area where each dog could have their own space, and a large outdoor enclosure, of which a small sec-tion, less than half the size of a basketball court, was fenced off for coital business. To study the beagles' sexual behavior, Beach and his researchers basically waited until the female dogs were in estrus—sexually receptive—which for dogs happens twice a year. Unlike nearly all wild canids, whose reproduction is seasonal, prompted by days getting longer, domestic dog reproduction is nonseasonal.* At those times the researchers let the males and females out on their half basketball court to frolic together, observing the goings-on from a small shed they built in the center of the field . . . which was certainly not noticed by any of the dogs.

In the beginning the researchers' method was to let a male into the field first, then (literally) toss a female out after him. It took a male dog approximately one second to mount a female, in these cases. Things got more interesting when, instead, females were let into the field first. Then the female dogs were choosy about whom they let mount them, preferring some partners and rejecting others outright.

As a child I felt that the only thing possibly more embarrassing than the act of sex itself was talking about sex—or anyone's writing about it. Beach had no such compunction: he describes the courtship and mating process in great detail. The male dog starts by sniffing and licking the female's vulvar area. He may chatter his teeth, a kind of flehmen behavior that helps these odors get absorbed and carried to his vomeronasal organ, below the nose, to be smelled. If she is so disposed, the female stands there agreeably and lets him sniff. That is about it for the courtship. The male mounts *a posteriori*, grabbing her around her waist with his front legs. His first pelvic thrusts are in "the general vicinity" of the vagina. Once he gets to the vicinity more specifically, he proceeds to thrust, clasps her strongly in her rear armpits, and pulls his tail down. Sometimes a male will bite the nape of a female dog's neck to either help stabilize himself or keep her from moving away. This ritual continues in a sometimes comic fashion. His legs, Beach

---

*The one exception is the basenji, who have one estrus annually and seasonally. This breed, with others including the Afghan hound and the Siberian husky, has been identified, via their genotype, as part of a genetic cluster that is perhaps more closely related to the distant wolf ancestors of all dogs. Among wild canids, bush dogs also do not reproduce seasonally, and dingos' behavior varies by population.

describes, "move spasmodically in what appears sometimes to be poorly coordinated stepping movements." Once in a while, in a particularly good moment, one presumes, his back feet both leave the ground at once. High-speed photography of the whole affair reveals male hip swiveling as well, too fast for the naked, or otherwise captivated, eye.

The female's role in this dance was initially described as: just hang out. As an aside, Beach mentioned that should she not like what she is feeling, or should he be thrusting off to the side, or otherwise ineffectively, the female may "whirl around" and "violently" dislodge the male. Several years on in watching coital behavior from the shed, the observers looked more closely, and amended their assessment of what the female dog was actually doing from "standing still" to engaging in a complex procedure having thirteen distinct "acts," including: sniffing or licking the male's rump, prancing in front of him, occasionally mounting the male herself, and, sometimes, forcibly rejecting the earnest male.

If all is going agreeably, and there is no dislodging or violent rejection, the male will proceed into tumescence, whereupon his penis is now too large to remove. At that point one of the pair swings a rear leg over the other so that both dogs have all four feet on the ground. Then the two dogs remain attached at their tushes, standing looking away from each other as they reflect, presumably, on their various choices that resulted in this state of affairs. This "copulatory tie" or "lock" can last from ten minutes to an hour. It is the time when the final batch of the up to five billion sperm is ejaculated, but is also a convenient way to ensure that some other male cannot come along and try to copulate with the female, too. Males of many species use this strategy, from bees, who literally leave their genitals inside the queen, to the house mouse, who plugs up the female with a kind of cork. Beach summed up much of his work in a paper entitled "Locks and Beagles."

He and his team recorded every consort, every rebuffed advance. They found that the females were discriminating, and that some males were popular with all the ladies. Thus we can report that in his first tests, Peggy never rejected Eddie, and Dewey had a special thing with Ken (whom Peggy, Spot, Blanche and Kate hated). Everyone liked Broadus, but Clark was regularly rejected—a total of 111 times by Blanche. You might be getting the sense that males are considered promiscuous and in most cases receptive to a female in estrus. The scientists did not speculate as to what was so alluring about Broadus, or what was off about Clark—but I think that if the team had included a female researcher, they might have.

What we know is that somehow Maize found a fella she could put up with for the several necessary minutes of intercourse. He more likely found her, as male dogs some distance away* are able to pick up the scent of a female in heat, detecting the change wrought by her rising levels of estrogen. In estrus, her urine has notes of acetophenone (smells to us like orange) and benzaldehyde (bitter almond), as well as less of the off-putting sulfide compounds than it usually does. Maize possibly consorted with more than one male: a litter can include pups who have different fathers. And, as the old story goes, two months later she was in a dark room in upstate New York, and something big was happening in her belly.

In fact the old story has changed significantly for dogs over the last few decades—at least, for some dogs. While it is easy enough for dogs to find one another and mate if left to their own devices, breeders of purebred dogs would rather not leave it to their devices. A champion dog's choice of mate may not—would likely not—comport with the choice that a breeder, with the breed's desired features in mind, would

---

*While anecdotal reports describe males coming from miles around to find a female in heat, exactly how far away they can detect the odors in her urine hasn't been scientifically investigated, surprisingly.

make. Purebred dogs' sex lives are all arranged marriages: matching good genes,* or good looks or temperament, with same. And many of these marriages happen without the dogs ever getting within sniffing distance of each other. Only their sperm and eggs meet.

Artificial insemination, one veterinary textbook states, "is an easy procedure. The difficulty," it continues, cagily, "is in collecting semen from the male." However, when it comes to it, the same book lays out the method as: "collect the sperm." One veterinarian who performs "AIs," as they are known, tells me that the method is "cleaner" than sex. "Breeders think that dogs don't want to tie," he says of his clients. In his practice, he says, 90 percent of artificially inseminated female dogs are successfully impregnated.

•   •   •

"I got a half hour from my house and realized I didn't have my ejaculator," Cheryl Asa says out loud to the people gathered at the Wolf Conservation Center in South Salem, New York, on a temperate day. She bounds in with enthusiasm, and the room comes to life: they have been waiting for her. The room is in a facility up an unmarked driveway, off a small highway that, after a drizzly night, was littered with sodden carcasses of small animals—raccoons, possums—who did not make it across the road. Had they, they might have encountered the twenty-one critically endangered Mexican gray wolves and twelve red wolves who live here, on thirty-two acres of mostly forested land. Today two of the gray wolves are going to encounter something new: artificial insemination day.

---

*The dog's genome has been mapped, and many inherited diseases can be traced to particular genes and rooted out. There are still breed standards that do not root out inherited diseases, if they come along with a feature of the breed thought to be desirable. (Hopefully the previous sentence will soon be incorrect.)

Dr. Asa—known as Cheri—is trim, with a full head of gray hair. A reproductive specialist retired from her position at the Saint Louis Zoo, she is on her "annual semen tour," as she calls it: part of a Mexican gray wolf recovery project that takes her to conservation facilities and zoos from Ohio to Minnesota to Julian, California. And today to a rural area an hour outside New York City. Thirty years ago she was asked by the U.S. Fish and Wildlife Service to start a semen bank for these endangered animals—part of a project managing their genetics for best reproduction and, ideally, reintroduction of the wolves into the wild. Today Cheri will collect the sperm of wolf M1133—aka Rhett—which will be injected into wolf F1538, Valentia: what the veterinarians and researchers gathered here call "AI with 'fresh' semen." It is not clear that Rhett and Valentia have any foreknowledge of this event.

When I arrive at the Center no one is manning the door. I step inside to a flurry of activity. A volunteer looks at me questioningly before disappearing with a load of towels. Maggie Howell appears from around the corner and greets me with a wide smile. Maggie is the executive director of the Center, an organization founded by the renowned pianist Hélène Grimaud that houses endangered wolves and runs educational programs about them. When I wrote to Maggie asking about the possibility of a litter this year—wolf pups are typically born in spring—she invited me to come to witness the artificial insemination process, as casually as asking me to brunch. To her it seemed perfectly natural that I would want to observe the moment of (possible) conception.

I did. And now I am watching as the AI team busy themselves in this makeshift surgical theater. At its center is a wolf on an exam table. Rhett, twelve years old, is a seventy-pound male born in captivity, who was successfully released into the wild. But he ran the wrong way and was recaptured—twice. Now he is here, and, on his own, without human intervention, paired with a wolf called Belle—with whom he had a litter. "He's a cute dad," Maggie says. Near the end of Belle's pregnancy he was worried, pacing back and forth in the manner familiar in obstetrics hallways everywhere. He left the den and returned with a deer head as a gift. She lay down on it.

The room is gradually filling with spectators—volunteers and staff and board members. It smells of forest, of animal breath, and the closeness of Rhett's body. He is lying on his side, slowly blinking. It feels eerie to be so close to a live wolf. His paws are huge and still. He is knocked out, but not all the way. Without delay Cheri starts trimming the fur around his penis. "The manscaping part," she says, just a faint smile on her lips. Veterinarians are moving around Rhett with a catheter and syringes; someone protrudes the shaft of the penis, inserts the catheter, then the syringe, pushing on his bladder to eject any urine. Cheri brings out the ejaculator, a surprisingly large probe that, in short order, she puts into the wolf's rump. The device's electric current is intended to stimulate the muscles around the prostate to contract and the pudendal nerve to prompt the expulsion of seminal fluid. A multi-person team descends upon Rhett: one to probe him, someone holding his penis, someone to collect the semen in a clear little plastic cup you might use for lemonade. Someone holds his back leg up, someone cradles his head and forebody, someone has a comforting hand on his belly. The first probe shorts the circuit. They reset it, then reapply what Cheri describes as a low "tingling" current, and suddenly there is a very small amount—on the order of drops—of lemonade.

Cheri looks at the cup and says, to no one in particular, "Sometimes there is junk in the first one." They repeat their procedure until a few cups have been not-filled. Afterward, Dr. Soon Hon Cheong—known as Cheong—an associate professor at Cornell's veterinary college, spreads a very small amount on a glass slide to examine the semen through a microscope. Cheri peers into the lens: "It's really dilute, but there are kickers"—vigorously swimming sperm. She is looking to see how many there are; how active they are; if they are shaped well; how many have heads. Cheong takes a video on his phone through the microscope lens. A few minutes later he brings it over for us to see, flipping past family photos on the album. Crazily jiggling sperm are racing across the screen, not having the faintest idea where they are heading in a few minutes. "They look good," he says: it is the "first ejaculation of the season." Cheri concurs: there are about 150 million sperm in that cup. Cheong sets about syringing the sample to spin in a centrifuge, concentrating it for the insemination.

Rhett is carried out in the arms of one of the larger men on the staff, and in short order Valentia is carefully carried in and placed on the table. She is a large wolf, about the size of Rhett, though with a much smaller head and smaller feet. A quick measurement finds her sixty-eight centimeters tall at her withers, or shoulders—about the height of a Doberman pinscher. Her fur is brush-tipped with black, and her ears are a pleasing brown-red. Were she a dog, her tail would be the main topic of conversation at the dog parks: it is ostentatiously bushy. Today marks fourteen days since a sustained-release hormone implant has been inserted, inducing ovulation; right now, her progesterone level is just where they want it. When breeding wolves with AI, ovulation is induced, as everyone wants to minimize the handling that would be necessary to see if they were ovulating; with compliant domestic dogs, by contrast, a veterinarian can simply check the blood work every few days. Caught at the right time in the estrus cycle, there is a high chance of success—higher when the male has "good quality" semen and the female is "relatively young" (meaning two to four years old), of course—language familiar to anyone who has looked into their own fertility. "The timing is pretty good," says a vet helping with the anesthetic, "at least, if she were a dog." It is his first wolf AI.

He ties her tail back and cinches a blanket under her. Someone pets her face and coos at her: "You're so pretty." It is hard not to put a hand on her. Rebecca Bose, a curator at the Center, gives me permission with a glance: "Now's your chance to pet a pretty endangered wolf," she says. I take it. Her fur is wiry but soft, not dog silky. Her brow is smooth, and I caress the soft edges of her ears.

"Put yourself in her position," Cheri says to everyone as they get ready to begin, asking for a little space for Valentia. I step away, respectfully. The team removes the hormone implant. Then they grab her front and back feet and reposition her on the mat. To inseminate dogs, veterinarians and breeders use a catheter and common syringe; here, too, Cheong uses an intravaginal endoscope to find the cervical opening to identify the best placement for the semen. In both dogs and wolves AI can be done surgically, through direct injection of the sample into the uterus via the abdomen, but that is more invasive than the method they are using today. In some cases, a dog will tolerate the procedure without sedation, simply standing cooperatively as a doctor with a steady hand investigates her nether regions. With wolves they cannot rely on such cooperativeness.

In a second the deed is done. In the wake of the insemination, Valentia is carried back out. She and Rhett will awaken apart, with dim memories of what has happened. The veterinarians and researchers start packing up their equipment, chatting about IVF methods and how to grow oocytes outside the uterus. The spectators disperse. Dirt and den bedding that came in on the wolves is left on the table, now wolfless.

Gale force ten

Outside, as summer fades to fall. Smells rise from the ground in layers, warmed by the morning sun, and emerging in great puffs and rivers from the forest of tall grasses at the side of the place we walk. She is with the one with the sometimes furrowed brow aimed in her direction. But soon she forgets if she is with Furrowed Brow or not, because there are things moving in the grasses. She plunges into them face first, bounding up to catch a glimpse even while her body charges forward. And then on the path is one of the thrilling new forms that is entirely still, then *hops!* tantalizingly back and forth in front of her, until completely disappearing in a non-path in the side forest. At the appearance of one of these, she flies toward it, determined to reach it before its disappearance, only to be stopped, shockingly, just as she is accelerating. Her body itself seems to stop her, but then clearly it has something to do with this body-touching thing that Furrowed Brow is always pulling over her head. She does not like it. Not only does it provide sensation in all sorts of places that do not want to have constant feeling, it abruptly stops her legs from running when she wants to run so, so fast.

This time Furrowed Brow makes a horrible sound—the sound her mother made when she nursed too hard, or that sibling who could not get out from under the puppy pile they loved. Both were frightening, and so is this, so she runs back to Brow and pads alongside her, forgetting the hopping form, just looking up at Brow's face with worry. After that Brow makes the noise much less often, and she runs after the forms much less often. Trotting next to her yields instead a flurry of small yums placed directly in her mouth, and a tinkling of good sounds from Brow's mouth.

I am running with Quid. We have had maybe a dozen runs together thus far. She has been surprisingly good: just running ahead of me on the park path, in pursuit of some real or imagined small animal, then, once they fly off or disappear in the brush, turning back around to wait for me to catch up. It is different from walking with her on these same paths, when she has the chance to not just run ahead but also run as far behind me and back again. But then the invisible rubber band between us begins getting stretched too taut: she is racing farther and farther away in her headstrong pursuit of a bird or bunny—either unaware of where I am, or perfectly aware but just comfortable with it.

I am less comfortable with it. She might run off, get lost, harass animals or people. So I begin taking her on leash for the runs. At first she deals with it by circling me and stepping directly in front of me or—expertly, I am not even sure how—tripping me from behind. Now she just mildly zigzags, but is still pulling hard, a little sled dog with an intransigent load.

Today, as she pulls suddenly at the sight of a rabbit minding his own business up ahead, I let out a yelp. I first heard myself making these kinds of sounds several years ago when I began to trip on a corner of rug. I hear it come out of me like an exhale, involuntarily, when I am hit or knocked by someone or something, or cut off in my path. At my yelp Quid is instantly alarmed. Her ears flatten on her head and she stops, looks back at me, and hurries to my side. Whether out of concern or through thinking my yelp was directed at her, it has the effect of reining her in.

The next time she pulls, I give a little yelp experimentally—almost a quote of my previous one: *Yelp?* Quid immediately slows and moves alongside me. And again, another time. Within a few minutes she is jogging by my side, looking up at me with a smile (wrought of eyes and tail), matching my pace—and continues to, without leash or yelp. Four bunnies cross our path; she pulls to not a one. It feels miraculous. She clearly could do this behavior all along; we just never asked her to in a way she understood. Whether my yelping feels to me like a polite way to ask or not, it conveys the message to her.

She's changing. She is more sensitive. She begins to startle at perfectly normal things. A container of laundry soap on the floor prompts ferocious barking (deterring the soap not at all). Even after a peaceful introduction to the bottle on its side, she remains unconvinced that it is not a threat. O., lying on his stomach, rhythmically kicking the closet door behind him, causes Quid to run under my chair with fear. The vacuum, which she formerly followed around like a duckling with her duck mom, suddenly concerns her.

At the same time, she is even more headstrong, and more vigilant at home. She watches the activities of the house with both ears, her right ear turned back to catch what is happening in the kitchen, her left ear toward me, across the room, and her eyes on the dogs in front of her. Every passing car must be barked at. Loudly. When the cat sidles up to her and starts licking, Quid snaps at her and walks away. Her previously magical ability to "wait" at the door before going in or out has turned into a new trick: I ask her to "wait," and she runs by me. Many mornings I call her name, she looks right at me, and she trots the other way. I can almost hear her slamming her bedroom door behind her.

The dog park, previously a place of much joy, turns sour. She has changed, or the community of dogs has changed, for on entrance this time she is targeted by a dog with a certain gleam in her eye: Surly

Dog. Every time Quid makes a gesture toward running, Surly Dog runs up to and over her, nipping. Quid shrieks, a new sound, and tries repeatedly to get back over to me in some way other than running. They both crash into me and bounce off. I get a whiff of a sharp smell coming from Surly Dog. Quid ninja-slinks back to the safety of my legs. But she never quite recovers, especially after chasing a greyhound with enthusiasm and causing another bout of bullying. Straight out of a Marvel movie, Surly Dog's energy seems to conjure a storm, which sweeps in with surprising speed and gusto—literal gusto, winds that cause the trees to dance profligately with their neighbors. With the darkening sky settling over us, Quid nearly leaps the fence trying to get out, with stick in mouth. We hustle home, wind-assisted, just making it before the clouds empty themselves.

We are inside. I look at Quid, still holding a stick from the dog park. She is whining, as she always does when grasping a stick, caught between the desires for possession and for breath. Maybe it is the charge in the air, but her fur looks electrified. The scruff around her ears and snout is longer; the hair on the back of her legs points backward, like fins on a fifties Chevy. Her tail looks as if it was snatched from a red fox, it has blossomed into bushiness. I feel a wash of pleasure to know her, even realizing how little I do know about her, how she is changing right before my eyes. She is looking back at me expectantly, so I do what she expects: I tickle her ears, gently ask for the stick, and we head down the hall to find her a treat.

•   •   •

Adolescence unites fruit flies, lobsters, zebras, and humans—only the duration of adolescence for the former is about five days, whereas in humans it is about seven years (between the ages of ten and seventeen). Quid has entered these golden years—thought to be, for dogs, from approximately six months old (varying by breed) through their second birthday. Just when we thought we were done with "sensitive periods" of development, another one races in—only this one is woefully understudied by researchers and often completely ignored by dog people.

But there is good reason to pay heed to this period in their life. As is widely acknowledged in humans, adolescence is a distinct stage of development: one is no longer a child, but far from an adult. It is a time of risk-taking, social and sexual experimentation, and roller-coaster emotions. No one looks at a fourteen-year-old boy's oddly distant yet needy behavior, his increasing independence and quarrelsomeness, and wonders what bit him. We know what bit him: he is a teenager. When we look at an adolescent dog suddenly refusing to come when called, seemingly willfully misbehaving, though, people are more disposed to think *Oh, they're a bad dog* than *Oh, they're going through a phase*. We acknowledge puppyhood in dogs, then race them into adulthood, but there is in fact a long transition getting from cute pup to mature adult. A primary reason for abandoning dogs in shelters is behavioral—they jump, bite, escape, soil the house. They are aggressive to animals, they are aggressive to people; they destroy things. And there is a severe uptick in relinquishments during adolescence, partly due to the uptick in these behaviors; moreover, since euthanization is still the result for many unadopted dogs, "simply being an adolescent can count as a fatal condition," write the authors of a book about adolescence, *Wildhood*.

Puberty is not a synonym for adolescence; rather, it can mark the beginning of it. Quid's pubertal heat is the start: it is the time in her reproductive cycle when her estrogen levels rise; she then moves through several stages, similar to those of the human cycle, during which her body prepares itself and she becomes fertile. It not only marks the occasion of her being able to become pregnant; it is also the beginning of a period of rapid growth. Dogs bound from half to nearly all of their final weight from puppyhood to late adolescence—a little earlier in small and toy breeds, a little later in giant breeds. They reach nearly their final height at the shoulder by seven months. The increase in hormones that leads to a dog's sexual maturation and a growth spurt also have secondary results, including increased sensitivities and less self-control. These hormones affect every system of the body— and incidentally, they are basically the same hormones in people as in anteaters, otters, and dogs. Adolescence also oversees a rewiring of the brain—especially, in mammals, in the areas of the cortex that regulate emotions and make judgments. The result is a changed mind and body; along the way, there can be turbulence. "Like waking up in your tent in the wilderness, in a gale force ten," as trainer Sarah Fisher put it—both for the pups and for their people.

This time is not quite as sensitive a sensitive period as the previous one, but it is still a significant time in dogs' early lives—and a reminder both that they are still developing, and that what happens now can affect their later behavior. Research has connected events and living situations of early adolescence with various personality traits and behaviors as young adults. For instance, being isolated (in a kennel, or left alone outdoors) or injured (through punishment or attack) during this period has been connected to later problems in interacting with other dogs or people. Dogs who have been threatened or attacked by an unknown dog as adolescents are significantly more likely to be fearful or aggressive toward dogs as young adults; similarly, being frightened by a person (known or unknown) during adolescence leads to more fear toward strangers. Their companions matter: dogs who grow up with other dogs are less aggressive in general, and those who grow up with any pets at all are more likely to succeed in training. At least in research with rats, having an enriched environment in adolescence completely undoes the negative effects of the early-life stressor of being separated from their mothers—such as might be experienced by a dog from a puppy mill or other adverse life beginning.

Getting through dog adolescence involves some bumps. What is called, flatly, "disobedience" seems to rise during this time: "a passing phase of carer-specific conflict-like behavior," one study finds. Part of the reason for this is that puppyhood involves learning, to some degree, what the rules of the house are; being trained, to whatever degree, to sit or come or shake a paw when asked. There is a license granted to puppies to err, to get things wrong now and then. As they grow, the expectations for their performance grow faster than they do. Plus, hormones. Just as one might expect an adolescent human child to possibly not "come here" with alacrity when called, or to not do the dishes or clean their room when asked, one research study found that dogs who learned to "sit" on command as puppies are less likely to do it as adolescents—and are more likely to sit when a stranger, not their person (read: parent), asks. How perfectly teenaged of them.

An adolescent dog is trying to expand their world, to become more adult—hence the seeming challenging of their person's "authority." Adolescent wolves may leave their natal pack at this time: notably, their puberty is very much delayed compared to dogs', arriving at about twenty-two months. They may be more equipped, physically and mentally, to skedaddle; still, one wonders if there is a vestigial urge in their domesticated cousins to leave the den. Pups starting this growth spurt might become sensitive to touch, alternating shying from you and clinging to you; they may start climbing or jumping on people or things. An increase in climbing furniture is not just a challenge of the rules (in homes with rules about such things); it is also a sign of a vestibular system challenging itself. As dogs explore the world partly with their mouths, there might be more chewing of undesired objects, of licking. All of these acts might read as "misbehavior," but in some cases they may actually be a way of self-medicating: chewing, for instance, may help lower stress hormone levels. Quid's sudden stick obsession falls squarely in this territory, as does her changing interaction with older dogs, now that she can't get away with being that cute puppy they all humored. Adolescent dogs may literally experiment with their voices, adding new vocalizations—the child testing out what happens when they mumble or scream. An adolescent wolf howls at a lower pitch than a pup, a kind of analog to a preteen boy's sudden voice drop.

As so often during early life with dogs, patience is due. Providing an acceptable outlet for their chewing, licking, climbing—as well as some time without demands—is recommended for a safe journey through the wilds of adolescence.

While paying so much attention to trying to get Quid to run with me, I almost overlook her *running*ness. It is masterful. From a newborn paddling with her front legs, unable to hold up her body or head, she has developed in seven months into the fastest runner in our family by leaps and bounds (and partially via leaping and bounding). She feels inexhaustible—and no wonder. When we look at the daily activity level of dogs' relations, it is quite unlike the sort of day most people have planned for their dogs. One study of Italian wolves tracked them as walking, typically, up to thirty-eight kilometers a night. Coyotes on Cape Cod travel up to thirty-two kilometers—which is a third of the length of the peninsula; those in Wyoming can journey much farther (making use, during winter, of any available snowmobile trails to increase distance when the snow is deep).

Their quadrupedal bodies, of course, are designed to travel distances. Yet young dog bodies are not simply tiny versions of adult forms: their proportions are much different. This is notable, since we lump them into the same environments with grown dogs, and assume there is little challenge in that—unlike what we do with infants, for

whom infant-sized environments with baby furnishings and para-
phernalia are a huge retail industry. Growth of bodily limbs is not
continuous or smooth. Pups, like infants, grow in fits and starts: they
may grow dramatically in one day, followed by weeks of no growth.
In adolescence, the skeleton is maturing, allowing the body to catch
up with itself, evening out the proportions.

Teenage pups continue to gain muscle mass, and their strength out-
paces their sense of their strength. Often one of the first experiences
adolescent dogs will have managing their newfound strength and size
is with any similarly aged infants in the house. Suddenly they can
topple a child—the same one who may have been pulling their tails
with impunity a month before. It is an occasion for dogs to learn to do
what older dogs have been doing with them all along: hold back. They
are not always skilled at restraint—just as the infant cannot help but
yank that tail. At this age, an infant may have evolved from sitting up
to a lopsided crawl, an achievement commemorated in home videos
across the world. Quid, meanwhile, is calculating the fastest route
between where she is and where that dog she spied over the hill is, in
real time—and, just as fast, covering that distance. The word "beeline" comes to mind. The sheer physical aptitude and grace of dogs
running at full throttle is viscerally satisfying to watch—in just the
way, incidentally, that an infant's movements, full of imbalance and
peril, are not. Parents hover behind their young charges, hands spread
outward in front of themselves ready to catch the child at the moment
of the inevitable teeter. Despite the fact that dogs are literally on their
tiptoes all the time—the design of their legs is such that their heels
never touch the ground, as if in the most ridiculous high heels—their
balance is impeccable from the start. With Quid, I stay on the side-
lines, laughing involuntarily with surprise and pleasure as she runs
zoomies around another dog. The joy of it!

There is one way the seven-month-old infant and pup are in a similar mental and physical space for the moment: their quadrupedality. Crawling, babies mostly see the world below them, on the floor, and show deep interest in the slightest objects they find there. Such, too, is the mindspace of every pup. Both will learn, of course, to crane their necks upward to look at us, to mind the world of faces more than that of feet—but for now they can bump hips and share an appreciation for the smaller world before their eyes.

At the Working Dog Center, the pups have recently faced the so-called "impossible task"—similar to the one used to gauge whether dogs look to us for assistance. The task is essentially to open a box that is, simply, unopenable without tools. Or not: "A couple of our dogs have broken into the impossible task box," Dana admits. These pups from past litters have found a way to wedge their teeth into it and crack it. The researchers have had to up their box security twice now. Now the box is essentially a thick wooden structure with a seal-able well in its belly in which a toy can be stashed.

At just over six months old, the V litter meets the box. A video recorder is trained on Vauk, excited to be in this room with her trainers, excited to see what's next. Dana pulls out an orange ball—the ball of many young pups' dreams—attached to a short rope, while a second trainer holds Vauk by her harness a few feet away. The pup is thrilled. She begins barking brightly, straining at the harness to get to the ball. Dana slips it in the well in the box and sits down. When released, Vauk beelines for it and pulls the ball out by the rope with a soft touch. The trainers erupt in congratulations, as though she'd shot the moon. As Vauk prances about with her prize, they additionally reward her with a short game of tug. Then they take the ball back, and the whole scenario is repeated several times, with a Plexiglas lid placed a bit more over the well each time. On the fifth go Dana *screws* the lid over the well, and Vauk is released to find her ball. She runs with enthusiasm, mouths the lid, steps back with surprise, and barks. And barks, and barks. She tries mouthing the lid again, but it is like a Frisbee glued to the ground: she can get her mouth on it, nearly around it, but it is immovable. She resorts to frantic digging of the box; in her efforts she circles around it seventeen times, as though trying to unscrew the lid with her body. More barking, more mouthing, more digging. It is the nightmarish behavior of any pet left at home alone who decides they must get that ball under the couch . . . and proceeds to chew through the couch until they reach it. But for Vauk, who continues trying to get into the box for the full five minutes allotted, it is a brilliant success. She is wildly persistent, never appealing to the two humans in the room to *just help her out a little bit*. In the end Dana unscrews the lid for her, and Vauk pulls the ball out with glee. She is on her way to being an excellent working dog.

Six of the eight pups persevere for the full five minutes. This time, none gets in—but, then, that was never the point of the test. Instead, it is a gauge of their persistence behaviors—which are impressive. They date back to the puppies' strong start pursuing toys, noises, and keys headlong, and getting all the praise for it. In a home, their behavior would be misbehavior, but here it is celebrated. Watching Vauk get to perform all these exceedingly doggy behaviors and get rewarded, not punished, for them is a reminder of how challenging it is for puppies to comport themselves in a way suitable to human, not dog, standards of behavior. Even with her frustration at not being able to get her ball, Vauk is the happiest-looking dog I have seen in a long while—just from having been allowed to do what comes naturally to her and her species.

Seeing us

Quid and I have struck a deal. Every morning she flies up the stairs, leaps onto our bed, and attacks my nose with her sharp little teeth. And I am awakened.

Oh wait, no: we don't have a deal. She just does that. It is vexing and charming at once. Just at the moment of nose-attack I can smell the sleep collected on her breath and fur. It mingles with the odor of the other dogs in the room and is beginning to smell to me like home. Since her heat, she has become more interested in contact with us of any sort. She minds where we are, beating a hasty path after us if we rise from a chair to leave the room, sometimes licking our ankles as we go. She lies next to me on the couch, her body contorted to maximize body-to-body contact—somewhat at odds with the expected adolescent behavior. She is sufficiently around that I have learned to multi-dog-task: scratching one dog with my toes, using one hand to alternate tossing a ball for her and stroking another's head in my lap, while holding my book in my other hand.

Just now she is lying on my feet as I sit at my desk—her recent discovery of how to remain touching when I am perched on a chair too small for gal *and* dog. The weight of her head on my foot is peak dog-human happiness. At the same time I find it impossible to move and displace her, so when I do need to rise, I text A. to phone me. She lifts her head at the sound of the ring and I make my escape.

It feels as if she has come to a different level of awareness of us. She is seeing us: she is minding us. With this she has developed a knowing look. Picking up a peanut butter jar lid on the floor, she gently mouths it and carries it over to a dog bed, the prey captured and brought back to her den. And then she looks directly at me as she begins to gnaw it. Outside she picks up a perfect maple leaf by the stem and lightly pads away inside with it, glancing backward until she is out of our view. Another day she hurries into O.'s room, then saunters out carrying his sock, lazily mouthing it, looking right at me. There is a real understanding going on there, between my seeing her and her seeing me see her (and now my seeing her see me see her). And it is not an understanding of the nested seeings; it's an understanding of who we are, and how we tend to react, and what that means for the actions she is doing at the moment. It is what causes puppies to discover that your tone of voice, when you catch them aiming their heads toward a pile of some other dog's poo in the park, will be followed by your interfering—so they hurry up and grab a mouthful and run.

I am accustomed to Quid's untrammeled excitement outdoors, but now she reveals some awareness that I am attached to the same leash she is. She has learned "go around"—more advanced than the "up" of several months ago—in the inevitable situations that arise with long leashes and trees in forests. Like all the dogs, she stares wide-eyed at me while she poos. *Yeah? I'm doing this right now*, their gazes seem to say. I register the absolute astonishment in Quid's look when I first go to pick up after her in a public park. Given the disgust she shows for her own excreta, she must think me dangerous, stupid, or equipped with smell-deflecting superpowers.

With her heightened attention to us, she knows right when we are about to leave the house. There is a reason she keeps her head on my foot: that way the foot can't walk me out the door. She has learned that we now might leave. It is reasonable that she might have thought otherwise. She was born on the cusp of a pandemic, and even as her world opened to include us, and eventually a city's worth of other people and dogs, we have been with her continually since birth. If one of us left, another stayed; there was no occasion on which we all had to leave. With the coming of fall, and the loosening of restrictions in response to the pandemic's waning, this changes: we leave the house. Without her. To acclimate her, we practice leaving—almost as much for us as for her. We all step out of the house together, go on an aimless five-minute walk, then step back in without fuss. Then we step out for twenty minutes. Then for an hour. And then we drive off in a car, only returning two hours later. She seems to handle separation from us well, in that on our return the house is an intact structure not held together with dog urine and tiny bits of couch stuffing. But she greets us with a new desperation, wiggling so hard the energy comes out of her mouth in the form of a continual cry.

Observing us, she has done a decent job of training us. If I presume to stop tickling her belly before she deems it time to stop, she looks at me with great seriousness of purpose, then paws me, requesting more tickles. I tickle her more. When I stop, she requests again. And again. Sadly, she finds that not everyone is so easily convinced by her conversational charms. As I sit on the couch one day responding to my mistress's every demand for tickles, the cat slowly wanders between us. I stop tickling, and Quid, per her wont, tries to paw me—pawing the cat instead. Edsel, having not been trained in fulfilling the puppy's every request, responds by calmly but firmly biting her on that paw. Quid looks completely surprised. She paws again. The cat bites again, more forcefully this time. Quid looks at her, and tries again. The cat bites with vehemence and a yowl that communicates even to the unschooled. Not only do I suddenly see how much more trainable I am than the cat, I realize that though I thought Quid had learned to "touch" me to make a request, what she has really learned is something slightly different: to "stretch your leg out" when you want something. The communication was not the touch; it was the feeling inside her when her leg moved—whether there is a cat in the way or not. As surprised as the cat is, Quid is no less surprised to learn that she is saying something she didn't know she was saying. Just as we credit a baby with using language when they say *googa* ("She said sugar! She's asking for sugar!"), what I assumed to be communication was really the result of happening to be nearby when she stretched her leg. She is just blowing air, but I credit her with a whistle.

When I was writing my first book on dog cognition, I asked my friend D. what he would like to know about a dog's mind. At the time, he lived with Maggie, a good-natured mixed breed with fetching eyebrows and a fearsome wag. *What does she know about me?* he said. His response has stayed with me, as it is not uncommon: people wonder not just what their dogs are thinking, but what they are thinking about *them*—whether they know our secrets, harbor any ill will; whether they see through our deceits or feel the love we feel for them. My answer then, and now, is usually the same: science is pretty quiet on the matter. But to be sure, they are thinking about us, and it is striking to be held in their gaze. They learn our habits well enough to show us when we veer from them; they anticipate our actions even before we are aware of them. And yet they level no judgment—as happy (or happier) to see you on the toilet as at the door, not flinching at your nakedness or weakness. We adopted a puppy, not thinking that she would see us so well.

•   •   •

Dogs' knowing anything at all about us begins with our taking them in—began with our domesticating of them (or our hitchhiking on their own self-domestication) thousands of years ago—and is extended by their tendency to care about our faces. Not only are they very good at looking at our faces, as we have seen; they are also skilled at using those faces to get information about the minds behind them.

As we greet our dogs, sharing a long gaze, we are tuned to see some recognition there. Their faces match ours mainly in the particulars—the somewhat-frontal eyes, the prominent (if more prominent in one of us) nose and mouth—but there are other, more subtle parallels that resonate with us. Researchers looking carefully at the facial muscle anatomy of canids have identified a muscle, known by the cumbersome name "levator anguli oculi medialis" or (no less cumbersomely) LAOM, that dogs have, but their wolf cousins do not. It enables dogs to raise their inner eyebrows in a beguiling way that is deeply familiar to humans: we do it, too. It is an expression that reads mostly as sadness, the poignant gesture of a creature too weary or crestfallen to even utter a sound—and this might be why, as the researchers found, shelter dogs who flexed their LAOM muscle and raised their inner eyebrows were more likely to get adopted than those who kept a stoic expression. A second eye muscle found in dogs, the RAOL ("retractor anguli oculi lateralis") muscle, pulls the outside corner of the eyelids toward the ears, enabling them to sweetly grin with their eyes when they see you. The researchers speculate that these muscles might work on us by prompting a nurturing response—but also have a role in communication with us, just as a person's eyes can give the lie to their words or emphasize their honesty.

When looking at our faces, dogs appear to see more than just an array of parts: they seem to understand that our eyes—and our gazes—hold meaning. Gazes relay emotion, convey attention, and impart information. At less than a year old, Quid can follow my gaze to find the food I have dropped, to quickly grok if I am about to head toward my sneakers or my chair—to know what I know, after a fashion. In this way she is doing what infants spend their infancy learning to do: make the connection between faces and minds. The youngest babies see faces for about fifteen minutes out of every hour—an immersive face-learning program. Given that infants are nearsighted and have generally poor vision, faces of people who are disposed to get very close to them and coo at them make up a substantial proportion of their early visual experience. Infants' poor vision means that these early faces—on average, the same three or so faces—are very compromised: infants register two eyeholes and a mouth hole centered below them. From these inauspicious beginnings they come to be highly skilled at face recognition by age two, able months later to recognize a face they have seen only once.

Comparing infants' rate of learning with what the typical owned dog encounters is humbling. For instance, by eight months Quid has cut through the huge amount of speech tossed at her and has sorted out: her name; the names of the other dogs and cat; maybe a dozen words for common objects; that "wait" is a shorter pause than "stay"; that "Do you want to go inside?" is a prompt for her to sit before charging through the open door; that "Let's go find your food ball" means it is mealtime; that "What's that?" is a request to find the new thing. And it is not even her native language! By all rights, the similarly developing human infant should distinguish individuals by the smell around their face and rump; be able to pick out the favorite tennis ball from all the identical non-favorites by odor alone; and recognize the smells of approaching thunderstorms.

By thinking about what we know, dogs become skilled at some very humanlike guile. One study found that dogs forbidden to eat a treat are pretty good at following those directions when a person is in the room with them, but steal treats right away if the lights are turned off (notably, dogs' night vision is exceptional, unlike ours); they are a little less likely to steal any treats if a spotlight is directed at the treat in an otherwise dark room. So they seem to be basing their theft on whether the person in the room with them can see them or the treat. (It is important to mention that in every situation most subjects stole at least *some* treats, so their cognition is tuned to "treats" at least as much as to "What does that person see?") If the person leaves the room, forget it: most dogs studied in the various experiments that have asked them to obey even in the person's absence just go right ahead and disobey as soon as the person is gone. Out of room, out of mind. When the person comes back into the room after this disobedience, they might react "guiltily"—ducking their head, looking away, frantically wagging low between their legs—but this reaction is not an indication of their guilt at disobedience, but of their sensitivity to whether *we* think they are guilty. For they show more of this guilty look when their person thinks they have eaten the treat—whether or not they have—than when the person thinks they haven't. Again, dogs read our minds—and in this case, our unconscious body language.

On reflection, a lot of dog cognition research relies on this kind of setup: asking a dog not to eat something scrumptious and then testing in what situations they go ahead and eat it anyway. Researchers have harnessed the power of small pieces of hot dog to motivate their subjects. Even without hot dogs, though, dogs in experimental studies have shown their sensitivity to what people know. One research group set up a slightly unusual scene for person and dog: the two sit on opposite sides of a room. Between them are two barriers—one transparent, one opaque; on the dog's side of each barrier is a dog toy. The toys are just about identical: allowed to grab either, dogs choose at random. But if asked to "fetch" by the person on the other side of the barriers, dogs choose the toy next to the transparent barrier: they think about which one the person can see. Dogs, not even language users, translate "fetch" into "fetch that one that I must be referring to because it's the only one I have visual access to." Not bad, pooch.

There are, we now know, many things that dogs know about us

that we ourselves do not, of course. In particular, dogs have been trained to detect various cancers, to notice precipitously low blood sugar levels or imminent seizures. The very first reported cases of dogs detecting cancers—a dachshund puppy who noticed a breast cancer and a Labrador who found a melanoma—happened with untrained dogs. In both cases the dogs were simply persistently sniffing at a part of their person's body (left armpit, left thigh); months later, their people realized the dogs might be onto something and went to their physicians. (This is not to say that your dog is an early-detection system for such diseases—but if my dogs were suddenly and doggedly keen on sniffing my big toe, I would probably check it out.) Within months of the novel coronavirus's spread, dogs were being trained to detect the virus in people who themselves did not yet know if they had contracted it. Would Quid know? We got a chance to find out when first A., then I, came down with the virus. There was no sign that Quid sniffed it out—or, at least, we did not notice her trying to tell us. And that's the rub: as interested as people profess to be in what their dogs know about them, we aren't often listening to what they might be saying.

Beliefs and knowledge of
an eight-month-old puppy

- The exact distance to wait outside the kitchen to get an occasional glimpse and toss of dinner prep from the chef
- Where everyone is in the morning, should you need to boop them on the mouth (which you do)
- That both inside and outside are "the place on the other side of that door," in the question "Do you want to go inside/outside?"
- Outside is for peeing

- If you continue to squirm on your back on the bed, you will eventually fall right off the bed (still: worth it)
- It's four turns, past the swallow field, past the straight-away with rabbits, next to the field with the giant birds, past the stream, past the second stream, before the curve, to meet up with the rest of the family
- The window upstairs to look out of to see who's outside, if you can't see them out of the first or second window you try
- The pleasure of catching one's own tail
- If you stay still near the door, you might get a halter put over your head. But you also get a small nugget of something tasty
- If you feel unsafe, first try to get on the large person's lap. If you determine that the lap is not available, between her legs will do
- When the door opens, run as fast as you can, keeping alert, and a squirrel will manifest to be chased
- If another small dog yaps at you, the proper response is to yap back, louder
- To get out of the building to the place with all the pigeons, with the ground spread with smells, you first need to enter a small room and stand still. There is nothing else you do in that room: there are no toys, there is no food, and there is no soft place to lie down. It makes a kind of hum, sometimes jostles, and then beeps. At the beep, look pensively at the people, and they will open the door for you to leave
- It doesn't look like it at first, but the steep cliffs in the house can be leapt to the top of. You may find another

cliff there! Just leap that one, too, and the next—
eventually, there is flatness again
- You can make the gate open by looking at people (first
choice) or vigorous touching with paws (if they don't
respond *right away*)
- Where the soft spaces in the house are
- Where the warm spaces in the house are
- Secret spaces where you might find the cat
- Before settling down someplace, it's useful to dig fran-
tically into the surface to make it nice for settling into

The thing about sleds

It snows all night, the sky unrelenting in its release. In the morning the air is crisp and the snow is high. The landscape is primed for navigation by sled. After a plow passes, the hill that is our driveway becomes a luge track, too sleek for driving but excellent for slipping down. We unbury two long plastic clamshells of sleds. Quid follows us up and down gamely—showing pleasure and confusion with our shape-shifting. The thing about sledding is that to the unschooled, it is not clear what the endpoint is. Quid, new to the concept, decides that it is about *being very fast*, and as we stop and turn to mount the hill again, she continues running very fast, past the edge of the driveway, through snow six inches higher than she is tall, until she catches wind of a trio of deer and disappears after them. We drop the sleds and run, too, calling her name into the indifferent bright morning.

Finnegan can no longer keep up with the sleds, and the slipperiness of hard-packed snow is tricky as he loses balance and strength. He was our initiator into the pleasure and terror of sledding with dogs: he was very sure that the sledder must be caught, must be brought to a stop. We had been transformed into creatures thrilling and horrible at once. He would race after us, mouth wide in a smile, barking and nibbling at our coat sleeves, until we crashed and he could come attack us properly.

Quid is no Finn. Her understanding of sledding is less about us and more about speed. We catch up with Quid well past the neighbor's house and carry her home, knowing we cannot impart to her how disappointing it is that she flees. So now I walk in the forest with her on leash, wishing that she could be off leash without running from me. But we are beginning to see her for who she is. She is with me, but even now, nine months on, she is *not* with me—not really. She is tuned to outside, to the world buzzing around her. Her body is tense and alert; her ears are erect, great satellite dishes receiving word of chipmunks in the wall and machines grumbling in the distance. She tracks invisible paths underfoot; she stops to sniff the most ordinary fallen branch for a full one hundred and ninety-seven seconds. (I counted.) She is in the forest in a way that I have never been in the forest: as though new to the world, receiving all its news at once.

And yet here I am struggling with her pulling on the leash. I realize that we have not followed trainers' counsel to always have great treats with us, in order to make ourselves "the most interesting thing" to her. We may have neglected to have treats on our person all the time; we may have all been irregular in our treating of her; we may have let her strain at the leash when we should not have—whatever it is, we were not excelling.

But as I contend with her willfulness, I see a great, obvious truth: we simply *aren't* the most interesting thing out here. There are the loping deer! Darting squirrels and chipmunks! Smells of dogs, birds, coyotes, and raccoons who have passed by. Smells on the breeze; smells on the ground; smells of death and new life and edible morsels. Little movements along the wall; something to roll in; people to greet.

As much as I would like Quid to have what the trainers call a bombproof recall—quickly and agreeably coming whenever I call for her—I see no reason to endorse and then perpetuate the myth that *we* are the most interesting things around. We're not. I mean, I am perfectly decent company for the length of a cocktail party, should you meet me and never have had anyone to ask all those questions about your dog. But I am not singularly interesting—more interesting *than anything else*. My goodness.

And also thank goodness! I do want Quid to be interested in us, in coming when we request it—for her sake, for our sake, and for the sake of anyone else around—but imagine if she never left our side. That is a pathology, that is a problem: we have to shower and leave the house and be by ourselves without her world ending. And she has to be a dog, to be herself: indeed, this is the very reason we wanted to know her—not because of her potential future adulation of us. What I want is to be "somewhat to moderately interesting" to my dog, and my big plan to get there does not involve always smelling of salmon treats.

I think of the poet Mary Oliver, who writes of a dog, Benjamin, who has run off, run away, run from being restrained by leashes. She resists the urge to insist he return to her at once, to call him to her side, forsaking the happy-making smells and sensations he's pursued. I want Quid to be like Benjamin—while not forgetting us completely.

I appreciate Quid's calling my attention to the chipmunks living in the stone wall and the rivulet of water across the path; her reminding me to notice the funky, fragrant, and fungal smells in the middle of a forest, and to look both up and down. A breeze hits us, and Quid angles her nose upward, nostrils working to pull in the air. She noisily exhales, jowls flapping *puhbapuhba*. Walking with the dogs in the forest is keeping their company, but they are also our guides to the animals that have been there before. Here is where a brace of deer slept last night; this is where a squirrel dug up a cherished acorn; this spot, the intersection of two invisible highways, is where the local coyote leaves messages in fur and pee. This is a new branch that was not there yesterday; there is a new burrow, a resting spot for a rabbit or porcupine. As she tugs at the leash, Quid is telling me that it is I who insisted she wear the silly thing—and that she has been pretty good-natured about it, given how nonsensical it is in her world.

The trainer Sophia Yin once wrote that "whether we're aware of it or not, every interaction we have with the pet is a training session." For "training" read "learning," and I might add: it is training for me as well. I learned something new about the puppy: she has a different pace than we do. It is not just that she moves more quickly—though she is a sprinter alongside our ambling. It is not just that she has grown into a teenager in the time it takes babies to learn to push themselves into a seated position. It is that her speed and growth are indicative of existing at her own tempo, one in which moments are not swollen and idle, as with our older dogs, but full of minutiae and anticipation.

Our walks with all the dogs have become comic, my arms pulled in three directions as Upton stands his ground, resolute nose in the air; Finn limpingly greets each stranger passing by; and Quiddity trembles with excitement to dart at everydogeverypigeoneverypersonwhatis-that. At last we figure out we should take the dogs on independent walks: Finn's vary between running and sniffing; Upton's are short meanders, following a scent on the breeze. Quid's allow her to take in great gulps of the world. We fence in a section of forest behind the house, creating a sub-forest within the forest where she can pursue her pace. I rake the generations of fallen leaves to make several serpentine, intersecting paths with neither reason nor rhyme. Within this area she is free to explore as she wants: she need not stay on path; she is not tethered to us; we are not going directly from point A to point B in the way that humans (but not dogs) walk. She takes to it immediately; or maybe it is just what the world would look like if mapped to her. On entrance she runs madly along the paths, in search of little furry things or for the mere pleasure of running flat-out. She minds the perimeter. She noses the holes that have appeared in the ground, and checks the hole in the apple tree into which she has seen chipmunks disappear.

One day I bring an old tennis ball out to her fenced forest and toss it. With that toss Quid found her raison d'être. Her reason for being is: to get that ball, to bring it back, and to get the next ball. We had no idea that hidden within this scruffy, long-eared pup there was a ball obsessive. This does not mark her as unusual: there are, of course, plenty of ball dogs living in homes across the United States. Just as there are dog dogs and people dogs, ball dogs are a devout class. They may have very specific ideas about practicing their religion, including but not limited to: type of ball, age of ball, color and size of ball, desirable level of filthiness of ball, squeakiness or squishability of ball, and ownership of ball (with, at times, other dogs' balls being the best balls). Quid turns out to be a *type: tennis ball*; *preference: slightly squishy* ball dog. I had never lived with a committed ball dog. I had a lot to learn.

I learn first that ball dogs are not made, they are born. She was not trained on balls in her first weeks of life; she did not watch ball dogs or sleep alongside her own too-big ball. Months into her life with us, we innocently began a game indoors with a ball (type: whatever squeaks). She spontaneously retrieved the ball, working her jaw on it to make it squeak, and dropped it when I held up my hand in a fist as though I were holding a second ball—a kind of representation of "ball": *Look! This is where the ball would be!* Now, outside, she simply brings it to me and drops it, stunningly. None of the retriever mixes I have known did this naturally. Oh, they liked balls; they just were less keen on retrieving and delivering them.

I learn that she is inexhaustible. In pursuing the erratically bouncing ball, poorly tossed by the tosser, she seems to be driven by the anticipation and the chase. One could stop there, satisfied with a

mouthful of fuzzy, moist, and dirt-spackled ball. But Quid has realized that the ball will go flying again if she brings it back. Dropping
one at my feet, she looks at me with anticipation and focus, the only
concession to anything non-ball in the world being her left ear, tuned
to the possibility of nearby chipmunks, just in case. For her patience,
she gets a second ball in the air: we can cycle through balls one-two
one-two and through and through until her tongue is almost completely out of her mouth. She shows no reasonableness about this: we
have to stop her before a cardiac event does.

Afterward, she lies on the cool floor on her side, her mouth open,
panting hard, tongue pulsing on the floor. Her warm breath pulses
over my bare foot. Splatters of dirt dot her beard. I know I have about
thirty minutes of her sheer exhaustion before she rises, gives a little
shake, and is raring to go again. A trainer friend of ours called her
"keen," which is a generous way of characterizing her hair-trigger
barking, zealous pursuit of moving things, and coiled energy. She is
nothing like who I thought she would be. And yet this might be the
pleasure of living with her. We have established a new game in the
mornings after she noses me awake. I race my fingers along the bed-
spread and, prone with her feet splayed behind her, she lunges after
them. I drop them to the floor, and she neatly jumps down; I lift them
up, she levitates. I raise them into the air, and she pauses, her hair
standing on end with anticipation. I turn her in a circle with my running fingers, up-and-down her from the bed a dozen times. She whines
with delight, her tail beating an allegro rhythm. As a nine-month-old
puppy, she may be the most responsive person I have ever met.

•   •   •

If I can say that there is any difficulty involved in being a dog cognition researcher (and really, there is not), it is simply that we can be too

close to our subjects to see them well. Once we start thinking we know what we will see, we stop seeing, and the science stops. We need to be agnostic, not ready to feel certain that we know what a dog means by a gesture, or what they might do next. An advantage of not knowing Quid well, even after nearly a year, is exactly that lack of closeness. I really do not know what is coming next. Even familiar behaviors benefit from this small distance from my subject. Watching her rise in anticipation of going out, I see her do a full-body shake. I then listen for her collar-jingling shakes for the next several weeks. I find out that, for the most part, they mark a change of activities—as from lying down to "Ready to go!" Indeed, songbirds do something similar: they ruffle their feathers before going from resting to actively exploring. In both dogs and birds, the shake also likely serves as a way to release tension.

Her ears, observed closely, turn out to be revealing about her frame of mind. Their comical giantness is what started me goggling at them. But whether satellite dishes or small felt triangles, each outer ear, or pinna, of a dog can move independently, enabling them to attend to both dinner-making in one room and stealthy cat behavior in an adjoining room, while also picking up any outdoor squirrel, rabbit, or pigeon activity within seventy feet of the house. The pinnae are also used emotionally—something we may overlook, given what researchers gently call our "gracile and vestigial" (read: thin and purposeless) outer ear muscles. It is widely known that dogs will flatten their ears back along their head if feeling frustrated, worried, or fearful. But that is not the only way they use them. When, by contrast, anticipating a treat or reward, they use their ear adductor muscles to bring their ears closer to the midline of their head. Watch for it: you will recognize the look: an earnest, hopeful face. Horses, whose ears are less variable in size across individuals than in dogs, have muscles to rotate their ears and bring them forward; dogs' ears tend in the same directions, to follow sound or show interest. In this posture you can clearly see the tiny fold of skin on the outer sides of the ears called the "marginal pouch" or, mysteriously (unless your dog is named Henry), "Henry's pocket." Anatomy books say that Henry's pocket has "no obvious function"—but the function is clearly to get you to admire your dog's improbable ears all the more closely. While the topic has yet to be studied in dogs, other species with similarly mobile ears, such as sheep, show high rates of "ear-posture change"—going from laid back to pointed forward—when something undesirable is happening, like being separated from their flock. When they are happily feeding on fresh hay, there are fewer ear-posture changes. I sit and watch Quid watching me, her left ear kinked to the side, her right ear smoothed back against her head, and I hope that she is having the happily-feeding-on-fresh-hay feeling, too.

All the dogs benefit from the new fenced space, not just the puppy. We lay out a kind of rudimentary nosework course for Finnegan, hiding scents or treats in a small area of the forest, prompting him to find them all (which he can). Our lab's own research found that practicing nosework daily for two weeks was enough to make dogs more optimistic—a feeling in diminishing supply at times with an older dog. Upton examines the far reaches of the fenced area, where the more daring local wildlife might have ducked in and left a trail (or other evidence). And Quid practices her object-permanence understanding with our tennis ball games. As we have seen, she and her littermates understood at six weeks of age that objects continued to exist even when they no longer saw them. (Infants are only reliably getting around to it by eight or nine months.) But dogs make the same A-not-B error that infants do, in general. Hide a toy under a pillow a few times, letting your dog find it each time, and then if you hide it under a second pillow—in full view of the dog—they usually, tragically, search again in the first spot. Are they simply not paying attention? Have they forgotten what they just saw? Human infants are usually given the benefit of the doubt: their failure is thought to be less a result of cognitive insufficiency than of various cognitive processes getting in one another's way when coming on line. The best explanation for dogs' behavior also reflects something other than a deficit. Their memory and attention are perfectly good. Instead, it is their cooperativeness—their willingness to follow a person's request—that leads to the error. They will follow the person's small glances and attention to the first spot more readily than even the squeaking of a toy hidden in the second location. Thus the ease with which many dogs can be fooled by a "fake" toss of a ball—the throw gesture without the ball following—after many actual tosses. It is not an error to be anticipatory. With dogs the error would more aptly be named the "*A* was a perfectly good spot; why would you move it?*" principle.

The pleasure of having a space where a dog can be off leash is felt by both the leash holder and the held. It can be viscerally satisfying to watch dogs run and play without human intervention—akin to the "nature effect," the de-stressing, happy-making result of being in nature. Just as researchers in the 1980s found that watching fish in an aquarium can lower people's blood pressure and heart rate, I suspect (but know no research demonstrating) that watching dogs play does, too. For dogs, of course, being off leash enables all sorts of free exploration, vital when most of their lives is controlled by people—down to where and when they get to walk, eat, excrete, and socialize. More than this, though, being off leash allows dogs to have choices. Some trainers talk about "opt in" or "opt out" work, in which dogs are allowed to decide to participate in an activity (or not). In most situations dogs reliably opt in, even when the activity is nail clipping, as long as it is made rewarding. Giving them an option to opt out is giving dogs the chance to have a tiny bit of control over their lives. Even the best-trained dogs are also encouraged to make some choices independently. Guide dogs, for instance, are asked to do what is called "intelligent disobedience": choosing to disobey their person if they see that it is not safe to obey them—such as if they see a car going through a red light. Being trusted enough to make good choices *for someone else* is a high level of understanding; but even for the un- or under-trained pet dog, being allowed to make choices improves their lives. I open the gate of the fence and let Quid choose what to do.

Ear Semaphore Code

alertness

sweetness

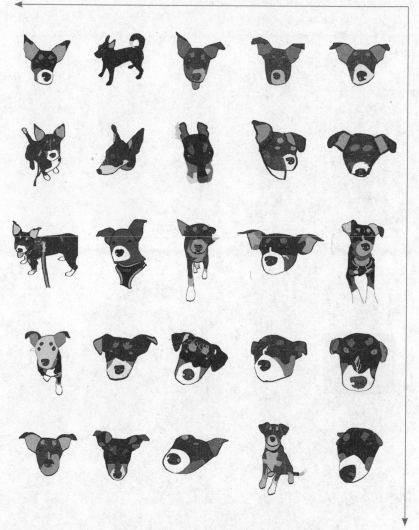

Illustration by Ogden Horowitz Shea

Face-first

We awaken to the aftermath of a late-season hurricane, which just brushed past us: trees are deconstructed, their limbs torn; branches and leaves are scattered on every surface. The day smells fresh, as though each molecule of air has been swapped out for a new one. For the dogs it is a universe to be explored by nose: each leaf is examined with the care of an art dealer flipping through newly found Picasso sketches—only at the end, the dogs usually let loose a declarative pee on one of the branches.

For Quid the world has been transformed with her in mind: it is not fallen trees, it is a world made of sticks. And each stick cannot only be admired—it can be possessed! Carried right away—until we immediately come across another stick, which should also be carried. She is burdened with her choices: Which stick to carry—the one in the mouth or the one on the ground? Is it possible to carry both sticks? And what about that third stick over there? The old adage "A stick in the mouth is worth two on the ground" does not apply to the puppy: closer might be "A stick in the mouth and two on the ground require that you try to get three sticks in the mouth." It is a physics lesson and a math lesson all at once.

She finally seems to settle on a beautiful broken birch branch, its bark peeling and mottled with lichen. As she walks off with it, I

applaud her aesthetic choice, but she promptly drops it at the side of
the path. Soon she grabs another, wider in her mouth than she is long,
and trots a bit until carefully placing it in what I must assume is its
correct place. I see what she is doing: she is redecorating the forest one
stick at a time.

Quid wears everything she encounters on her beard—tree debris,
the mud, the pollen from the grasses, the river algae, the snow—
reminding me how much of what she does is face-first. Of course, we
are face-first animals, too, our broad hairless visages beaconing where
we are headed. But dogs are deeply and truly face-first: the face not
only leads, it commits. To see where that chipmunk went in the tree
hollow one does not just *gaze,* eyeballs a safe distance from the hole;
one *dives in.* The leaf pile, the dirt pile: for dogs, perception is wrapped
up with action. One might stick a nose right up into another dog's
scruff: their personal space in greeting is not an arm's length away, but
full-body contact. Their enthusiasm is massive: they not only give the
burrow a sidelong glance, they leap face-first into the burrow. They are
that one chemistry teacher you had who rubbed their hands gleefully,
managing a little half-jump in the air, before combining combustible
elements; who peeked over your shoulder as you followed directions,
eyes knowingly wide.

Their whole experience of life is defined by contact. So many of
Quid's encounters with the world are *touching* the world: rolling on
the bed gleefully; using her paws to nudge a ball along while one is in
her mouth; play punctuated by biting and full-body blows. In rest she
settles her head on a nearby foot or hand; she stretches her body to
align with ours, weaned on her pile of siblings. And we want to touch
her back. It is outrageous to imagine not touching a dog. We reach
for her scruff, for the felty tips of her ears; we lay our hands on her
warm belly, and tickle our fingers on her neck under her collar, mak-

ing her lips extend back into a kind of smile. Strangers reach to touch her straightaway, and though she ducks a touch on the top of her head, she will herself bridge the span between them with a quick nose poke.

She first became aware of her own tail when it grew long enough to curl over and tickle her back, surprising her. Now I see her at times lying on her side watching her own tail wag, and grabbing at it. Over the months it has grown more voluminous, almost ostentatious: a feathery sickle dangerously on the move. Because I have a son who might take ten photos of the puppy in a second, I have evidence of precisely how her tail wags. Left to right, of course, but not just left-right. On each side, the final moment of wag has the white tip of her tail curling almost to touch her back, then slingshotting back to wag the other way. She will complete just two steps—right foot, left foot— during a cycle of her normal, merrily-walking-around-the-house wag. Her someone-is-definitely-at-the-door wag is almost twice as fast. Her it's-morning-oh-my-god-hello-I've-missed-you wag is impossible to capture on film, seeing as her entire body is a wiggling jelly.

As Quid's tail ramps up, Finnegan's tail has stopped wagging. He has been diagnosed with a degenerative disease that progressively paralyzes from the rear forward. His run is a hop, not unlike Quid's first attempts at running: the back legs operating together, the front body doing all the work. I see the frustration on his face as he cannot climb the stairs without assistance and is slow to attack Quid as she runs by. We are assured that, by definition, paralysis is not painful. But I mourn the loss of his tail wag, and lament all the quiet pauses where a tail thump used to be: on greeting us, running with me, sniffing out a treat, in play, in dreams. On my desk where I write, a photo of young Finnegan smiles at me, his tail mid-wag, as he heads straight for my camera. Now Quid will have to wag for two.

• • •

Apart from our inability to fly, the absence of a tail in humans is, to me, our greatest evolutionary sorrow. Worse, we had tails at one point, and now have only a vestigial tailbone, the coccyx. Human embryos of four weeks have a tail that curls toward their head; it is typically lost by nine weeks (although there are rare instances of babies born with a "caudal appendage"). The canid tail has up to twenty-three vertebrae—nearly as many as the rest of their spine. It is truly a multitasking limb, involved in movement, balance, communication, and expression of emotion.* Happily there is a small field of tail-wag science, which looks at the context and meaning of various tail postures and velocities. They tell us that six stages of tail "dorso-ventral elevation and depression"—tail height—can be measured, from the highest (straight up from the base) through a forty-five-degree decrease to the third highest (straight back), then relaxing, going under the body, and curling around the body when lying on the ground. Tails are used differentially in everything from "upright trot" and "investigative approach" (highest), to "gambolling" or "sexual approach" (second highest), to "fear" (under the body) and sleep (around the body). What scientists call "lateral tail movements"—what everyone else calls "tail wagging"—add additional meaning. Far from just showing happiness, the rate of tail wagging changes in different contexts: part of happy greetings, as a threat, before mating, in play,

---

*This is one reason why tail docking—literally cutting off much or nearly all of the tail—is being banned in more countries, although not yet in the United States, where a docked tail is still part of many purebred dogs' "breed standards," for antiquated reasons. Docking is painful, can lead to chronic pain, and results in loss of this hugely expressive and important limb.

when alarmed, when finishing stretching, and even waiting to be let outside.

Look even more closely, and the tail wags' message is more specific. When dogs see their person, or someone else they are eager to greet, their tail wag is more right-wag than left-wag; when they see an unknown dog, tail wagging veers left. Most of the body is mapped cross-laterally to the brain, so a left-wagging tail is connected to the right side of the brain—specializing in hesitation or withdrawal. The right-wagging tail connects to the left hemisphere, associated with approach behavior. Watching a dog's tail in slow motion gives a little peek into their mind.

In another study, when dogs are placed in front of a video of other dogs' tail wagging (a kind of weird movie for them), the emotion conveyed by the wag laterality was contagious: if watching more left-wagging (withdrawal) dogs, the subjects' heart rates rise—as though they're wagging that tail themselves.

Wags are sufficiently tuned to dogs' internal experience that researchers can count wags to determine how excited dogs are. Highly excited dogs might wag an average of 125 times in a minute, or 2 wag-laps a second. (Quid's tail, sometimes zooming into a blur, clearly skews this average.)

Watch a bird dog track their bird and you will see a wag rate indicative of tremendous excitement. Though it has not been studied as closely as social interaction, the tail is surely a glimpse into what dogs experience through smell as well. While humans are perfectly good smellers, we leave the deepest sniffs to the dogs, and thus mostly miss the parallel universe they are living in: smelling the weather upcoming and the recent history of the block or path. They smell where you have been, who you have been with, and what other dog you have petted. Their tails, keeping a thoughtful tempo, tell us how they might feel about that dog you were tickling.

One of the greatest pleasures of the puppy is her willingness to be tickled, petted, and rubbed; her solicitation of contact. With the pandemic, social contact was foreclosed; dogs became proxies for other people in our homes, and our outlet for literal connection. We might forget how it feels to sit close enough to someone that your legs are touching, or you can smell their shampoo; but the puppy naturally stretches out her body to achieve full contact with mine (and will suffer my cozying up to her). That contact is a reminder of the pleasure of the simplest of human contact, too: the hug or slight touch from family and friends; the helping hands and shaking of hands (though I now prefer an elbow bump). From the time we are newly born, one of the most acute senses we have is touch. Dogs, allowing themselves to be available as touch magnets—singular petting zoos—could not have been more perfectly designed to scratch that itch.

Petting a dog is, in fact, salubrious: it increases levels of immunoglobulin A, important to immune function, anxiety levels, cortisol levels, blood pressure, and heart rate—you name it. The pleasurable rush of endorphins from the touch of a loved one can be reproduced by reciprocating with a dog. The dog you pet need not even be your own, just a fur-covered, doe-eyed member of the species. (The dogs' willingness to participate in these studies was not measured.) There is a small sub-literature asking if petting makes the dog feel better, too. Unfortunately, as with much mid-twentieth-century research, scientists tried to make their subjects feel bad first. When they shocked a dog's paws, then petted the dog, petting decreased the big spike in heart rate that the shock induced. *Bad researchers.* More enlightened researchers find naturally distressing situations and simply see if they can make the dogs feel better about them. Now we know that petting blocks the spike in cortisol—an indicator of stress—dogs show when having blood drawn, and before their person leaves them home alone; a big bout of petting can raise endorphins and oxytocin in dogs. Army dogs and shelter dogs preferred petting to praise as a reward—sometimes more than food. What counts as "petting" varies in these studies: it is usually a variation on "long firm strokes" from head to rump. Less easy to characterize, for person and dog alike, is the affection that is conveyed from person to dog and back again via the petting hand. That's the magic bit.

Lick, memory

It is one week shy of a year since the day the puppy was squirted onto a towel and met her mother on the outside. Plunged out in a rush of bodily fluids, tumbled about by persistent, long licks from her mother that completely covered her body, smoothing her very short, fresh hair. That little black form, eyes pressed shut, ears but a gesture, ruddy eyebrows straining—it was Quiddity.

I remember not knowing her, but my memories of her are already changed by the dog I know now. I wonder if we, in turn, have completely supplanted the memory of her actual mother, of the constant company of her siblings. Those first weeks of her life were full of such impulses and frustrations, noise and smell, body upon body. Now she hops neatly up on the sofa and orients herself toward me, watching me with surprising avidity while I eat a pear. She has ordered the confusion of sensations for the newly born into coherent layers of the world. She has figured out, with very little help, how to be a dog among dogs, and how to be a dog among people. Sometime in there she became herself.

And we became able to see her for who she is. It is hard to see, initially. In today's culture, puppies come to us, from breeder or shelter, with the reputation of their breed or parents already seeming to define who they are. And so we all come to the experience of having a puppy with ideas about how it's going to go: who that puppy is going to be. We prepare with books that claim to inform us about "how puppies behave"—not unlike the user's manual for our new tablet or coffee maker. We think we're ready. We think it will be an innocent, sweet, easy addition to our lives. We think she will sleep through the night, will understand us, will want what we want. We're wrong, of course. Worse, our expectations distract us from seeing the delicious new, difficult, and budding personality that is there.

With this in mind, I have made a new list of What You Need to Be Prepared for Your Puppy. Are you ready? Do you have somewhere you can write this down? A pen? Okay, then. Here is the list.

> ### Requirements
>
> 1. Expect that your puppy will not be who you think, nor act as you hope.

That's it! That's the list.

Of course, I was glimpsing some of who she was when I first met her. The farther she is from her natal litter, the more I see in Quid vestiges of her time among her blood relatives. The way she lies with us—her body tracing the length of my leg, her head resting on my lap, or sometimes all of her resting on my lap—recapitulates the time of her youth, huddled up next to, on top of, and under her siblings. It began as a way to keep warm; it became a sign of affection and affiliation. Alongside one another she and Upton dig their noses deep into each other's fur, evocative of that time before vision was on line— when other dogs were defined only by their smell and warmth, and to get more of both you burrowed closer.

In quiet moments, when I peek over the top of my book and see her lying with her eyes open, gazing nowhere, I wonder if she is reminiscing about her young puppyhood. If she is thinking back, as I am, to the day when she was one week old, and wormed around the edge of a dog bed, probing for some familiar smell and finding only my knee. If she looks for her mother in the dog she spots approaching on the sidewalk or coming over the hill. If she thinks about the day she arrived home, on a leash for the first time, and huddled under our feet as the dogs probingly sniffed her. If she pines for her siblings, remembering running alongside them, proudly parading a long stick together; following one pup into trouble and calling out for another pup when scared.

One day, we find out. The sky is unnaturally blue, wide-eyed; the air expectant. Over Quid's head we have talked about this day for weeks: two of her faraway siblings are coming to see her. O. swoons with pleasure at the prospect; Quid betrays no suspicion, no premonition. She pads alongside me through my morning ministrations, lying down at my feet with a sigh when I sit at my desk—up until the moment that a car from a neighboring state pulls up the driveway. It's followed by a second, from yet another state.

She lifts her head, her ears satellite dishes tuned to the arrival. The first car quiets; a door opens. She barks, and the car barks back: it is Luna, *née* Persimmons, one of the puppies I remember as sweetly predisposed to lap-sitting. As we greet them, I take her in: she is Quid-sized, her coat merle gray, and she sports a splash of blue in one eye, giving her a look of perpetual alarm. She hops out of the car gracefully and noiselessly (as Quid does), then looks with uncertainty at her person holding her leash (as Quid does not). We start walking to the house, talking/barking as we go. The pups walk astride each other, both light on their toes, both loud of voice. They are aware of each other, to be sure, but do they recognize each other?

What would recognition look like? Well, Quid certainly recognizes us when we return home; she recognizes the cat; she recognizes canine friends. With us, recognition is visible in the speed with which an alarm bark morphs into a friendly warble; in the softening of her ears from erect and alert to pressed back against her head. Her tail is enthusiastic in all cases with people and dogs, but her wag is looser with friends. I look at her and Luna. Both wear a stiff-wagged, perked-eared pose, their barks pointed exclamation marks. While there is much resemblance between the two, I don't see any immediate signs of familiarity. And yet, over several minutes, they become comfortable with each other—considerably more quickly than usual with an unknown dog. It is as if they see themselves in each other—and soon become less concerned with "this strange dog" beside them.

Similarly when Coren—previously Cholla Cactus—joins the pair. He is 50 percent bigger than the two girls, with a natural smile. As they circle one another, I enumerate the features they have in common: each one's head a little smaller than befits their size; they all sport white tips to their tails and white paint-dipped feet; feathering graces the backs of their legs. But for his abundant tail and cream-colored coat, he is another doppelgänger. And, more strikingly, they are similar of style, with the same intent gaze, the same gazelle-like running and explosive energy. And yet he, too, shows no clear acknowledgment of these pups with whom he shared the first, formative weeks of life. They mill around one another, more interested than engaged, alternating small bouts of play with exploration (Coren), entreaties to their owner (Luna), or fixation on getting a tennis ball tossed (Quid).

At one point, when I have ducked inside, I hear Quid barking—her shrill, piercing bark. I peek out the window to see what she's announcing. What I see is Quid lying down, her eyes on a ball, her pose serene and focused. She makes not a sound. To my delight, it is the two others barking her bark. For once, our pup is not the loudest in the scene.

• • •

By the age of one year, young dogs are the equivalent of thirty-year-old adolescents: their bodies have mostly developed but their brains (and their behavior) have not. The signs of raw youth have waned: blue eyes have nearly all darkened, the pink pads of their feet turned spotted and then darkened with age. Bodies have grown into proportion with heads; faces with eyes. Compared with the first year of a person's life, dogs are high performers. An infant of this age is taking her first steps, unassisted; can sit down from standing, unassisted; is about a third of the way toward mastering bowel control; and has figured out how to coordinate her jaw muscles to chew food. An average active puppy will have taken millions of steps in their first year; sits on request; and, thank goodness, has been eating and excreting on their own for eleven months. Yet they are still works in progress, just on the edge of familiarity with their place in our world.

This year, this dreadful year for the world, brought more dogs than ever into people's homes. While adoptions from shelters actually went down somewhat from the previous year, it was a year for buying dogs, as we bought so many things—hand sanitizer, masks, bicycles, canned beans, bulk paper goods—as our cultural response. In a survey by our lab of people who adopted dogs in the months after the pandemic became globally recognized in March 2020, a third had not been planning to add a dog to their family. Why now? "Everyone was home to help with the transition," one respondent said; another reflected many people's feelings of the desirability of having a dog when working from home. Among people filling out the survey, the experience was challenging—"hardest thing I've ever done"—but rewarding—"she has kept me sane"; "they've changed the lives of everyone in this house"; "great for our mental health." "Saved my life," one person said, simply.

Nonetheless, the chance that some of these pups will wind up "returned" to a shelter or breeder, or even abandoned or electively euthanized, is not trivially small. One busy animal shelter, the Charleston Animal Society in South Carolina, homed almost ten thousand dogs in four years (from 2015 to 2019), but saw more than fifteen hundred returned in that time—and that was pre-pandemic. The highest rates of return were of young adults around Quid's age: the adolescents who test boundaries and have grown out of their deep puppy cuteness. A third of them were returned because of the dog's "behavior"— especially their activity level, perceived aggression to people or other animals, and their destructive behavior. Exactly zero people said they returned their dog because the dog was "not friendly."

This shelter's experience jibes with another large-scale study, in which so-called "behavioral problems" were cited by 40 percent of people who gave up their dog. Our own puppy has been full of "behavioral problems." She is active, can bark rudely at people and animals, and continues to eat various non-edible, and sometimes valuable, items. But she is Quid. I am already starting to forget the long nights, the frustrations, the troubles.

For a year as full of moment as the first year of life is, it is not obvious that the one-year-old (puppy or child) has much memory of it at all. Surely there is implicit memory of how to be, how to move, of where (in the case of the puppy) the dog treats are kept. They know *how* and *where* and *what*: Researchers have confirmed that dogs have memories of specific events—what they call "episodic memory." One group trained their subjects to imitate a person's actions, whatever they did. Then the dogs were shown a brand-new action—like touching an opened umbrella, or walking around a bucket—and the dogs were asked to replicate it after a delay. Nearly all of them remembered the novel actions and could perform them (to the best of their canid abilities) themselves.

But the kind of memory we wonder about is, of course, the one we treasure ourselves: autobiographical memories. I can think back to my fiftieth birthday, joined by friends and family on a walk down the length of Manhattan—and I can also think back to my fifth birthday, joined by littler friends and my natal family, eyeing a well-frosted cake on a picnic table. Do dogs remember their lives in this way? No research has confirmed that they do, yet—not because dogs cannot, but because it is difficult to ask non-language-using subjects to recall something earlier in their past for you. But the episodic-memory studies hint strongly at the prospect that dogs do remember. And given how evocative of the past odors can be—and how central odors are to dogs' lives—one might imagine that some of these memories are encoded in smells. The preference puppies show for the smell of their siblings, and the ease with which they interact with those long-lost siblings when reunited, is suggestive. Research has shown that odors present at the time of learning something (such as where treats are hidden in a room) can serve as a cue to help dogs find those hidden treats again later. It is possible that their memories of their own past rush back—just as a whiff of talcum powder transports me into a decades-old scene: watching my powder-wearing grandmother slice tomatoes into segments, arrange them on a cool white plate, and dollop mayonnaise alongside them.

By the age of one year, those thirty-year-old adolescent pups are part of the human family: they will turn to their people over their natal siblings; they know the habits, style, and treat-giving potential of each of their family; they are attached. One of the elements that keeps sleep-deprived parents going as their babies' schedules and needs addle their brains is the swell of feelings of love and attachment that rise at the same time. Oxytocin, a neuropeptide, is widely held to be the neurological reason for parents' bond with their infants; the same hormone can be produced by gazing, touching, or interacting in any way with a dog. Even without either party consciously trying, the dog-person bond is forged. One day I look up at the face biting my nose and I find it delightful—something I've come to expect and await. She is no longer a stranger; she is ours, and we are hers.

•　•　•

On the morning of her birthday, Quid arrives on the bed as if cannon-shot, and beelines for my face to lick my mouth. Then she circles around and delivers mouth-licks to Finnegan, to Upton, to A., and to Edsel, who has been unwise enough to follow Quid upstairs. Then she races downstairs and mouth-licks our son.

I know intellectually what she is doing. She is greeting us; she is showing her affection for us; she is trying to get our attention: all of those things at once. Her manner is so professional, though—so completely efficient and thorough—that as I lie there, hiding my face under the sheet against the second round, I get another idea of what she is doing. Each morning Quid faces what to her are a series of unresponsive, still bodies. Perhaps she believes that she is giving us life with her licks. With each life-giving lick, we slowly stir from our comas and rejoin the living. Indeed, an exceptionally good lick brings a whole lot of life all of a sudden: we may rise straight out of bed, uttering a great sound. She knows best to back away then, to stand vigilant over this new life she has created—and definitely not to lick again, for fear of its potency exceeding that of all known life forms.

This is like nothing more than what Maize did a year ago today, as she licked her puppies into life. On a walk with my family, as Quid checks in on everyone, nosing each of us in turn, I see her mother again, poking her nose into the pen holding eleven mewling eggplant-shaped pups to count that everyone is there.

And hasn't she given us life? Our family's story of the pandemic, like those of innumerable other families, includes sickness and loss and fear. But the story is also entangled with the chaos and joy brought by this complex furry character whom we have come to know. When the world kept its distance, she walked right up to the world and licked it in its face. My alarm about the future was regularly displaced by the simple need to help this puppy survive into her future. Days took form by her passage through them, saving us from weeks of undifferentiated hours. She reminded us of—she embodied—the pleasure of life.

At the same time, I only later realized—after her energy became organized; after the pandemic released us from its grip—that it was her very vitality that had made it hard for me to love her. I was watching the vitality slip from Finnegan and inhabit Quid. Finn, who spent years running by my side—or sometimes running away, with a stolen ball in his mouth (sorry, Moose, for that ball we stole); Finn, whose tail wagged the most exuberant greetings; who leapt on the bed to find me under the covers; who rolled on his back with pleasure in the perfect dirt patch; who charged into puddles with his mouth wide and tail high—Finn was suddenly unable to run, to wag, to leap, to roll, to charge. I lamented his losses, and felt his chagrin as he watched Quid seem to take his place. While he could move less each day, she could do every sort of move: neatly leap from a stand to the top of the dining table; launch herself into the air, mouth-first, after a high-bouncing ball; relax her shoulders to shimmy under the couch, back legs splayed; roll on her back in the grass. It is as though she has taken those movements from him, stolen them. I would not let her steal my love from him, too.

And she did not. Yet one day I find myself talking about "the dogs"—and meaning her to be among them. Slowly, reluctantly, over the year, two has become three. Somehow it has taken this long for us to realize that we didn't get *just* "another dog." While there are plenty

of resemblances between Quid, Finn, and Upton—they are all quadrupedal sniffers with kind faces, long tails, and a shared genetic
history—we were really adding an entirely different person to the
family. One who is not only a different age, with its consequent re-
quirements and abilities, but also a different personality, with a different set of skills, drives, concerns, sensitivities. And now, our family
has one bearded lady.

I smile at that beard. At her eyebrows, her spectacular ears; at the
raoh-rooo! she says to me in the morning. Our relationship bloomed
despite my resistance. Dogs have, after all, evolved with us—may even
have evolved us as a species. They sneak into our hearts, because our
hearts are tuned to their frequencies. Over the year I removed my scientific cap more often, and just let her be.

Quid, in her being who she is, and not who I hoped or imagined
she would be, reminds me that it is less who I want our puppy to be
than who I want to be with our puppy. I return from a trip and open
the door, happy to see her. I invite her for naps and belly rubs; I put
down my work to toss a tennis ball for her to go bananas over. I welcome her changeability, her enthusiasms. I look forward to what mercurial spirit will grab her next.

Do I love her?

How could I ever have not?

Illustration by Ogden Horowitz Shea

Postscript

It's one year later: Quid has turned two. And we have just lost Finnegan and Upton, four weeks apart. Our family is suddenly changed and a yawning hole is at its center.

The dogs filled every second of our days, and now their absence is felt in all those moments. It takes form in longing, in grief that they are gone, in melancholic remembrance. I miss Finn's winsome smile, formed of his panting mouth, soft eyes, and wagging tail. I miss Upton's howl at dinnertime, his akilter tail, and his gangly run. In the house, I miss sharing the space with them: hearing them shake when rising, their toenails on the floorboards, their cadence up the stairs, their breath and muffled noises in sleep. Outside, I miss following them on their explorations, feeling the invisible rubber band that joined us as we moved at our respective paces through a forest or park—Finn always circling back to us, Upton pulled farther by distant scents. I miss them galloping down the hall when I came home, circling around me and knocking my legs with their tails. I miss the way Finn would push his nose into my hand to guide me to pet his face and tickle his ear; I miss Upton's pawing of the air to ask us to continue rubbing the soft folded fur on his chest.

These dogs were worked into the fabric of our lives, into the sinews of our bodies. Quid lies on her back next to me now, head thrust backward, legs reaching to the ceiling, quiet. I stroke her ear aimlessly. These dogs.

Acknowledgments

Could I have written this book without you all? Quiddity, I literally could not have written it without you. But—and this holds extra for Finnegan, Upton, and Edsel—what I moreover appreciate is your letting us keep your company.

And all the people around Quid! I want to thank Amy Hershberger, who fostered the litter—not only for her incredible generosity in taking in so many dogs being rehomed, but also for entertaining my visits on those early weeks, and into the pandemic. Thank you to Kara Gilmore, who runs the Hudson Valley Dog Farm, for connecting us with Amy and for her sage ideas. Thank you to the other families who adopted Maize and her puppies—Pumpkin (Romeo), Acorn, Blue Camas (Blü), Cranberry, Fiddlehead, Persimmons (Luna), Chaya, Flint, Pawpaw (Chutney), Cholla Cactus (Coco/Coren)—for glimpses of the parallel universes of these young sprites.

Seung Suh and Bob Caccamise—and Caine and Bullitt—you were essential parts of this year. Alison Curry and Layla, thank you for city picnics and treasured companionship. Gayle Edgerton and Jaxx, thanks for the pandemic walks. Susan and Georgie, sorry about the barking. Thank you to people whom I consulted along the way: Maggie Howell, Cheri Asa, Soon Hon Cheong; Roxanne Bok and Linda Seaver; Amy Attas and Karen Becker. Thank you to Jesse Freidin for photography tips, to Pat Goodman and Karen Davis at Wolf Park for wolf tips, and to those working at or with the WDC family: Jenny

Essler, Dana Ebbecke, Amritha Mallikarjun, Cindy Otto, and Alice Barnhart. Thanks to Anna Lai at Muddy Paws and Mike Rose, foster to Viola and her pups, and dad to Boots.

Thank you to my agent and friend, Kris Dahl, for boosting the good book ideas and gently stamping out the bad ones. Thanks to Wendy Walters, Betsy Carter, Aryn Kyle, Maira Kalman, Jennifer Vanderbes, Sally Koslow, and Elizabeth Kadetsky for regular writerly inspiration at our obligatory distance, and to Maneesha Deckha and Daniel Hurewitz for keeping me honest—both to the story and to the schedule. Thank you to Brad Mehldau for unwittingly providing the soundtrack to many, many paragraphs.

To Rick Kot and everyone at Viking, thank you for welcoming this puppy. Your enthusiasms and ideas have simply made this book what it is.

Thank you to my natal family, Damon and Elizabeth: every story comes from you originally. Most of all, Ammon and Ogden, thank you for reading drafts, entertaining sentences, and egging me on— and thank you for how you love Quiddity.

Notes

WEEK 0: DEAR GOD, THAT'S A LOT OF PUPPIES

14 **just five tiny vertebrae:** Mudasir Bashir Gugjoo et al., "Vertebral Heart Score in Dogs," *Advances in Animal and Veterinary Sciences* 1, no. 1 (2013): 1–4.

14 **220 beats a minute:** Flávia Gardilin Vassalo et al., "Topics in the Routine Assessment of Newborn Puppy Viability," *Topics in Companion Animal Medicine* 30, no. 1 (2015): 16–21.

16 **they prefer the middle ones:** Lourdes Arteaga et al., "The Pattern of Nipple Use before Weaning among Littermates of the Domestic Dog," *Ethology* 119, no. 1 (2013): 12–19; Julie Hecht, "The Common Wisdom about Dog Nipples Is Wrong," *Scientific American*, August 12, 2016.

17 **interval between births:** Bonnie V. Beaver, *Canine Behavior: Insights and Answers*, 2nd ed. (St. Louis, MO: Saunders Elsevier, 2009).

18 **male-like traits:** Robert L. Meisel and Ingeborg L. Ward, "Fetal Female Rats Are Masculinized by Male Littermates Located Caudally in the Uterus," *Science* 213 (1981): 239–42; Brice C. Ryan and John G. Vandenbergh, "Intrauterine Position Effects," *Neuroscience and Biobehavioral Reviews* 26, no. 6 (2002): 665–78.

18 **The newborns then prefer:** Deborah L. Wells and Peter G. Hepper, "Prenatal Olfactory Learning in the Domestic Dog," *Animal Behaviour* 72, no. 3 (2006): 681–86.

18 **stress during pregnancy:** James Serpell, Deborah L. Duffy, and J. A. Jagoe, "Becoming a Dog: Early Experience and the Development of Behavior," in *The Domestic Dog*, ed. James Serpell, 2nd ed. (Cambridge, UK: Cambridge University Press, 2017), 93–117.

18 **unfairly ugly term "placentophagia":** Daniel Mota-Rojas et al., "Consumption of Maternal Placenta in Humans and Nonhuman Mammals: Beneficial and Adverse Effects," *Animals* 10, no. 12 (2020): 2398.

18 **When researchers remove:** Maurice L. Abitbol and Steven R. Inglis, "Role of Amniotic Fluid in Newborn Acceptance and Bonding in Canines," *Journal of Maternal-Fetal Medicine* 6, no. 1 (1997): 49–52.

18 **the fright of cold air:** Clement A. Smith, "The First Breath," *Scientific American* 209 (October 1963): 27–35.

18 **kills off *E. coli*:** Benjamin L. Hart and Karen L. Powell, "Antibacterial Properties of Saliva: Role in Maternal Periparturient Grooming and in Licking Wounds," *Physiology and Behavior* 48, no. 3 (1990): 383–86.

19 **puppies share the microbiome:** Maja Zakošek Pipan et al., "Do Newborn Puppies Have Their Own Microbiota at Birth? Influence of Type of Birth on Newborn Puppy Microbiota," *Theriogenology* 152 (2020): 18–28.

19 **mothers who got the extra pheromone:** Natalia R. Santos et al., "Influence of Dog-Appeasing Pheromone on Canine Maternal Behaviour during the Peripartum and Neonatal Periods," *Veterinary Record* 186, no. 14 (2020): 449.

19 **puppy Apgar also tests:** M. Batista et al., "Neonatal Viability Evaluation by Apgar Score in Puppies Delivered by Cesarean Section in Two Brachycephalic Breeds (English and French Bulldog)," *Animal Reproduction Science* 146, nos. 3–4 (2014): 218–26; Maria Cristina Veronesi, "Assessment of Canine Neonatal Viability—the Apgar Score," *Reproduction in Domestic Animals* 51, suppl. 1 (2016): 46–50.

19 **average weight at birth:** Amélie Mugnier et al., "Birth Weight as a Risk Factor for Neonatal Mortality: Breed-Specific Approach to Identify At-Risk Puppies," *Preventive Veterinary Medicine* 171 (2019): 104746.

20 **five ounces of milk:** Beaver, *Canine Behavior.*

20 **the kneading-suckling rhythm:** Craig F. Ferris et al., "Pup Suckling Is More Rewarding Than Cocaine: Evidence from Functional Magnetic Resonance Imaging and Three-Dimensional Computational Analysis," *Journal of Neuroscience* 25, no. 1 (2005): 149–56.

20 **pups are themselves the reward:** Gerald S. Hecht, Norman E. Spear, and Linda P. Spear, "Changes in Progressive Ratio Responding for Intravenous Cocaine throughout the Reproductive Process in Female Rats," *Developmental Psychobiology* 35, no. 2 (1999): 136–45.

WEEK 1: SWEET POTATOES

23 **close to the 101.5:** Rachel Moxon and Gary England, "Care of Puppies during the Neonatal Period: Part 1, Care and Artificial Rearing," *Veterinary Nursing Journal* 27, no. 1 (2012): 10–13.

25 **"bloom of confusion":** William James, *The Principles of Psychology*, vol. 1 (New York: Henry Holt, 1890), 496; online at psychclassics.yorku.ca/James /Principles/prin13.htm.

26 **They can *do* almost nothing:** Julie Hecht and Alexandra Horowitz, "Introduction to Dog Behavior," in *Animal Behavior for Shelter Veterinarians and Staff*, ed. Emily Weiss, Heather Mohan-Gibbons, and Stephan Zawistowski (Ames, IA: Wiley-Blackwell, 2015), 5–30; John Paul Scott and John L. Fuller, *Genetics and the Social Behavior of the Dog* (Chicago: University of Chicago Press, 1965); Steven R. Lindsay, *Handbook of Applied Dog Behavior and Training*, vol. 1: *Adaptation and Learning* (Ames, IA: Iowa State Press, 2000).

26 **motor skills are few:** Moxon and England, "Care of Puppies during the Neonatal Period."

27 **choose sleeping on cloth:** G. J. Igel and A. D. Calvin, "The Development of Affectional Responses in Infant Dogs," *Journal of Comparative and Physio-

logical Psychology 53, no. 3 (1960): 302–5. *Note: *problematic study; welfare and validity concerns.*

27 **They find some smells disgusting:** Michael W. Fox, *Behaviour of Wolves, Dogs, and Related Canids* (New York: Harper & Row, 1971); Lindsay, *Handbook of Applied Dog Behavior.*

27 **Their sleep is active:** Lindsay, *Handbook of Applied Dog Behavior,* 36, 46; M. W. Fox, "Postnatal Development of the EEG in the Dog—1, 3, 3," *Journal of Small Animal Practice* 8, no. 2 (1967): 71–111.

27 **bursts in slow-wave sleep:** Michelle Lampl and Michael L. Johnson, "Infant Growth in Length Follows Prolonged Sleep and Increased Naps," *Sleep* 34, no. 5 (2011): 641–50.

27 **should double their birth weight:** Isabel Alves, "A Model of Puppy Growth during the First Three Weeks," *Veterinary Medicine and Science* 6, no. 4 (2020): 946–57.

28 **repugnant anise oil:** Lindsay, *Handbook of Applied Dog Behavior,* 35ff.

28 **swabbed from their own armpits:** Trevor Turner, *Veterinary Notes for Dog Owners* (London: Stanley Paul, 1990).

28 **strength of their suckle:** Sherman Ross, "Sucking Behavior in Neonate Dogs," *Journal of Abnormal and Social Psychology,* 46, no. 2 (1951): 142–49. *Note: problematic study; welfare and validity concerns.*

28 **mom's diet during pregnancy:** Peter G. Hepper and Deborah L. Wells, "Perinatal Olfactory Learning in the Domestic Dog," *Chemical Senses* 31, no. 3 (2006): 207–12.

28 **"Super Dog" program:** Carmen L. Battaglia, "Periods of Early Development and the Effects of Stimulation and Social Experiences in the Canine," *Journal of Veterinary Behaviour: Clinical Applications and Research* 4, no. 5 (2009): 203–10.

29 **rat pups are less stressed:** Juan Francisco Núñez et al., "Effects of Postnatal Handling of Rats on Emotional, HPA-Axis, and Prolactin Reactivity to Novelty and Conflict," *Physiology & Behavior* 60, no. 5 (1996): 1355–59.

29 **compulsive blanket-suckers:** Angelo Gazzano et al., "Effects of Early Gentling and Early Environment on Emotional Development of Puppies," *Applied Animal Behaviour Science* 110, nos. 3–4 (2008): 294–304.

30 **"vertical" nursing style:** Emily E. Bray et al., "Effects of Maternal Investment, Temperament, and Cognition on Guide Dog Success," *Proceedings of the National Academy of Sciences* 114, no. 34 (2017): 9128–33.

30 **The kind of maternal care:** Lisa Dietz et al., "The Importance of Early Life Experiences for the Development of Behavioural Disorders in Domestic Dogs," *Behaviour* 155 (2019): 83–114.

30 **Your dog's nose-bump:** Fox, *Behavior of Wolves, Dogs and Related Canids.*

30 **high-pitched "alone" barks:** Sophia Yin and Brenda McCowan, "Barking in Domestic Dogs: Context Specificity and Individual Identification," *Animal Behaviour* 68, no. 2 (2004): 343–55; Péter Pongrácz, Csaba Molnár, and Ádám Miklósi, "Acoustic Parameters of Dog Barks Carry Emotional Information for Humans," *Applied Animal Behaviour Science* 100 (2006): 228–40.

30 **virtually no color vision:** Russell J. Adams and Mary L. Courage, "Human Newborn Color Vision: Measurement with Chromatic Stimuli Varying in

Excitation Purity," *Journal of Experimental Child Psychology* 68, no. 1 (1998): 22–34.

31 **through their transparent lenses:** Charles Fernyhough, *A Thousand Days of Wonder: A Scientist's Chronicle of His Daughter's Developing Mind* (New York: Avery, 2009).

31 **they are wildly nearsighted:** Amy R. Koehn, ed., *Neonatal Nurse Practitioner Certification Intensive Review* (New York: Springer, 2020).

31 **vision is involuntary:** Greg D. Reynolds and Alexandra C. Romano, "The Development of Attention Systems and Working Memory in Infancy," *Frontiers in Systems Neuroscience* 10 (2016): 15.

31 **creatures of taste and smell:** Koehn, *Neonatal Nurse Practitioner Certification.*

31 **moms started drinking carrot juice:** Julie A. Mennella, Coren P. Jagnow, and Gary K. Beauchamp, "Prenatal and Postnatal Flavor Learning by Human Infants," *Pediatrics* 107, no. 6 (2001): E88.

31 **both newborns and their mothers:** Richard H. Porter, "Olfaction and Human Kin Recognition," *Genetica* 104, (1998): 259–63.

31 **a small set of reflexes:** Koehn, *Neonatal Nurse Practitioner Certification.*

31 **equivalent of the "handling" tasks:** I got this idea from Suzanne Clothier.

31 **mixes wiring up:** Fernyhough, *A Thousand Days of Wonder.*

WEEK 2: YOUNG BLUE EYES

35 **ears will be completely open:** Rachel Moxon and Gary England, "Care of Puppies during the Neonatal Period: Part 1, Care and Artificial Rearing," *Veterinary Nursing Journal* 27, no. 1 (2012): 10–13.

35 **chorus of the puppy pile:** Michael W. Fox, *Behavior of Wolves, Dogs, and Related Canids* (New York: Harper & Row, 1971).

39 **their skull proportions:** Robert K. Wayne, "Cranial Morphology of Domestic and Wild Canids: The Influence of Development on Morphological Change," *Evolution* 40, no. 2 (1986): 243–61.

40 **wobbly crawl-walking:** Steven R. Lindsay, *Handbook of Applied Dog Behavior and Training,* vol. 1: *Adaptation and Learning* (Ames, IA: Iowa State Press, 2000), 36.

40 **still entirely reflexive:** Jan P. Piek, *Infant Motor Development* (Champaign, IL: Human Kinetics, 2005).

41 **three spontaneous blink types:** Sadahiko Nakajima et al., "Spontaneous Blink Rates of Domestic Dogs: A Preliminary Report," *Journal of Veterinary Behavior Clinical Applications and Research* 6, no. 1 (2011): 95.

41 **rate of human blinking:** Anna Rita Bentivoglio et al., "Analysis of Blink Rate Patterns in Normal Subjects," *Movement Disorders* 12, no. 6 (1997): 1028–34.

41 **the average gorilla:** Akiko Matsumoto-Oda et al., "Group Size Effects on Inter-Blink Interval as an Indicator of Antipredator Vigilance in Wild Baboons," *Scientific Reports* 8 (2018): 10062.

41 **nearly non-blinking guinea pig:** W. P. Blount, "Studies of the Movements of the Eyelids of Animals: Blinking," *Experimental Physiology* 18, no. 2 (1927): 111–25; Katrin Trost, M. Skalicky, and Barbara Nell, "Schirmer Tear Test,

Phenol Red Thread Tear Test, Eye Blink Frequency and Corneal Sensitivity in the Guinea Pig," *Veterinary Ophthalmology* 10, no. 3 (2007): 143–46.

42 **dogs who unblink:** Sadahiko Nakajima et al., "Spontaneous Blink Rates of Domestic Dogs: A Preliminary Report," *Journal of Veterinary Behavior Clinical Applications and Research* 6, no. 1 (2011): 95.

42 **described by tongue scientists:** Hironori Takemoto, "Morphological Analyses of the Human Tongue Musculature for Three-Dimensional Modeling," *Journal of Speech, Language, and Hearing Research* 44, no. 1 (2001): 95–107.

42 **dogs' considerable tongue musculature:** Nazim Keven and Kathleen A. Akins, "Neonatal Imitation in Context: Sensorimotor Development in the Perinatal Period," *Behavioral and Brain Sciences* 40 (2017): e381

42 **full of capillaries:** Ádám Miklósi, *The Dog: A Natural History* (Princeton, NJ: Princeton University Press, 2018).

42 **the tongue-flick:** Alexandra Horowitz, *Inside of a Dog: What Dogs See, Smell, and Know* (New York: Scribner, 2009).

42 **"intense, strident, and prolonged":** G. J. Noonan et al., "Behavioural Observations of Puppies Undergoing Tail Docking," *Applied Animal Behaviour Science* 49, no. 4 (1996): 335–42.

WEEK 3: THE WEEK OF POOP

47 **reflex to eliminate:** Trevor Turner, *Veterinary Notes for Dog Owners* (London: Stanley Paul, 1990).

48 **suckling has turned noisy:** Bonnie V. Beaver, *Canine Behavior: Insights and Answers*, 2nd ed. (St. Louis, MO: Saunders Elsevier, 2009).

49 **"the most influential nine weeks":** Steven R. Lindsay, *Handbook of Applied Dog Behavior and Training*, vol. 1: *Adaptation and Learning* (Ames, IA: Iowa State Press, 2000), 43.

49 **commercially bred or puppy-mill dogs:** James Serpell and J. A. Jagoe, "Early Experience and the Development of Behaviour," in *The Domestic Dog: Its Evolution, Behaviour and Interactions with People*, ed. James Serpell (Cambridge, UK: Cambridge University Press, 1995): 79–102.

50 **a brood of young goslings:** Konrad Z. Lorenz, "The Companion in the Bird's World," *The Auk* 54, no. 3 (1937): 245–73.

50 **socialization period lasts:** John Paul Scott and John L. Fuller, *Genetics and the Social Behavior of the Dog* (Chicago: University of Chicago Press, 1965).

50 **sensory and motor cortices:** See, e.g., Michael W. Fox, *Behavior of Wolves, Dogs, and Related Canids* (New York: Harper & Row, 1971).

51 **Chihuahua puppies with a cat:** Fox, *Behavior of Wolves, Dogs, and Related Canids*; Lindsay, *Handbook of Applied Dog Behavior*, 34.

51 **play and social interactions:** Raymond Coppinger and Lorna Coppinger, *Dogs: A Startling New Understanding of Canine Origin, Behavior and Evolution* (New York: Scribner, 2001).

51 **Literature on livestock guarding:** Jeffrey S. Green and Roger A. Woodruff, "Livestock Guarding Dogs: Protecting Sheep from Predators," *Agriculture Information Bulletin* 588 (Washington, DC: United States Department of Agriculture Animal and Plant Health Inspection Service, 1990); Orysia

Dawydiak and David E. Sims, *Livestock Protection Dogs: Selection, Care and Training*, 2nd ed. (Wenatchee, WA: Dogwise Publishing, 2004).

52 **sleep with their sibling smell:** Victoria Mekosh-Rosenbaum et al., "Age-Dependent Responses to Chemosensory Cues Mediating Kin Recognition in Dogs (*Canis familiaris*)," *Physiology and Behavior* 55, no. 3 (1994): 495–99.

53 **young wolves would not grow up:** Personal correspondence, Pat Goodmann, Head Animal Curator, Wolf Park, April 26, 2021; K. M. Davis et al., "Improving Socialization Methods for Wolf Ambassadors: Preparing Captive Wolves (*Canis lupus*) for a Life of Complexity and Change Starts in Infancy," poster, 2018.

WEEK 4: PROFESSIONAL WAG

59 **Finally able to maintain:** Rachel Moxon and Gary England, "Care of Puppies during the Neonatal Period: Part 1, Care and Artificial Rearing," *Veterinary Nursing Journal* 27, no. 1 (2012): 10–13.

59 **rapidly improving sensorium:** Linda P. Case, *The Dog: Its Behavior, Nutrition, and Health*, 2nd ed. (Ames, IA: Blackwell, 2005).

59 **just wrong to say:** Kathryn Lord, "A Comparison of the Sensory Development of Wolves (*Canis lupus lupus*) and dogs (*Canis lupus familiaris*)," *Ethology* 119, no. 2 (2013): 110–20.

59 **rampant generation of neurons:** Charles Fernyhough, *A Thousand Days of Wonder: A Scientist's Chronicle of His Daughter's Developing Mind* (New York: Avery, 2009), 14.

60 **the "visual cliff" experiment:** Karen E. Adolph and Sarah E. Berger, "Physical and Motor Development," in *Developmental Science: An Advanced Textbook*, ed. Marc H. Bornstein and Michael E. Lamb, 6th ed., 241–302 (New York: Psychology Press/Taylor and Francis, 2010); Karen E. Adolph, "Specificity of Learning: Why Infants Fall over a Veritable Cliff," *Psychological Science* 11, no. 4 (2000): 290–95.

61 **Puppies are much speedier:** Richard D. Walk and Eleanor J. Gibson, "A Comparative and Analytical Study of Visual Depth Perception," *Psychological Monographs: General and Applied* 75, no. 15 (1961): 1–44; Richard D. Walk, "The Influence of Level of Illumination and Size of Pattern on the Depth Perception of the Kitten and the Puppy," *Psychonomic Science* 12 (1968): 199–200.

61 **"social facilitation" enables them:** Steven R. Lindsay, *Handbook of Applied Dog Behavior and Training*, vol. 1: *Adaptation and Learning* (Ames, IA: Iowa State Press, 2000), 45.

62 **"really still a beached fetus":** Fernyhough, *A Thousand Days of Wonder*, 35.

62 *several* **sucks before one swallow:** Nazim Keven and Kathleen A. Akins, "Neonatal Imitation in Context: Sensorimotor Development in the Perinatal Period," *Behavioural and Brain Sciences* 40 (2017): e381.

62 **months from being able:** Adolph and Berger, "Physical and Motor Development," 258.

63 **just** *seeing* **a puppy tail:** John Paul Scott and John L. Fuller, *Genetics and the Social Behavior of the Dog* (Chicago: University of Chicago Press, 1965).

WEEK 5: MOUTHS WITH TAILS

67 **there is a genetic connection:** George M. Strain, "Genetics of Deafness in Domestic Animals," *Frontiers in Veterinary Science* 2 (2105): 29.

68 **weaned off their mother's milk:** Lisa Dietz et al., "The Importance of Early Life Experiences for the Development of Behavioural Disorders in Domestic Dogs," *Behaviour* 155 (2019): 83–114.

68 **milk production peaked:** Bonnie V. Beaver, *Canine Behavior: Insights and Answers*, 2nd ed. (St. Louis, MO: Saunders Elsevier, 2009).

69 **The occasional male contributes:** Kerstin Malm, "Regurgitation in Relation to Weaning in the Domestic Dog: A Questionnaire Study," *Applied Animal Behaviour Science* 43, no. 2 (1995): 111–22.

69 **Survival is not assured:** Sunil Kumar Pal et al., "Pup Rearing: The Role of Mothers and Allomothers in Free-Ranging Domestic Dogs," *Applied Animal Behaviour Science* 234 (2021): 105181.

69 **survival rates for dogs' cousins:** See, e.g., Dave Mech, quoted in Doug Smith, "Wolf Pup Survival a Fragile Thing," *Star Tribune*, March 5, 2015; Vadim Sidorovich et al., "Wolf Denning Behaviour in Response to External Disturbances and Implications for Pup Survival," *Mammalian Biology* 87 (2017): 89–92.

69 **pseudopregnancy can even include lactation:** Pat Goodmann, Head Animal Curator, Wolf Park, personal correspondence, 4/26/2021. Also, Cheryl S. Asa and Carolina Valdespino, "Canid Reproductive Biology: An Integration of Proximate Mechanisms and Ultimate Causes," *American Zoologist* 38 (1998): 251–59.

70 **their mother often scolds them:** Rudolf Schenkel, "Submission: Its Features and Function in the Wolf and Dog," *American Zoologist* 7, no. 2 (1967): 319–29; Robert L. Trivers, "Parent-Offspring Conflict," *American Zoologist* 14, no. 1 (1974): 249–64.

70 **Two puppies playing together:** John W. S. Bradshaw, Anne J. Pullan, and Nicola J. Rooney, "Why Do Adult Dogs 'Play'?," *Behavioural Processes* 110 (2015): 82–87; Alexandra Horowitz, "Attention to Attention in Domestic Dog (*Canis familiaris*) Dyadic Play," *Animal Cognition* 12, no. 1 (2009): 107–18; Rebecca Sommerville, Emily A. O'Connor, and Lucy Asher, "Why Do Dogs Play? Function and Welfare Implications of Play in the Domestic Dog," *Applied Animal Behaviour Science* 197 (2017): 1–8.

70 **Pups weaned too early:** Steven R. Lindsay, *Handbook of Applied Dog Behavior and Training*, vol. 1: *Adaptation and Learning* (Ames, IA: Iowa State Press, 2000), 43.

71 **approach their siblings first:** Peter G. Hepper, "Sibling Recognition in the Domestic Dog," *Animal Behaviour* 34, no. 1 (1986): 288–89.

71 **Perceiving an object depends:** James J. Gibson, *The Ecological Approach to Visual Perception*, Classic Edition (New York: Psychology Press, 2014; orig. pub. Boston: Houghton Mifflin, 1979).

71 **Daisy, Ollie, and Truffles:** Ashley Prichard et al., "The Mouth Matters Most: A Functional Magnetic Resonance Imaging Study of How Dogs Perceive Inanimate Objects," *Journal of Comparative Neurology* 529 (2021): 2987–94.

72 **With fully working ears:** Rachel Moxon and Gary England, "Care of Puppies during the Neonatal Period: Part 1, Care and Artificial Rearing," *Veterinary Nursing Journal* 27, no. 1 (2012).

72 **lasting wariness of people:** Tiffani J. Howell, Tammie King, and Pauleen C. Bennett, "Puppy Parties and Beyond: The Role of Early Age Socialization Practices on Adult Dog Behavior," *Veterinary Medicine* (Auckland, NZ) 6 (2015): 143–53; John Paul Scott and John L. Fuller, *Genetics and the Social Behavior of the Dog* (Chicago: University of Chicago Press, 1965).

WEEK 6: LITTLE BRUISERS

79 **a nearby human pointed:** Brian Hare and Michael Tomasello, "Domestic Dogs (*Canis familiaris*) Use Human and Conspecific Social Cues to Locate Hidden Food," *Journal of Comparative Psychology* 113, no. 2 (1999): 173–77.

79 **Human babies of ten months:** George Butterworth, "Joint Visual Attention in Infancy," in *Theories of Infant Development,* ed. Gavin Bremner and Alan Slater, 317–54 (Malden, MA: Blackwell, 2004).

79 **follow a person's guidance:** Alexandra Horowitz, Julie Hecht, and Alexandra Dedrick, "Smelling More or Less: Investigating the Olfactory Experience of the Domestic Dog," *Learning and Motivation* 44, no. 4 (2013): 207–17; Emanuela Prato-Previde, Sarah Marshall-Pescini, and Paola Valsecchi, "Is Your Choice My Choice? The Owners' Effect on Pet Dogs' (*Canis lupus familiaris*) Performance in a Food Choice Task," *Animal Cognition* 11 (2008): 167–74.

80 **80 percent of six-week-old puppies:** Julia Riedel et al., "The Early Ontogeny of Human–Dog Communication," *Animal Behaviour* 75, no. 3 (2008): 1003–14.

80 **They get better at point-following:** Emily E. Bray et al., "Early-Emerging and Highly Heritable Sensitivity to Human Communication in Dogs," *Current Biology* 31, no. 14 (2021): 3132–36.e5.

82 **But in their sixth week:** Sylvain Gagnon and François Y. Doré, "Cross-Sectional Study of Object Permanence in Domestic Puppies (*Canis familiaris*)," *Journal of Comparative Psychology* 108, no. 3 (1994): 220–32.

82 **the bars of her crib:** Daniel N. Stern, *Diary of a Baby: What Your Child Sees, Feels, and Experiences* (New York: Basic Books, 1992).

WEEK 7: ADVENTURE PUPS

86 **observing puppies solved it quickly:** Lenore L. Adler and Helmut E. Adler, "Ontogeny of Observational Learning in the Dog (*Canis familiaris*)," *Developmental Psychobiology* 10, no. 3 (1977): 267–71.

86 **understand the idea of imitation:** Friederike Range, Zsófia Viranyi, and Ludwig Huber, "Selective Imitation in Domestic Dogs," *Current Biology* 17, no. 10 (2007): 868–72.

87 **"do as I do":** József Topál et al., "Reproducing Human Actions and Action Sequences: 'Do as I do!' in a Dog," *Animal Cognition* 9, no. 4 (2006): 355–67; Claudia Fugazza and Ádám Miklósi, "Deferred Imitation and Declarative Memory in Dogs," *Animal Cognition* 17 (2014): 237–47.

87 opening a "puzzle box": Claudia Fugazza et al., "Social Learning from Conspecifics and Humans in Dog Puppies," *Scientific Reports* 8 (2018): 9257.

88 much more scolding from mom: Steven R. Lindsay, *Handbook of Applied Dog Behavior and Training*, vol. 1: *Adaptation and Learning* (Ames, IA: Iowa State Press, 2000), 47.

89 a trained drug-detection dog: J. M. Slabbert and O. Anne E. Rasa, "Observational Learning of an Acquired Maternal Behaviour Pattern by Working Dog Pups: An Alternative Training Method?," *Applied Animal Behaviour Science* 53, no. 4 (1997): 309–16.

89 parents stay with their pups: Sunil Kumar Pal, "Parental Care in Free-Ranging Dogs, *Canis familiaris*," *Applied Animal Behaviour Science* 90, no. 1 (2005): 31–47.

89 the dogs tend to disperse: Sunil Pal et al., "Dispersal Behaviour of Free-Ranging Dogs (*Canis familiaris*) in Relation to Age, Sex, Season and Dispersal Distance," *Applied Animal Behaviour Science* 61, no. 2 (1998): 123–32.

89 more time with the mom towel: Peter G. Hepper, "Long-Term Retention of Kinship Recognition Established during Infancy in the Domestic Dog," *Behavioural Processes* 33, nos. 1–2 (1994): 3–14.

90 dogs intently sniffing: Marianne Heberlein and Dennis C. Turner, "Dogs, *Canis familiaris*, Find Hidden Food by Observing and Interacting with a Conspecific," *Animal Behaviour* 78, no. 2 (2009): 385–91.

90 newborn babies imitate an adult: Andrew N. Meltzoff and M. Keith Moore, "Newborn Infants Imitate Adult Facial Gestures," *Child Development* 54, no. 3 (1983): 702–9.

90 this "tongue protrusion": Susan S. Jones, "The Development of Imitation in Infancy," *Philosophical Transactions of the Royal Society B* 364, no. 1528 (2009): 2325–35.

90 stopped imitating this gesture: Meltzoff and Moore, "Imitation of Facial and Manual Gestures by Human Neonates," *Science* 198, no. 4312 (1977): 75–78.

90 nine-month-olds matched: Meltzoff, "Infant Imitation and Memory: Nine-Month-Olds in Immediate and Deferred Tests," *Child Development* 59, no. 1 (1988): 217–25.

90 they often over-imitate: Andrew Whiten et al., "Imitative Learning of Artificial Fruit Processing in Children (*Homo sapiens*) and Chimpanzees (*Pan troglodytes*)," *Journal of Comparative Psychology* 110, no. 1 (1996): 3–14.

WEEK 8: YOUR CHOICE OF MODELS

95 each dog's identifying "noseprint": Hyeong In Choi et al., "The Formation and Invariance of Canine Nose Pattern of Beagle Dogs from Early Puppy to Young Adult Periods," *Animals* 11 (2021): 2664.

98 bigger eyes, smaller jowls: Julie Hecht and Alexandra Horowitz, "Seeing Animals: Human Preferences for Dog Physical Attributes," *Anthrozoös* 28, no. 1 (2015): 153–63.

98 the impossibly cute form: Nadine Chersini, Nathan J. Hall, and Clive D. L. Wynne, "Dog Pups' Attractiveness to Humans Peaks at Weaning Age," *Anthrozoös* 31, no. 3 (2018): 309–18.

99 **Dogs with longer noses:** Mary Morrow et al., "Breed-Dependent Differences in the Onset of Fear-Related Avoidance Behavior in Puppies," *Journal of Veterinary Behavior* 10, no. 4 (2015): 286–94.

99 **why pet-store puppies:** James Serpell, Deborah L. Duffy, and J. A. Jagoe, "Becoming a Dog: Early Experience and the Development of Behavior," in *The Domestic Dog*, ed. James Serpell, 2nd ed. (Cambridge, UK: Cambridge University Press, 2017).

99 **secure attachment to an adult:** Emanuela Prato-Previde et al., "Intraspecific Attachment in Domestic Puppies (*Canis familiaris*)," *Journal of Veterinary Behavior* 4, no. 2 (2009): 89–90.

99 **Recordings of the electrical activity:** Steven R. Lindsay, *Handbook of Applied Dog Behavior and Training*, vol. 1: *Adaptation and Learning* (Ames, IA: Iowa State Press, 2000), 44, 46.

100 **They can leave the nest:** Lindsay, *Handbook of Applied Dog Behavior and Training*, vol. 1: *Adaptation and Learning*; Linda P. Case, *The Dog: Its Behavior, Nutrition, and Health*, 2nd ed. (Ames, IA: Blackwell, 2005); Daniel G. Freedman et al., "Critical Period in the Social Development of Dogs," *Science* 133 (1961): 1016–17.

100 **adopters' top reasons for choosing:** Emily Weiss et al., "Why Did You Choose This Pet?: Adopters and Pet Selection Preferences in Five Animal Shelters in the United States," *Animals* 2, no. 2 (2014): 144–59.

100 **dogs who lay down:** Alexandra Protopopova and Clive David Lawrence Wynne, "Adopter-Dog Interactions at the Shelter: Behavioral and Contextual Predictors of Adoption," *Applied Animal Behaviour Science* 157 (August 2014): 109–16.

101 **approximately *eight* minutes:** Protopopova and Wynne, "Adopter-Dog Interactions at the Shelter: Behavioral and Contextual Predictors of Adoption."

101 **chose a single piece:** Maria Elena Miletto Petrazzini, Fabio Mantese, and Emanuela Prato-Previde, "Food Quantity Discrimination in Puppies (*Canis lupus familiaris*)," *Animal Cognition* 23, no. 4 (2020): 703–10.

101 **called "sticky fixation":** Greg D. Reynolds and Alexandra C. Romano, "The Development of Attention Systems and Working Memory in Infancy," *Frontiers in Systems Neuroscience* 10 (2016): 15.

ARRIVAL OF THE STORM

115 **"Make time for exercise":** Victoria Stilwell, *The Ultimate Guide to Raising a Puppy: How to Train and Care for Your New Dog* (New York: Ten Speed Press, 2019).

116 **people who return their dogs:** Francesca Mondelli et al., "The Bond That Never Developed: Adoption and Relinquishment of Dogs in a Rescue Shelter," *Journal of Applied Animal Welfare Science* 7, no. 4 (2004): 253–66.

117 **they don't yet look to us:** Emily E. Bray et al., "Dog Cognitive Development: A Longitudinal Study across the First 2 Years of Life," *Animal Cognition* 24, no. 2 (2021): 311–28.

119 **young human learns "doggy":** Stan A. Kuczaj, Martyn D. Barrett, ed., *The Development of Word Meaning: Progress in Cognitive Development Research* (New York: Springer, 1986).

(IM)PERFECT PUPPY

130 **"He just loved Christmas":** Clinton R. Sanders, "Understanding Dogs: Caretakers' Attributions of Mindedness in Canine-Human Relationships," *Journal of Contemporary Ethnography* 22, no. 2 (1993): 220.

132 **the "alone" bark:** Julie Hecht and Alexandra Horowitz, "Seeing Animals: Human Preferences for Dog Physical Attributes," *Anthrozoös* 28, no. 1 (2015).

132 **trained pigeons to play ping-pong:** "BF Skinner Foundation—Pigeon Ping Pong Clip," Youtube video, :36, April 1, 2009, youtube.com/watch?v=vGazy H6fQQ4.

132 **pilot a guided missile:** Joseph Stromberg, "B. F. Skinner's Pigeon-Guided Rocket," *Smithsonian Magazine*, August 18, 2011.

133 **turn in a counterclockwise circle:** "BF Skinner Foundation—Pigeon Turn," Youtube video, 1:21, April 1, 2009, youtube.com/watch?v=TtfQlkGwE2U.

134 **pulling on the reins:** Andrew N. McLean, "The Positive Aspects of Correct Negative Reinforcement," *Anthrozoös* 18, no. 3 (2005): 245–54.

135 ***Training You to Train Your Dog:*** Blanche Saunders, *Training You to Train Your Dog* (Garden City, NY: Doubleday, 1946), 19.

135 **"holding his jaws together":** Saunders, *Training You to Train Your Dog*.

135 **"grasp it by the throat":** *Mine and Tunnel Dog Training and Employment*, Field Manual 7-41 (Washington, DC: U.S. Department of the Army, 1973).

136 **"but no flogging":** William Dobson, *Kunopaedia. A Practical Essay on Breaking or Training the English Spaniel or Pointer* (London: C. Whittingham, 1814).

136 **"a leathern strap":** Thomas Burgeland Johnson, *The Shooter's Companion*, 2nd ed. (London: Sherwood, Jones, & Co., 1823).

136 **"without a single blow":** Stephen T. Hammond, *Practical Dog Training, or, Training vs. Breaking* (New York: Forest and Stream Publishing Company, 1882).

136 **"This trick is exceedingly funny":** William E. Sterling, *A System of Dog Training and Complete Medical Guide* (New York: The American News Company, 1881).

GHOSTS

142 **Sophia Yin's list:** Sophia Yin, *Perfect Puppy in 7 Days: How to Start Your Puppy Off Right* (Davis, CA: CattleDog Publishing, 2011).

142 **Swedish working dog community:** Kenth Svartberg and Björn Forkman, "Personality Traits in the Domestic Dog (*Canis familiaris*)," *Applied Animal Behaviour Science* 79, no. 2 (2002): 133–56.

146 **the marshmallow test:** Walter Mischel, Ebbe B. Ebbesen, and Antonette Raskoff Zeiss, "Cognitive and Attentional Mechanisms in Delay of Gratification," *Journal of Personality and Social Psychology* 21, no. 2 (1972): 204–18.

147 **involves the frontal cortex:** Sandra Aamodt and Sam Wang, *Welcome to Your Child's Brain: How the Mind Grows from Conception to College* (New York: Bloomsbury, 2012).

147 **white matter, the myelin:** Bill Gross et al., "Normal Canine Brain Maturation at Magnetic Resonance Imaging," *Veterinary Radiology and Ultrasound* 51, no. 4 (2010): 361–73.

147 **big-dog electrical activity:** Lisa Dietz et al., "The Importance of Early Life Experiences for the Development of Behavioural Disorders in Domestic Dogs," *Behaviour* 155 (2019): 83–114.

147 **if the dog had found food:** Marianne Heberlein and Dennis C. Turner, "Dogs, *Canis familiaris*, Find Hidden Food by Observing and Interacting with a Conspecific," *Animal Behaviour* 78 (2009): 385–91.

148 **Chaser, a Border collie:** John W. Pilley and Alliston K. Reid, "Border Collie Comprehends Object Names as Verbal Referents," *Behavioural Processes* 86, no. 2 (2011): 184–95.

148 **putting in the effort:** Attila Andics and Ádám Miklósi, "Neural Processes of Vocal Social Perception: Dog-Human Comparative fMRI Studies, *Neuroscience and Biobehavioral Reviews* 85 (February 2018): 54–64.

148 **the "cocktail-party effect":** Amritha Mallikarjun, Emily Shroads, and Rochelle S. Newman, "The Cocktail Party Effect in the Domestic Dog (*Canis familiaris*)," *Animal Cognition* 22, no. 3 (2019): 423–32.

149 **responsive to this kind of speech:** Tobey Ben-Aderet et al., "Dog-Directed Speech: Why Do We Use It and Do Dogs Pay Attention to It?," *Proceedings of the Royal Society B* 284, no. 1846 (2017): 20162429.

150 **a strong relationship with their dogs:** Pinar Thorn et al., "The Canine Cuteness Effect: Owner-Perceived Cuteness as a Predictor of Human-Dog Relationship Quality," *Anthrozoös* 28, no. 4 (2015): 569–85.

150 **fifty things you should notice:** Michael Sorkin, *Two Hundred and Fifty Things an Architect Should Know* (Hudson, NY: Princeton Architectural Press, 2021).

PUPPY'S POINT OF VIEW

154 **270-degree visual field:** Alexandra Horowitz, *Inside of a Dog: What Dogs See, Smell, and Know* (New York: Scribner, 2009), 124.

157 **"one of the most robust findings":** Patricia J. Bauer, "Amnesia, Infantile," in *Language, Memory, and Cognition in Infancy and Early Childhood*, ed. Janette B. Benson and Marshall M. Haith (San Diego, CA: Academic Press/ Elsevier, 2009), 1–12.

157 **"Kin recognition," the unsexy name:** Peter G. Hepper, "Long-Term Retention of Kinship Recognition Established during Infancy in the Domestic Dog," *Behavioural Processes* 33, nos. 1–2 (1994): 3–14.

158 **Male dogs were particularly adept:** Carisa Gillis et al., "Scent-Mediated Kin Recognition and a Similar Type of Long-Term Olfactory Memory in Domestic Dogs (*Canis familiaris*), in *Advances in Chemical Signals in Vertebrates*, ed. Robert E. Johnston et al. (New York: Kluwer Academic/Plenum, 1999), 309–14.

158 **separated from their person:** Gillis et al., "Scent-Mediated Kin Recognition."

158 **attachment to their entire pack:** József Topál et al., "Attachment to Humans: A Comparative Study on Hand-Reared Wolves and Differently Socialized Dog Puppies," *Animal Behaviour* 70, no. 6 (2005): 1367–75.

158 three ten-minute visits: Márta Gácsi et al., "Attachment Behavior of Adult Dogs (*Canis familiaris*) Living at Rescue Centers: Forming New Bonds," *Journal of Comparative Psychology* 115, no. 4 (2001): 423–31.

159 certain abilities are set: Angelina S. Lillard and Alev Erisir, "Old Dogs Learning New Tricks: Neuroplasticity beyond the Juvenile Period," *Developmental Review* 31, no. 4 (2011): 207–39.

159 failed because they were frightened: C. J. Pfaffenberger and J. P. Scott, "The Relationship between Delayed Socialization and Trainability in Guide Dogs," *Journal of Genetic Psychology* 95 (1959): 145–55.

159 juvenile period living in a kennel: Naomi D. Harvey et al., "Test-Retest Reliability and Predictive Validity of a Juvenile Guide Dog Behavior Test," *Journal of Veterinary Behavior Clinical Applications and Research* 11 (2016): 65–76.

159 busy urban environment: David L. Appleby, John W. S. Bradshaw, and Rachel A. Casey, "Relationship between Aggressive and Avoidance Behaviour by Dogs and Their Experience in the First Six Months of Life," *Veterinary Record* 150, no. 14 (2002): 434–38.

159 Captive wolf cubs: Lisa Dietz et al., "The Importance of Early Life Experiences for the Development of Behavioural Disorders in Domestic Dogs," *Behaviour* 155 (2019): 83–114.

159 given a chance to socialize: Tiffani J. Howell, Tammie King, and Pauleen C. Bennett, "Puppy Parties and Beyond: The Role of Early Age Socialization Practices on Adult Dog Behavior," *Veterinary Medicine* (Auckland, NZ) 6 (2015): 143–53.

161 holding their heads up: Karen E. Adolph and Sarah E. Berger, "Physical and Motor Development," in *Developmental Science: An Advanced Textbook*, ed. Marc H. Bornstein and Michael E. Lamb, 6th ed., 241–302 (New York: Psychology Press/Taylor and Francis, 2010).

IN AND UP

167 pretty desirable behaviors: Kathy Sdao, *Plenty in Life Is Free: Reflections on Dogs, Training and Finding Grace* (Wenatchee, WA: Dogwise Publishing, 2012).

169 "three-segmented limbs": Daniela Helmsmüller et al., "Ontogenetic Allometry of the Beagle," *BMC Veterinary Research* 9 (2013): 203.

170 trying to get through a doorway: Alexandra Horowitz et al., "Can Dogs Limbo? Dogs' Perception of Affordances for Negotiating an Opening," *Animals* 11, no. 3 (2021): 620.

170 Dogs can limbo: Horowitz et al., "Can Dogs Limbo?"

171 step of the rear leg: Rachel Page Elliott, *Dogsteps—a New Look: A Better Understanding of Dog Gait through Cineradiography—"Moving X-rays,"* 3rd ed. (Mount Joy, PA: CompanionHouse Books/Fox Chapel, 2014).

171 dogs are a little more "sloppy": Paul Rezendes, *Tracking and the Art of Seeing: How to Read Animal Tracks and Sign*, 2nd ed. (New York: HarperCollins, 1999).

171 five-month-olds might be accomplished: Karen E. Adolph and Sarah E. Berger, "Physical and Motor Development," in *Developmental Science: An Advanced*

Textbook, ed. Marc H. Bornstein and Michael E. Lamb, 6th ed., 241–302 (New York: Psychology Press/Taylor and Francis, 2010).

172 **330,000 fewer animals:** "Shelter Animals Count: The National Database," accessed June 22, 2021 at shelteranimalscount.org/american-pets-alive -blog-the-datas-in-no-pandemic-pets-werent-returned-to-shelters-but-shelters -do-need-help.

172 **the smell of their persons:** Alexandra Horowitz, "Discrimination of Person Odor by Owned Domestic Dogs," *International Journal of Comparative Psychology* 33 (2020).

173 **Dogs are much better readers:** Catia Correia-Caeiro, Kun Guo, and Daniel Mills, "Bodily Emotional Expressions Are a Primary Source of Information for Dogs, but Not for Humans," *Animal Cognition* 24, no. 2 (2021): 267–79.

173 **distinguishing happy faces:** Miho Nagasawa et al., "Dogs Can Discriminate Human Smiling Faces from Blank Expressions," *Animal Cognition* 14, no. 4 (2011): 525–33.

173 **happy from angry faces:** Corsin A. Müller et al., "Dogs Can Discriminate Emotional Expressions of Human Faces," *Current Biology* 25, no. 5 (2015): 601–5.

173 **can match a photo:** Natalia Albuquerque et al., "Dogs Recognize Dog and Human Emotions," *Biology Letters* 12, no. 1 (2016): 20150883.

173 **person opening a box:** David Buttelmann and Michael Tomasello, "Can Domestic Dogs (*Canis familiaris*) Use Referential Emotional Expressions to Locate Hidden Food?," *Animal Cognition* 16, no. 1 (2013): 137–45.

173 **can identify these expressions:** Müller et al., "Dogs Can Discriminate."

THE TROUBLES

182 **a lot of broadband sound:** Kathryn Lord, Mark Feinstein, and Raymond Coppinger, "Barking and Mobbing," *Behavioural Processes* 81, no. 3 (2009): 358–68.

183 **barks convey a lot:** Nikolett Jégh-Czinege, Tamás Faragó, and Péter Pongrácz, "A Bark of Its Own Kind—the Acoustics of 'Annoying' Dog Barks Suggests a Specific Attention-Evoking Effect for Humans," *Bioacoustics* 29, no. 2 (2020): 210–25.

183 **right smack in the frequency:** Jégh-Czinege, Faragó, and Pongrácz, "A Bark of Its Own Kind."

183 **homology between baby crying:** Péter Pongrácz et al., "Human Listeners Are Able to Classify Dog (*Canis familiaris*) Barks Recorded in Different Situations," *Journal of Comparative Psychology* 119, no. 2 (2005): 136–44.

184 **four-and-a-half-month-old children:** Denise R. Mandel, Peter W. Jusczyk, and David B. Pisoni, "Infants' Recognition of the Sound Patterns of Their Own Names," *Psychological Science* 6, no. 5 (1995): 314–17.

185 **found her live person:** "Vara (7-19-21)," Penn Vet Working Dog Center, Youtube video, 2:41, July 19, 2021, youtube.com/watch?v=RksUU7ErPcc.

186 **"sawdust and cleaning supplies":** Amritha Mallikarjun, personal correspondence, August 15, 2021.

186 **compound was designed:** Kenneth G. Furton et al., "Advances in the Use of Odour as Forensic Evidence through Optimizing and Standardizing Instru-

ments and Canines," *Philosophical Transactions of the Royal Society B* 370, no. 1674 (2015): 20140262.

186 **allows the trainers to teach:** Cynthia M. Otto, "Implementing Early Odor Training," 2019 AKC US Detection Dog Conference, August 27–29, 2019, Durham, NC.

186 **a specially designed room:** See, e.g., Bob Dougherty's UCD imprint training with puppy Dozer, "Dozer udc imprint 3 elbows 12 10 2020 1," Youtube video, 9:37, January 14, 2021, youtube.com/watch?v=y6C1MALJonM.

187 **"How do [we] accomplish this task?":** Julia Parish-Morris, Roberta Michnick Golinkoff, and Kathryn Hirsh-Pasek, "From Coo to Code: A Brief Story of Language Development," in *The Oxford Handbook of Developmental Psychology*, vol. 1, ed. Philip David Zelazo, 867–908 (New York: Oxford University Press, 2013).

TO SLEEP, PERCHANCE

192 **"A reversible state of immobility":** Rachel Kinsman et al., "Sleep Duration and Behaviours: A Descriptive Analysis of a Cohort of Dogs up to 12 Months of Age," *Animals* 10, no. 7 (2020): 1172.

192 **memory and learning consolidation:** Kinsman et al., "Sleep Duration and Behaviours."

192 **a healthy immune system:** Matthew Walker, *Why We Sleep: Unlocking the Power of Sleep and Dreams* (New York: Scribner, 2017), 74.

193 **teach their dogs to "touch":** Veronica Leifer et al., "Memory for Learned Tricks: Do Dogs (*Canis familiaris*) Remember a Learned Behavior Better after an Overnight Sleep?," poster, Association of Professional Dog Trainers virtual conference, September 29–30, 2021.

194 **not only to the furnishings:** Edouard Cadieu et al., "Coat Variation in the Domestic Dog Is Governed by Variants in Three Genes," *Science* 326 (2009): 150–53.

LONGING

200 **until fourteen months:** Cindy Otto, personal correspondence, July 13, 2020.

200 **"as long as possible":** Karen Becker, personal correspondence, July 14, 2020.

202 **studied dog sex in earnest:** Frank A. Beach and Burney J. LeBoeuf, "Coital Behaviour in Dogs. I. Preferential Mating in the Bitch," *Animal Behaviour* 15 (1967): 546–58; Donald A. Dewsbury, *Frank Ambrose Beach, 1911–1988, Biographical Memoirs* 73 (Washington, DC: National Academies Press, 1998).

202 **Unlike nearly all wild canids:** Jennifer B. Nagashima and Nucharin Songsasen, "Canid Reproductive Biology: Norm and Unique Aspects in Strategies and Mechanisms," *Animals* 11, no. 3 (2021): 653; Heidi G. Parker et al., "Genetic Structure of the Purebred Domestic Dog," *Science* 304 (2004): 1160–64.

204 **forcibly rejecting the earnest male:** Frank A. Beach, "Coital Behavior in Dogs: VI. Long-Term Effects of Castration upon Mating in the Male," *Journal of Comparative and Physiological Psychology* 70, no. 3, part 2 (1970): 1–32.

204 **leave their genitals:** Olivia Judson, *Dr. Tatiana's Sex Advice to All Creation: The Definitive Guide to the Evolutionary Biology of Sex* (New York: Metropolitan Books/Henry Holt, 2002).

205 **pups who have different fathers:** Sunil Kumar Pal, "Mating System of Free-Ranging Dogs (*Canis familiaris*)," *International Journal of Zoology* 2011 (2011): 314216.

206 **"collecting semen from the male":** Rita Payan-Carreira, Sonia Miranda, and Wojciech Niżański, "Artificial Insemination in Dogs," in *Artificial Insemination in Farm Animals*, ed. Milad Manafi, 51–78 (Rijeka, Croatia: InTech, 2011), inte chopen.com/chapters/16099; Stefano Romagnoli and Cheryl Lopate, "Transcervical Artificial Insemination in Dogs and Cats: Review of the Technique and Practical Aspects," *Reproduction in Domestic Animals* 49, no. s4 (2014): 56–63.

206 **"collect the sperm":** Sophia Yin, *The Small Animal Veterinary Nerdbook*, 3rd ed. (Davis, CA: CattleDog Publishing, 2010).

206 **artificial insemination day:** Cheryl Asa, "The Role of Reproductive Management in Mexican Gray Wolf Recovery," Wolf Conservation Center webinar, 2020, nywolf.org/learn-scientific-webinar-series-reproductive-management -mexican-gray-wolves/.

GALE FORCE TEN

214 **duration of adolescence:** Barbara Natterson-Horowitz and Kathryn Bowers, *Wildhood: The Epic Journey from Adolescence to Adulthood in Humans and Other Animals* (New York: Scribner, 2019); Naomi D. Harvey, "How Old Is My Dog? Identification of Rational Age Groupings in Pet Dogs Based upon Normative Age-Linked Processes," *Frontiers in Veterinary Science* 8 (April 2021): 643085.

215 **approximately six months old:** Harvey, "How Old Is My Dog?"; James A. Serpell and Deborah L. Duffy, "Aspects of Juvenile and Adolescent Environment Predict Aggression and Fear in 12-Month-Old Guide Dogs," *Frontiers in Veterinary Science* 3 (2016): 49.

215 **often completely ignored:** Serpell and Duffy, "Aspects of Juvenile and Adolescent Environment."

215 **a time of risk-taking:** Natterson-Horowitz and Bowers, *Wildhood*.

215 **primary reason for abandoning dogs:** M. D. Salman et al., "Human and Animal Factors Related to Relinquishment of Dogs and Cats in 12 Selected Animal Shelters in the United States," *Journal of Applied Animal Welfare Science* 1, no. 3 (1998): 207–26; Gillian Diesel, David Brodbelt, and Dirk U. Pfeiffer, "Characteristics of Relinquished Dogs and Their Owners at 14 Rehoming Centers in the United Kingdom," *Journal of Applied Animal Welfare Science* 13, no. 1 (2010): 15–30.

215 **"simply being an adolescent":** Natterson-Horowitz and Bowers, *Wildhood*, 50.

216 **final height at the shoulder:** Daniela Helmsmüller et al., "Ontogenetic Allometry of the Beagle," *BMC Veterinary Research* 9 (2013): 203.

216 **increased sensitivities and less self-control:** Naomi D. Harvey, "Adolescence," in *Encyclopedia of Animal Cognition and Behavior*, ed. Jennifer Vonk and Todd Shackelford (Cham, Switzerland: Springer, 2019).

216 oversees a rewiring of the brain: Harvey, "Adolescence."
216 "waking up in your tent": Sarah Fisher, "Creating a Support Bubble for Adolescent Dogs," Dog Behavior Conference, Victoria Stilwell Academy for Dog Training and Behavior, April 17, 2021.
216 later problems in interacting: James Ha, in Natterson-Horowitz and Bowers, *Wildhood*, 143.
216 grow up with other dogs: Serpell and Duffy, "Aspects of Juvenile and Adolescent Environment Predict Aggression and Fear."
216 an enriched environment in adolescence: Darlene D. Francis et al., "Environmental Enrichment Reverses the Effects of Maternal Separation on Stress Reactivity," *Journal of Neuroscience* 22, no. 18 (2002): 7840–43.
217 "a passing phase": Lucy Asher et al., "Teenage Dogs? Evidence for Adolescent-Phase Conflict Behavior and an Association between Attachment to Humans and Pubertal Timing in the Domestic Dog," *Biology Letters* 16, no. 5 (2020): 20200097.
217 dogs who learned to "sit": Asher et al., "Teenage Dogs?"
217 Adolescent wolves may leave: Cheryl S. Asa and Carolina Valdespino, "Canid Reproductive Biology: An Integration of Proximate Mechanisms and Ultimate Causes," *American Zoologist* 38, no. 1 (1998): 251–59.
218 lower stress hormone levels: Kin-ya Kubo, Mitsuo Iinuma, and Huayue Chen, "Mastication as a Stress-Coping Behavior," *BioMed Research International* (2015): 876409; Fisher, "Creating a Support Bubble."
218 adolescent wolf howls: Fred H. Harrington and L. David Mech, "Wolf Vocalization," in *Wolf and Man: Evolution in Parallel*, ed. Roberta L. Sharp and Henry S. Hall, 109–32 (New York: Academic Press, 1978).
218 outlet for their chewing: Fisher, "Creating a Support Bubble."
218 study of Italian wolves: Paolo Ciucci et al., "Home Range, Activity and Movements of a Wolf Pack in Central Italy," *Journal of Zoology* 243, no. 4 (1997): 803–19.
218 Coyotes on Cape Cod: Jonathan G. Way, Isaac M. Ortega, and Eric G. Strauss, "Movement and Activity Patterns of Eastern Coyotes in a Coastal, Suburban Environment," *Northeastern Naturalist* 11, no. 3 (2004): 237–54; Eric M. Gese, Jennifer L. B. Dowd, and Lise M. Aubry, "The Influence of Snowmobile Trails on Coyote Movements during Winter in High-Elevation Landscapes," *PLoS ONE* 8, no. 12 (2013): e82862.
218 young dog bodies: Helmsmüller et al., "Ontogenetic Allometry of the Beagle."
219 grow dramatically in one day: Karen E. Adolph and Sarah E. Berger, "Physical and Motor Development," in *Developmental Science: An Advanced Textbook*, ed. Marc H. Bornstein and Michael E. Lamb, 6th ed., 241–302 (New York: Psychology Press/Taylor and Francis, 2010).
219 the skeleton is maturing: Fisher, "Creating a Support Bubble."
220 Crawling, babies mostly see: Kari S. Kretch, John M. Franchak, and Karen E. Adolph, "Crawling and Walking Infants See the World Differently," *Child Development* 85, no. 4 (2014): 1503–18.

SEEING US

226 **our domesticating of them:** James A. Serpell, "Commensalism or Cross-Species Adoption? A Critical Review of Theories of Wolf Domestication," *Frontiers in Veterinary Science* 8 (April 2021): 662370.

227 **"levator anguli oculi medialis":** Juliana Kaminski et al., "Evolution of Facial Muscle Anatomy in Dogs," *Proceedings of the National Academy of Sciences* 116, no. 29 (2019): 14677–81.

227 **shelter dogs who flexed their LAOM muscle:** Bridget M. Waller et al., "Paedomorphic Facial Expressions Give Dogs a Selective Advantage," *PLoS ONE* 8, no. 12 (2013): e82686.

228 **The youngest babies see faces:** "Linda B. Smith: Word Learning from the Infant's Point of View," PsychologicalScience, Youtube video, 56:27, August 14, 2018, https://www.youtube.com/watch?v=_v-M5H67FQI.

228 **steal treats right away:** Juliane Kaminski, Andrea Pitsch, and Michael Tomasello, "Dogs Steal in the Dark," *Animal Cognition* 16 (2013): 385–94.

229 **as soon as the person is gone:** Josep Call et al., "Domestic Dogs (*Canis familiaris*) Are Sensitive to the Attentional State of Humans," *Journal of Comparative Psychology* 117, no. 3 (2003): 257–63; Christine Schwab and Ludwig Huber, "Obey or Not Obey? Dogs (*Canis familiaris*) Behave Differently in Response to Attentional States of Their Owners," *Journal of Comparative Psychology* 120, no. 3 (2006): 169–75.

229 **they might react "guiltily":** Alexandra Horowitz, "Disambiguating the 'Guilty Look': Salient Prompts to a Familiar Dog Behavior," *Behavioural Processes* 81, no. 3 (2009): 447–52.

229 **which one the person can see:** Juliane Kaminski et al., "Domestic Dogs Are Sensitive to a Human's Perspective," *Behaviour* 146, no. 7 (2009): 979–98.

230 **dogs detecting cancers:** I describe this ability more fully in *Being a Dog: Following the Dog into a World of Smell* (New York: Simon and Schuster, 2016).

THE THING ABOUT SLEDS

235 **who writes of a dog, Benjamin:** Mary Oliver, "The Dog Has Run Off Again," *Dog Songs* (New York: Penguin Press, 2013), 33.

236 **"every interaction we have":** Sophia Yin, *Perfect Puppy in 7 Days: How to Start Your Puppy Off Right* (Davis, CA: CattleDog Publishing, 2011), 45.

236 **babies to learn to push themselves:** Karen E. Adolph and Sarah E. Berger, "Physical and Motor Development," in *Developmental Science: An Advanced Textbook*, ed. Marc H. Bornstein and Michael E. Lamb, 6th ed., 241–302 (New York: Psychology Press/Taylor and Francis, 2010).

239 **songbirds do something similar:** Elina Mäntylä, Silke Kipper, and Monika Hilker, "Insectivorous Birds Can See and Smell Systemically Herbivore-Induced Pines," *Ecology and Evolution* 10, no. 17 (2020): 9358–70.

239 **"gracile and vestigial":** Jen Wathan et al., "EquiFACS: The Equine Facial Action Coding System," *PLoS ONE* 10, no. 8 (2015): e0131738.

239 **ear adductor muscles:** Annika Bremhorst et al., "Differences in Facial Expressions during Positive Anticipation and Frustration in Dogs Awaiting a Reward," *Scientific Reports* 9, no. 1 (2019): 19312.

239 muscles to rotate their ears: Wathan et al., "EquiFACS."

240 Henry's pocket has "no obvious function": Lynette K. Cole, "Anatomy and Physiology of the Canine Ear," *Veterinary Dermatology* 20, nos. 5–6 (2009): 412–21.

240 feeding on fresh hay: Nadine Reefmann et al., "Ear and Tail Postures as Indicators of Emotional Valence in Sheep," *Applied Animal Behaviour Science* 118, nos. 3–4 (2009): 199–207.

240 make dogs more optimistic: Charlotte Duranton and Alexandra Horowitz, "Let Me Sniff! Nosework Induces Positive Judgment Bias in Pet Dogs," *Applied Animal Behaviour Science* 211 (February 2019): 61–66.

240 the same A-not-B error: Anna Kis et al., "Does the A-not-B Error in Adult Pet Dogs Indicate Sensitivity to Human Communication?," *Animal Cognition* 15 (2012): 737–43; Zsófia Sümegi et al., "Why Do Adult Dogs (*Canis familiaris*) Commit the A-not-B Search Error?," *Journal of Comparative Psychology* 128, no. 1 (2014): 21–30.

241 watching fish in an aquarium: Aaron Honori Katcher et al., "Looking, Talking, and Blood Pressure: The Physiological Consequences of Interaction with the Living Environment," in *New Perspectives on Our Lives with Companion Animals*, ed. A. H. Katcher and Alan M. Beck, 351–59 (Philadelphia: University of Pennsylvania Press, 1983); Mary M. DeSchriver and Carol C. Riddick, "Effects of Watching Aquariums on Elders' Stress, *Anthrozoös* 4, no. 1 (1990): 44–48.

241 "opt in" or "opt out" work: E.g., Jean Donaldson, Kristi Benson, and many others.

242 what is called "intelligent disobedience": Southeastern Guide Dogs, guidedogs.org.

FACE-FIRST

248 up to twenty-three vertebrae: Tim Lewis, "Canine Biology Learning Lab," Association of Professional Dog Trainers, virtual conference, October 21–22, 2020.

248 "dorso-ventral elevation and depression": Marthe Kiley-Worthington, "The Tail Movements of Ungulates, Canids and Felids with Particular Reference to Their Causation and Function as Displays," *Behaviour* 56, nos. 1–2 (1076): 69–115.

249 right-wagging tail: Angelo Quaranta, Marcello Siniscalchi, and Giorgio Vallortigara, "Asymmetric Tail-Wagging Responses by Dogs to Different Emotive Stimuli," *Current Biology* 17, no. 6 (2007): R199–R201.

249 placed in front of a video: Marcello Siniscalchi et al., "Seeing Left- or Right-Asymmetric Tail Wagging Produces Different Emotional Responses in Dogs," *Current Biology* 23, no. 22 (2013): 2279–82.

249 an average of 125 times: Emily E. Bray, Evan L. MacLean, and Brian A. Hare, "Increasing Arousal Enhances Inhibitory Control in Calm but Not Excitable Dogs," *Animal Cognition* 18, no. 6 (2015): 1317–29.

250 important to immune function: Carl J. Charnetski, Sandra Riggers, and Francis X. Brennan, "Effect of Petting a Dog on Immune System Function," *Psychological Reports* 95, no. 3 part 2 (2004): 1087–91.

250 **anxiety levels:** Shoshana Shiloh, Gal Sorek, and Joseph Terkel, "Reduction of State-Anxiety by Petting Animals in a Controlled Laboratory Experiment," *Anxiety, Stress and Coping* 16, no. 4 (2003): 387–95.

250 **cortisol levels, blood pressure:** J. S. J. Odendaal and R. A. Meintjes, "Neurophysiological Correlates of Affiliative Behaviour between Humans and Dogs," *Veterinary Journal* 165, no. 3 (2003): 296–301; Linda Handlin et al., "Associations between the Psychological Characteristics of the Human-Dog Relationship and Oxytocin and Cortisol Levels," *Anthrozoös* 25, no. 2 (2012): 215–28.

250 **rush of endorphins:** R. I. M. Dunbar, "The Social Role of Touch in Humans and Primates: Behavioural Function and Neurobiological Mechanisms," *Neuroscience and Biobehavioral Reviews* 34, no. 2 (2010): 260–68.

250 **shocked a dog's paws:** James J. Lynch and John F. McCarthy, "The Effect of Petting on a Classically Conditioned Emotional Response," *Behaviour Research and Therapy* 5, no. 1 (1967): 55–62.

251 **when having blood drawn:** Michael B. Hennessy et al., "Influence of Male and Female Petters on Plasma Cortisol and Behaviour: Can Human Interaction Reduce the Stress of Dogs in a Public Animal Shelter?," *Applied Animal Behaviour Science* 61, no. 1 (1998): 63–77.

251 **leaves them home alone:** Chiara Mariti et al., "Effects of Petting before a Brief Separation from the Owner on Dog Behavior and Physiology: A Pilot Study," *Journal of Veterinary Behavior* 27 (September–October 2018): 41–46.

251 **raise endorphins and oxytocin:** Odendaal and Meintjes, "Neurophysiological Correlates of Affiliative Behaviour."

251 **Army dogs and shelter dogs:** Roger W. McIntire and Thomas A. Colley, "Social Reinforcement in the Dog," *Psychological Reports* 20, no. 3 (1967): 843–46; Erica N. Feuerbacher and Clive D. L. Wynne, "Most Domestic Dogs (*Canis lupus familiaris*) Prefer Petting to Food: Context, Schedule, and Population Differences in a Concurrent Choice," *Journal of Experimental Analysis of Behavior* 101, no. 3 (2014): 385–405; Feuerbacher and Wynne, "Shut Up and Pet Me! DomesticDogs (*Canis lupus familiaris*) Prefer Petting to Vocal Praise in Concurrent and Single-Alternative Choice Procedures, *Behavioural Processes* 110 (January 2015): 47–59.

251 **What counts as "petting":** Hennessy et al., "Influence of Male and Female Petters."

LICK, MEMORY

257 **equivalent of thirty-year-old adolescents:** Tina Wang et al., "Quantitative Translation of Dog-to-Human Aging by Conserved Remodeling of the DNA Methylome," *Cell Systems* 11, no. 2 (2020): 17685; Claudia Kawczynska, "How to Calculate Your Dog's Age in Human Years," The Wildest, June 1, 2021, see https://thebark.com/content/about-us.

257 **an infant of this age:** Karen E. Adolph and Sarah E. Berger, "Physical and Motor Development," in *Developmental Science: An Advanced Textbook*, ed. Marc H. Bornstein and Michael E. Lamb, 6th ed., 241–302 (New York: Psychology Press/Taylor and Francis, 2010).

257 **An average active puppy:** Imagining about twenty thousand steps a day, Quid's average, for three hundred days, would be six million. Even a relatively under-walked, sedentary pup who managed four thousand steps a day would walk over a million steps by a year.

257 **adoptions from shelters actually went down:** Andrew Rowan, "Companion Animal Demographics: When Are They Good Enough?," *WellBeing International* newsletter, February 26, 2021, wellbeingintl.org/companion-animal -demographics.

258 **the highest rates of return:** Lauren Powell et al., "Characterizing Unsuccessful Animal Adoptions: Age and Breed Predict the Likelihood of Return, Reasons for Return and Post-Return Outcomes," *Scientific Reports* 11, no. 1 (2021): 8018.

258 **"behavioral problems" were cited:** James Serpell, Deborah L. Duffy, and J. A. Jagoe, "Becoming a Dog: Early Experience and the Development of Behavior," in *The Domestic Dog*, ed. James Serpell, 2nd ed. (Cambridge, UK: Cambridge University Press, 2017).

258 **dogs have memories of specific events:** Claudia Fugazza, Ákos Pogány, and Ádám Miklósi, "Recall of Others' Actions after Incidental Encoding Reveals Episodic-Like Memory in Dogs," *Current Biology* 26, no. 23 (2016): 3209–13.

259 **odors present at the time:** Angelo Quaranta, Serenella d'Ingeo, and Marcello Siniscalchi, "Odour-Evoked Memory in Dogs: Do Odours Help to Retrieve Memories of Food Location?," *Animals* 10 (2020): 1249.

259 **reason for parents' bond:** Eric E. Nelson and Jaak Panksepp, "Brain Substrates of Infant-Mother Attachment: Contributions of Opioids, Oxytocin, and Norepinephrine," *Neuroscience and Biobehavioral Reviews* 22, no. 3 (1998): 437–52.

260 **gazing, touching, or interacting:** Miho Nagasawa et al., "Oxytocin-Gaze Positive Loop and the Coevolution of Human-Dog Bonds," *Science* 348 (2015): 333–36.

Index

Italicized page numbers indicate material in tables or illustrations.